Death Passage on the Hudson

DEATH PASSAGE ON THE HUDSON

THE WRECK OF THE HENRY CLAY

KRIS A. HANSEN

PURPLE MOUNTAIN PRESS
Fleischmanns, New York

To my husband, Kornel, for his love, encouragement and continuous assistance

And, Max, my faithful writing buddy

Death Passage on the Hudson: The Wreck of the Henry Clay
First Edition 2004

Published by
Purple Mountain Press, Ltd.
P.O. Box 309, Fleischmanns, New York 12430-0309
845-254-4062, 845-254-4476 (fax), purple@catskill.net
www.catskill.net/purple

ISBN 1-930098-56-1
Library of Congress Control Number 2004097004

Photography, cover design, title page design by Kornel A. Krechoweckyj.

Front Cover:
"Burning of the Henry Clay Near Yonkers," lithographic print by Nathaniel Currier, The Mariners' Museum, Newport News, Virginia.

Back Cover:
Model of the steamboat Armenia, built by F. Van Loon Ryder for the Historical Society of Newburgh in the 1950s. Collection of the Historical Society of Newburgh Bay, model photographed at the Hudson River Maritime Museum, Kingston, New York.

Title Page:
Painting of the steamboat *Henry Clay*, by James Bard (1851), The Mariners' Museum, Newport News, Virginia.

Manufactured in the United States of America on acid-free paper
5 4 3 2 1

Table of Contents

Preface

INITIALLY, I did not set out to find a historical event to use as a topic for a book. I stumbled across this story while working on my family history, and it aroused my interest to a point where I began to research the incident more thoroughly. There were only a few pieces written about the *Henry Clay* disaster. To my knowledge, there had not been an entire book written on the subject.

I was intrigued that a person whom I strongly believe to be one of my direct ancestors was on the steamboat the day of the disaster. I wanted to confirm this, so my quest began. After reading the few pieces written about the *Henry Clay*, I endeavored to search further. My research for the book spanned three years, not including the previous six years looking into my family history.

However, I must add that history is written as those who recorded it remember. Therefore, although I have researched to the best of my ability, I am captive to the written documents of the 1850s. I am influenced not only by the facts presented, but also by the thoughts and feelings that were put to paper more than a century and a half ago.

In my research, I found discrepancies about the facts and the spelling of names among the various newspaper reports, witness testimonies, and documents. I have tried to sort them out and make the best decision about what information to incorporate in the book.

By using the information about the people involved, I have attempted to bring to life a few of the stories from the *Henry Clay*. There must be missing pieces—more untold stories of those who perished and those who survived.

Thus, I present my own first book and the first book written about the *Henry Clay* disaster. This journey, one I never expected to take, brought me to the Hudson River again. It allowed me to see the river from another perspective, one that I had not seen while growing up near its waters. I was taken to the river's past and my own past as well.

During my research, I journeyed up and down the Hudson's east and west shores, researching and uncovering bits of information. I saw sights that I had seen before in my youth, but perhaps really had not seen at all. I found a past that I had no idea I was looking for.

This was a remarkable journey for me. I wish you the same as you enter the pages of the *Death Passage on the Hudson*.

K.A.H.

Book 1: Tragedy

Prologue

THE PATINA OF THE GOLD WATCH was weathered with age, as was the ruddy face of the old man who held this treasure in his ancient hand. Although many years had passed, this watch was still a prized possession to him. The passage of time had not dulled his memory of events that occurred long ago, and his precious watch served as the reminder.

His name was Edward, and his life on the river, once known as the North River, commenced decades before, in the early 1800s, when he was a young man. It was a time when river boating had a magic of its own and inspired young boys to leave their small hometowns and head toward the boats for adventure. The hard work and long days away from home forced many to abandon their dreams. Only those strong enough to withstand the years of strenuous work would survive, and those who did, often passed their professions on to their own sons.[1]

Edward spent more than sixty years of his working life on riverboats and much of that time on steamboats. The job kept him where he wanted to be—on the river. This was a river that flowed for hundreds of miles, from the upper reaches of New York State down to New York City, meandering through the graciously beautiful Hudson Valley.[2]

The old man knew the river as well as another would know his own backyard. So much so that he affectionately called it "the brook." Today, this river is known as the Hudson. It was on those waters, years before, that a tragic course of events altered his life and that of hundreds of others.[3]

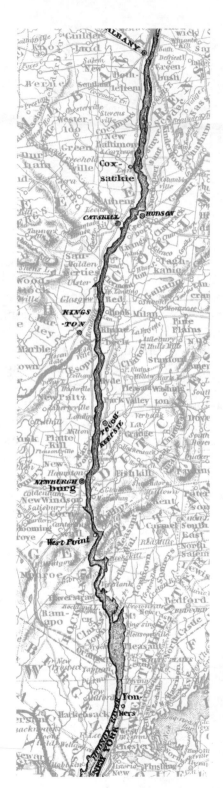

From the Map of the State of New York
by J. Calvin Smith
New York
J. Disturnell
1842
Engraved on steel by Sherman and Smith

Courtesy of the Local History Room
at the Newburgh Free Library,
Newburgh, New York

Chapter 1

Strife!

FIRES were common on the Hudson River, so it was no surprise that something catastrophic would eventually happen. It was a matter of time. The circumstances leading to disaster had escalated after 1824. Until that time, Robert Fulton and his business partner Robert Livingston essentially controlled the steamboats on the Hudson River.

The year 1807 was almost two centuries since Henry Hudson made his exploratory trip up the Hudson River in his *Halve Maen*. In August of that year, Robert Fulton followed in the same path of the great explorer by taking, not a sailing vessel, but his first commercial steamboat from New York City to Albany. The vessel, originally named the *North River Steamboat of Clermont*, was later referred to as simply *Clermont* after Robert Livingston's country home.[1]

Livingston, who inherited his family's working manor, provided the money to back Fulton and his steamboat. Together, Fulton and Livingston successfully opened the doors to steamship travel on the Hudson River. Fulton's historic steamboat trip from New York City to Albany took thirty-two hours, an average of five miles per hour. Shortly thereafter, the steamboat partners had a scheduled run for the *Clermont* from New York to Albany with several stops including Newburgh, Poughkeepsie, Esopus, Hudson, and lastly, Albany. The trip took thirty-six hours. Passengers paid a hefty price at seven dollars for the trip, providing a lucrative income for these two partners when multiplied by the number of paying travelers.[2]

To further solidify their relationship and strengthen their North River Steamboat Company, Livingston and Fulton were successful in obtaining a twenty-year monopoly that the New York State legislature had granted. Thanks to that deal, the two men with their business enterprises had virtual control of steamboat lines on the Hudson River for the next fifteen years. This was the era in which the old man, Edward, was born. It was a time of faster travel, a faster pace, and a faster life.[3]

The Fulton-Livingston monopoly would have lasted longer but it was not popular with other steamboat owners and shipbuilders. They too wanted a piece of the shipping business on the Hudson River. This resulted in years of venomous legal jurisdictional battles between New York and New Jersey that plagued the Hudson River steamboat industry. The fights over the monopoly on the Hudson River continued both on the river waters and in the courts.[4]

In one noteworthy business deal that riled the tempers of other steamboat operators, Fulton and Livingston allowed the governor of New Jersey (before he was voted out by the state's voters) Aaron Ogden to run a ferry route using his own boat, the *Sea Horse*, from Elizabethtown, New Jersey, to New York City. The deal would operate under the monopoly for ten years. To muddy the waters, Thomas Gibbons from Savannah, who happened to be a part owner in Ogden's ferry, set up a rival operation, in competition against Ogden. The captain of one of Gibbons' two steamboats was "Commodore" (Cornelius) Van Derbilt (Vanderbilt). He brazenly defied the monopoly and took the *Belona* into protected waters from New Jersey to New York City, often hiding to avoid arrest.[5]

The legal battle finally climaxed with the help of the "Commodore" and Gibbons who retained the famous Daniel Webster to argue against the Fulton-Livingston monopoly. They had their day in the U.S. Supreme Court, in 1824 with the case Gibbons vs. Ogden. Under Chief Justice John Marshall, the court decided that the monopoly was unconstitutional because the federal government was the only body allowed to govern waterways. Fulton and Livingston would never learn of the outcome of the judgment that would impact their business operations. The two, who for years owned Hudson River steam boating, both had died a decade earlier.[6]

The monopoly was gone in an instant, and other steamship operators, who had waited years for their chance, finally could grab a piece of Hudson River enterprise. Steamboat fever created competition and brought about a boom time on the river. With it came the opportunity for jobs for those young men, including Edward, who wanted to try their luck at working on the many boats that would come to the Hudson.

By 1825, Fulton's business was gone, and competing Hudson River steamboat lines were born. There were sixteen steamboats running on the river, and by the 1830s the number of steamboats increased to forty-five. The North River Line, Hudson River Line, and Newburg Line all vied for passenger fare. Among the shipbuilders that moved in was the famous Stevens shipbuilding family from

New Jersey. John Stevens and Robert L. Stevens both set up operations along the river. Robert established a New York to Albany run, and his boat, the *New Philadelphia,* set a speed record to Albany of twelve hours and twenty-three minutes in 1826. Travel time had been cut to a third of the *Clermont*'s time and travel speed had more that doubled.[7]

Passage by steamboat travel was further expanded with the completion of the Erie Canal in 1825 from Albany through Buffalo to Lake Erie. It helped swell the numbers of the traveling public. By 1850, about twenty thousand immigrants came to New York City each year from overseas. The population in that city jumped from ninety thousand in 1800 to five hundred thousand by 1850. Many of the immigrants traveled up the Hudson River by boat to Albany and continued their journey to Ohio and beyond, settling in the Midwest.[8]

Steamboats initially needed wood for fuel, before conversion to coal, and a vast amount of forest was cut for that purpose. Agriculture, once a staple of the old manor system, was converted to dairy farming. The once flowing wheat and grain fields that covered the Hudson Valley disappeared and were moved west. In its place came the fragrant scents of spring fruit blossoms that covered the masses of apple, plum, and pear trees that were planted.[9]

Although the commercial scenery changed, the Hudson River valley still retained its native beauty. Word spread about the area, and oil painters arrived to record the majestic wonders on canvas. A new genre of painting, the Hudson River School, was developed. These paintings inspired others to come and see the wonders of the river region.[10]

Man had traveled up the Hudson for centuries before. First it was the Native American, followed by the explorer, the colonist, the British enemy, and the traveler. Now there was a new kind of traveler—the tourist. Resort hotels and country estates began to dot the landscape along the Hudson. To the north, the Catskill Mountain House appeared on the scene in the 1820s and Cozzens' Hotel was built on a cliff in the central region around Buttermilk Falls (now named Highland Falls). Cozzens' Hotel was one of a trio of better-known resorts in the Hudson Highlands area including the Tappan Zee House in Nyack and Monk's Hotel at Lake Mahopac.[11]

The steamboat entered a new era of providing relaxation. The "Sunday Excursion" became popular with passengers taking a day to travel up the Hudson River to enjoy the pretty riverside scenery and beautiful estates. Passengers traveling on these "floating palaces" could wash away the hustle and bustle of city life with a wisp of fresh country breeze in their faces and a deep breath of country air in their lungs. Both day and night boats became popular. With the help of lighthouses that started to spring up after 1826, the waters were guided for nighttime travel. By 1840, there were a hundred steamboats on the river.[12]

The scene was a far different life than in the centuries before the European had set foot in the new world. Then it was a time of quiet. The river was witness to centuries of Native American Algonquin, Iroquois, and Mohawk life. The Mahican name for the river was "Muhheakunnuk" meaning "great waters constantly in motion." An apt description, as the river flow moves in more than one direction. Runoff originating from the Adirondacks flows downstream, while the tides of the Atlantic Ocean travel northward for more than 150 miles. Somewhere in between, the two forces meet.[13]

Local names like Manhattan, "the island," Sintsink, "stone upon stone," Poughkeepsie, "safe harbor," and Esopus meaning "river" bear testament to the native peoples who once populated these lands. We are reminded of the legacy of those many tribes like Manhattas of the more southern region, the Sint Sint to the north, and Wappingers farther upstream, whose tribes made their homes and livelihood off the river valley's lands.[14]

Thick forests of oak, chestnut, and hickory trees were home to wild turkey, deer, and grouse. The native peoples grew corn and ate the local fruit. They fished for bass and harvested oysters from the river; navigating the waters in boats powered by human strength alone. Only the soft brush of paddle strokes native man made as his canoe glided through the shimmering waters of the mighty river interrupted the quiet of nature, from the rustling of the wind to the wildlife in the forest.[15]

Too soon the quiet was gone. The European man had arrived and the pristine silence along the Hudson River eroded away. Populated farmlands replaced the native village and the Native American way of life was gone. River transportation became, not the methodical paddle of canoes, but the movement of large multi-manned boats designed to carry a heavier cargo. Noisy docks and chattering hoards of people lined the river's shores.[16]

The Dutch made the first strong European foothold along the river's lands. The French, Germans, then later the English, and others who established their own settlements followed. Settlers from each country left their own legacy alongside that of the native tribes. Sprinkled among the native named spots are those of the Europeans, like the Dutch named Peekskill, the French Huguenot towns of New Rochelle and New Paltz, and the German settled Rhinebeck and Newburgh.[17]

The names for the river changed over the years as well. First named the "Grand River" by Giovanni de Verrazano, then, "Manhattes" by Henry Hudson, among the many other names, the Dutch later named it the "River of Prince Mauritius," the "Nassau River," and the "Manhattan River." However, it was the name of "North River" that stuck until 1664 when the English took control and permanently changed the name to the Hudson River. Although, for years the section of the river along Manhattan still retained the name of the North River. Boat pilots in their day frequently referred to the Hudson as the North River as well.[18]

In Dutch New York, the Hudson River proved a more reliable travel route than the dirt roads that quickly turned to mud with the rain or froze in cold weather. In addition, the location of New Amsterdam (now known as Manhattan) at the southern mouth of the river served as a major port and stopping point for boats. Fort Orange (now named Albany), located 150 miles to the north, served the same purpose for the upper parts of the river.[19]

The Dutch became master sailors on the Hudson River, adapting ocean sailing vessels that would develop into the favored Dutch sloop with hulls reaching to ninety feet. They learned to navigate the Hudson with their sloops by using the sails, capturing the available breezes to power the vessel forward. They also used the tides, which could be felt as far north as Troy, to their advantage.[20]

For navigation purposes, the Dutch divided the Hudson River between New Amsterdam and Fort Orange into fourteen reaches. These reaches were stops on the river where one could see the next designated stop while traveling upstream or downstream. Thus, the next stop was always visible from the current stop. This system provided the first foundations from which would evolve the steamboat landings along the river from New York City to Albany. Tappan Zee, Haverstraw, and Hunter are a few names that survive to this day.[21]

Throughout the early years, the Dutch remained superior in their sailing expertise. Even after the English gained control of the Hudson's lands, the skilled Dutch sailors navigated the river's waters for several years to follow. English control lasted until the time of the American Revolution, and much of the land along the Hudson River had, generations before, been granted to a handful of families with names like Philipse and Van Cortlandt along the southern end and Livingston and Van Renssalaer to the north. A feudal system was established on those land patents with a clench that intermarriage strengthened among those quasiaristocratic families.[22]

The American Revolution began to change all that. Loyalist manor lords (loyal to British rule) like Frederich Philipse III would find themselves on opposite sides from the patriot manor lords like Pierre Van Cortlandt and the upriver Livingstons. It became Loyalist versus patriot colonial, and, inevitably, the Hudson River itself was embroiled in battle. The British burned homes, boats, and entire towns during its siege to the north on the river. The British tried to take West Point, but the attempt failed. After years of conflict, the patriots prevailed and the British lost control of the colonies as well as the Hudson River.[23]

After the war, Loyalists, like the Phillipse family, had little choice. They could stay on American soil and have the American patriots despise them. Or, the Loyalist could leave to a more hospitable land under British rule. New York State passed anti-Loyalist laws, which took away their voting rights, the ability to hold public office, or own land. Loyalists evacuated either overland to Canada or departed New York City on seagoing vessels for their journey to British soil. Some went to the West Indies or England but the majority fled to Nova Scotia. In one year alone, in 1783, there were over twenty-eight thousand Loyalists who left New York. There were more than one hundred thousand Loyalists who fled.[24]

The massive flight changed the complexion, once again, of the Hudson River valley. Many of the feudal lands were broken up. Phillipsburg Manor, dissected after the Loyalist Philipse family fled to their new home in England, became Westchester County and part of the Bronx. New York State found itself the holder of forfeited lands that fleeing Loyalists had left. Once feudal workers were free in the new America, they bought some land for themselves, the land they once paid rent to work. There were patriot manors remaining but the antirent strikes put a virtual end to them by the 1840s.[25]

New towns, new land ownerships, and new farms and businesses evolved as a result of the breakup of the manors. Besides agriculture, commercial endeavors in lumbering, cement, and brick making and quarrying became profitable, as well as staples of the river's economy. The Hudson River itself became a huge resource for ice harvesting. Boatyards for the building of sloops sprung up along the Hudson River from the time of the end of the American Revolution to the mid-nineteenth century. Whaling was attempted in Hudson, a settlement created by whalers from Nantucket and other New England ports. Newburgh and Poughkeepsie served as homeports for whaling companies, but after a few years, unable to sustain profitability, the whaling trade disappeared from the region.[26]

The means of river travel changed as well. The steamboat out powered and outran the popular sloop, dependent on available wind and tides. With the demise of the steamboat monopoly in 1824, rival companies were empowered to get a piece of their own action on the river. As new steamboat companies grew in number and size, so did the rivalry between them. Boatmen tried their own share of monopoly schemes. Fare wars between steamboat lines and price fixing were common and standard practice. Agents or "runners" for the steamboats would run along the docks prior to departure attempting to entice or even kidnap unsuspecting passengers for their boats. Owners lied or publicly ridiculed the competition. Unscrupulous tactics were used, like offering free fares for travel to get the passenger on board but then excessively price meals and staterooms to make up the difference.[27]

Rivalry expanded to towns and residents of those towns as well, like that of the two upriver towns, Troy and Albany. New Englanders had settled Troy to compete with Albany, which had thrived since the time of the Dutch (as Fort Orange). Both cities situated upriver on the Hudson shared a distain for one another when it came to the river. Travelers from either Troy or Albany would not set foot on a boat that had first stopped at the rival city's docks on its run from New York City. The steamboat captain could leave many a passenger stubbornly standing on the docks if he had made the error of stopping at the rival city first.[28]

In 1832, several steamboat lines combined to form the North River Steamboat Association. Three years later, Daniel Drew along with A. P. Saint John and other investors founded the People's Line and then built the *Rochester*. The North River Line ran the *Swallow*. Both of these boats were used for the New York City to Albany run, and the lines raced against each other for years, with wins for each about even.[29]

Racing like this became common, and, at times, it was a sport to win at all costs. To promote safety for the river traveling public, the 1838 Act of Congress had provided for the inspection of steamboats. Unfortunately, the legislation could not be enforced. Inspections of the hull were supposed to take place every twelve months and inspections of the boiler, every six. But boats were never stopped from running; the amount of steam allowed was the only restriction to their operations. Not a problem for enthusiastic racers, as the safety valves were adjusted to allow for more steam whether legal or not. The result was unbridled steamboat racing to an extent that passengers' lives were endangered.[30]

The operators of the boats had other devices up their respective sleeves. Steamboat crews would get very close to competing boats, thus crowd them and cause them to slow down or stop. Sometimes the crews would skip scheduled landings. The unsuspecting passenger was put in the middle of these feuds, missing his landing because the boat never stopped. In some cases, the passengers were let off the steamboats into small boats tethered to the landing by a rope, so the steamboat could save time by not docking. This practice ended when the New York legislature outlawed it after several incidents of loss of life.[31]

The competition between boats and passenger demands for improved travel time resulted in the building and running of faster and faster boats. By the 1840s travel time on the New York to Albany run had been reduced to less than eight hours. The *Alida*, built in 1847 by William H. Brown with a vertical beam engine by Henry R. Dunham, timed at seven hours and fifty-six minutes, running south to New York City from Albany on May 5, 1848. The *Reindeer*, built in 1850 by Thomas Collyer, reduced the running time to seven hours and forty-four minutes on July 1, 1851. Whenever a speed record was set, there were captains and ship-builders ready to beat it. On June 30, 1852, the *Francis Skiddy*, built by George Collyer, timed the New York to Albany run in seven hours and thirty-minutes.[32]

Making speed even more important, to the chagrin of the steamboat operators, was commencement of the construction of the New York & Hudson Railroad in 1845. Trains easily surpassed the travel times for steamboats. By 1851, a New York to Albany run took just four hours on an express train, nearly half the fastest steamboat time. In that year, a million passengers traveled on the Hudson River in boats, so the stakes were high to compete with train travel.[33]

For whatever the reason, to win passengers, ease boredom, company rivalry, captain ego, or railroad competition, steamboat racing was a common sight on the

From the New York Herald.

Steamboat Accidents in the United States in 1852.

January 9th.—Boiler of Steamer Magnolia exploded at St. Simon's Island, Ga. 13 persons killed; 11 injured.

14th.—Boiler of Steamer George Washington explo'd near Grand Gulf. Miss. 16 lives loss; 10 persons injured.

14th.—Steamer Martha Washington, Memphis, Tenn. 5 lives lost.

33d.—Steamer Pitzer Miller's boiler exploded at the mouth of the White river. Seven persons killed.

25th.—Steamer De Witt Clinton struck a snag, near Memphis, Tennessee. Forty lives lost.

31st.—Steamer General Warren wrecked, at Astoria, Oregon. 40 lives lost.

February 14.—Steamer Caddo sunk, near New Orleans. Five lives lost.

29th.—Steam Tow Boat Mary Kingsland's boiler burst, below New Orleans. 5 lives lost; 3 persons injured.

March 26th.—Steamer Pocahontas collapsed her flues, near Memphis, Tenn. 8 lives lost; 18 persons severely scalded.

26th.—Steamer Independence wrecked, in Matagorda Bay. Texas. 7 lost.

April 3d.—Steamer Redstone's boiler exploded near Carrollton, La. 21 lives lost; 25 persons injured.

3d.—Steamer Glenence blew up at St. Louis. Number of lives lost unknown.

9th.—Steamer Saluda's boiler exploded at Lexington, Mo. 100 lives lost.

11th.—Steamer Pocahontas burnt near Choctaw Bend. 12 lives lost.

25th.—Steamer Prairie State collapsed her flues on the Illinois, killing and wounding twenty persons.

May 19th.—Steamer Pittsburg's cylinder heads broke, killing one and injuring 3 persons.

June 14th.—Steamer Forest City collapsed a flue at Cleveland. Three lives lost.

July 5th.—Steamer St. James' boiler exploded near New Orleans. 40 lives lost.

12th.—Propeller City of Oswego run into by another steamer near Cleveland, and sunk. 20 lives lost.

28th.—Steamer Henry Clay burnt near Yonkers, on the Hudson. About 80 lives lost, and 20 more or less injured.

THE MELANCHOLY RESULT IN FIGURES.

	NUMBER OF STEAMERS.	LIVES LOST.	PERSONS INJURED.
January · · · · · · ·	6	119	21
February · · · · ·	2	10	3
March · · · · · · ·	2	15	18
April · · · · · · · ·	5	143	35
May · · · · · · · · ·	1	1	3
June · · · · · · · · ·	1	3	
July · · · · · · · · ·	3	140	20
Total · · · · · ·	20	431	100

The numbers lost by the disaster to the Pitzer Miller and Glencoe, not being known, are not included in the foregoing list; but there can be little doubt that if added to the other cases which have been ascertained, the aggregate would amount to at least five hundred human beings sent prematurely to their account, with all their imperfections on their heads. We give this frightful table in order to draw the attention of members of Congress to the subject, in connection with the bill now before them.

The Eagle (Poughkeepsie), Saturday 14 August 1852.
Steamboat disasters in the United States were common, and 1852 was no exception.
By July there had been several.

Hudson River. In 1847, George Law's steamboat the *Oregon* won a race against Cornelius Vanderbilt's, *C. Vanderbilt* because *Oregon*'s crew resorted to burning furniture and boat fixtures after the coal supply was exhausted. Another notable race occurred between the *Hendrik Hudson* and the *Alida* in 1849 when both raced from Albany to New York City. Both boats left New York at 7:00 A.M. with the *Alida* reaching Albany at 2:55 P.M., only fifteen minutes before her competitor.

Boiler explosions were common, and notable wrecks became folklore. The *Swallow* was wrecked in 1845 during her race with the *Express* and the *Rochester* near Athens, New York. More than fifty people perished.[34]

In 1852, the Hudson River day boating season commenced on the spring morning of May 1. The *Reindeer* was running with the *Armenia* against her. The *Henry Clay* started its route a week later, but in mid-May was taken out of service for a number of weeks because she "broke her shaft." Once back in service, she continued in her place as an opposition boat. The *Francis Skiddy* was running on the river as well. That steamboat became a regular competitor to the *Alida* on the New York to Albany run. The *Henry Clay*, along with the *Armenia* and the *Francis Skiddy*, were listed as "Oppositon Day Boats" for the 7:00 A.M. run.[35]

The season commenced on the Hudson River with faster boats and river racing from the start. The weeks passed as quickly as the boats, and accidents happened on waterways around the country.[36]

The stage was set by July 28, 1852, for
DISASTER.

Change of Hour.

ON and after MONDAY, June 14th, 1852. MORNING BOAT for NEW YORK, landing at Milton, Newburgh, Cornwall, Cold Spring and Cozzen's Dock (West Point.) Fare 50 cents Meals served on board.

The Steamer ARMENIA, Captain J. P. SMITH, will leave Poughkeepsie every Morning at 6 o'clock; Newburgh at 6¼; Cornwall, 7; Cold Spring and Cozzens' at 7½ o'clock arriving in New York at 10½ o'clock. Sundays excepted.

Returning, will leave New York, at foot of Jay Street, every Afternoon at Four o'clock, landing at the above named landings, and arriving at Poughkeepsie from 8 to 8½ o'clock.
42

The Eagle (Poughkeepsie), Saturday 24 July 1852.

Chapter 2

Wednesday, July 28, 1852—An Ordinary Day

THE DAY began as usual at the river port of Albany, New York. Large and strategically situated on the western shores of the Hudson River, the port served for centuries as a final destination for boats making the 150-mile journey upriver from New York City. Like bookends, New York City and Albany each sat at opposite points and held between them the life flow of that great waterway, its lands, its people, and its boats.

Competition was fierce and riverboat agents were busying themselves, scurrying up and down the creaky wooden walkways of the docks. Running past heavy trunks and parcels that took up precious space, the ticket sellers yelled, pushed, and deceived their way to winning passengers for their boats. It was all part of the frenzied daily ritual.

Eager passengers, loaded down with luggage and dressed for travel, purchased their tickets from the agents and approached the gangways. For some travelers, the choice of which boat to take may have been a split-second decision, depending on which ticket runner approached them first. For others, the choice had been planned well in advance. On this day, by chance, the steamboats moored at the docks were the *Armenia* and the *Henry Clay*, the same reputable builder Thomas Collyer having built both. He was a member of the famous Collyer shipbuilding dynasty that collectively had operations spanning the globe from New York City, up the Hudson River, to the Great Lakes, and as far away as China.[1]

In 1847, Thomas Collyer built the *Armenia*. It was a majestic steamboat for the time. At 185 feet in length, the steamboat allowed for extensive side railings and ample seating for passengers to view the sights along the Hudson River. This also was true for the pilothouse situated a level above the main deck. It offered the pilot a bird's-eye view of the Hudson River.[2]

Taking up the midsection behind the pilothouse was the smoke pipe. The furnace room housed the iron boiler and engine that Henry R. Dunham & Company had built. Huge wooden waterwheels, whose rotating action moved the massive steamboat forward, flanked each side of the steamboat. The stern section of the *Armenia* held two decks for passenger seating. In the boat's interior was a dining room with a waitstaff ready to accommodate passengers with a midday meal.[3]

Like a marquis announcing a star, the boat's name, *Armenia*, was painted on the paddle boxes on both the port and starboard sides. The *Armenia* was truly a shining star on the river. The steamboat initially had been built for the shorter Peekskill route on the Hudson River, but it proved too fast a boat to be wasted on such short trips. The *Armenia* was later transferred to the New York City to Albany run where she set a speed record of seven hours and forty-two minutes.[4]

Captain Collyer's ownership of his prize *Armenia* was short-lived; he sold her to Captain Isaac Smith in 1849. Collyer went on to pursue the completion of his newest endeavor, the steamboat *Henry Clay*, launched in August 1851. At a length of over 198 feet, this steamboat was almost 15 feet longer than the *Armenia*. The smoke-pipe reaching upward to the sky accentuated the *Henry Clay*'s profile. Forward of the black column was the pilothouse, aft was the walking beam. The hurricane deck took up the remainder of the aft section. The promenade deck ran the entire length from bow to stern, an awning partially covering it. The *Henry Clay* was a showcase of a steamboat on the river and was advertised as "the new and swift steamer." It quickly earned a reputation as a fast boat and became a favorite with the traveling public. Both the *Henry Clay* and the *Armenia*, had a history of racing with their rivals on the Hudson River.[5]

On this Wednesday morning, by circumstance, these two steamboats, which rival lines now owned, were docked at Albany and scheduled for the Albany to New York City run. To learn the *Armenia* was on this route was a surprise to many. As recent as July 24, a newspaper ad stated that the *Armenia* was scheduled for the Poughkeepsie to New York City route with a departure at 6:00 A.M. every morning, and arrival in New York City at 10:00 A.M. In a total change from its advertised schedule, the *Armenia* was now docked in Albany as the replacement boat for the steamboat *Reindeer*, which was undergoing repairs.[6]

The *Reindeer*, its hull also built by Thomas Collyer, was itself quite famous, noteworthy for transporting Jenny Lind, a popular singer of the time, to Albany. Famous also for its speed, the *Reindeer* had many rivals. The *Henry Clay* had tried before but had not succeeded in outracing her. Interest would have been very high if the *Reindeer* was on its scheduled run today. A match between the two boats would have been inevitable.[7]

As the passengers boarded, the crews of both steamboats busied themselves preparing for departure. The firemen shoveled black coal and stoked up the furnace fires. The engineers readied the equipment for the day's trip and the pilots, up in the pilothouse, prepared to navigate their respective boats. The cooks and servants made the midday meal in the kitchen below deck, while on deck, the crews, muscular from their work of loading luggage and cargo, moved quickly to avoid any delay in the scheduled departure. The time was nearing 7:00 A.M., and ticket agents for the two steamboats were madly attempting to snatch each last remaining passenger from the docks. As the last few travelers were hurried on board, they were unaware that the normal captain of each boat was indisposed, both for different reasons.

Two days before, on Monday, William Radford, Esq. of Radford & Co., owner of a one-fourth share of the *Henry Clay* was in his New York City office. He had learned that the *Armenia*, not the *Reindeer*, was scheduled to run the same trip as his *Henry Clay*. The boats were scheduled to depart from New York City on Tuesday for travel to Albany. After an overnight stay in Albany, the two boats were scheduled for a return trip back to New York City on Wednesday. Radford knew that the *Armenia* and the *Henry Clay* were fierce rivals, and he sensed possible trouble between both crews.[8]

Hoping to prevent the two steamboats from running together on the same route, Radford spoke to Captain Isaac P. Smith, the owner of the *Armenia*. He asked Smith to cancel the *Armenia* as the replacement boat for the *Reindeer*. The request was an impossible one. Smith had chartered his *Armenia* to Mr. Bishop of Bishop & Co. of Beaver Street in New York City. Contractual agreement obligated the *Armenia* to run.[9]

Radford, still trying to prevent a confrontation on the river between the two boats, suggested to Captain Smith, "Won't you go with me to Mr. Bishop, and we will try and prevent it." Together, the two men met with Bishop, who had subscribed the boat. Radford asked Bishop to keep the *Armenia* on the Poughkeepsie run for Tuesday and Wednesday. In desperation, Radford offered to give Bishop half of the *Henry Clay's* profits for those two days as an incentive to keep the *Armenia* off the Albany route.[10]

Bishop would have none of it and refused Radford's offer with an indignant response saying it would, "derange his business." The meeting was not going well for Radford. As he and Smith started to leave, Smith remarked, "Well, Mr. Bishop, if you insist on my boat running to Albany, she shall not race." To that incisive comment, Mr. Bishop snapped, "I do not wish her to race."[11]

Bishop's terse comment allowed for more discussion among the men, as apparently none of the parties wanted a race between their respective boats. In the meantime, Thomas Collyer had arrived. Collyer's participation in the meeting was more than just as the builder of the two boats. He owned a majority share of the *Henry Clay*, a five-eighths interest.[12]

The discussions between the men carried on into the evening, and by the next morning, they finally struck a deal. Radford, Bishop, Captain Smith, and Collyer all agreed that there would be no racing between the *Armenia* and the *Henry Clay*. Captain Smith also agreed that the *Henry Clay* would lead in front of the *Armenia* on the Tuesday run to Albany and again on the return trip to New York City on Wednesday.[13]

On Tuesday morning, Radford and Collyer traveled together north on the *Henry Clay* from New York City as far as Newburgh. The *Armenia* steamed along the same route. So far there were no problems with the boats running together. During the trip, Radford noticed that the *Henry Clay*'s commander, Captain John F. Tallman, who happened to hold a one-eighth interest in the boat as well, was suffering from some sort of illness. Since Radford had planned to get off at Newburgh, he suggested that Collyer continue with the *Henry Clay* all the way to Albany and then on the following day for the return trip back to New York City. Collyer agreed to the suggestion and stayed on board the *Henry Clay* to keep an eye on things, especially to make sure the officers of the *Armenia* kept with the deal. The two boats continued their trip up the Hudson River to Albany and finished the day without incident. The agreement had been upheld and trouble avoided.[14]

The sun broke through in the early hours of the next morning as Thomas Collyer stood on the docks waiting to embark on his return trip to New York City on the *Henry Clay*. It was Wednesday, July 28, 1852, a "fine, clear morning." Collyer knew that Captain Tallman was still quite sick. Normal protocol called for the commander or captain of a boat to give all the orders, but Tallman was obviously not up to the task. That being the case, the ship's clerk may have the authority to act as second captain. The duty would fall to the young James L. Jessup from Newburgh. However, the lines in the chain of command were somewhat clouded because Collyer, the owner of the boat, was on board.[15]

Owner William Radford had hired most of the officers on the *Henry Clay*. He believed in giving each of the officers the responsibility to perform their own duties properly in order to provide for the safe operation of the boat. He also gave them the directive to carry out requests of the captain when reasonable. But today, Radford was not on the boat for the Albany to New York City run; he departed at Newburgh the day before.[16]

Owner Isaac P. Smith normally commanded the *Armenia*. However, Smith had left the boat without explanation, and his post remained vacant for this day's trip. Thus, by default, the *Armenia* was left in the hands of Mr. Bishop, the subscriber of the boat. As the situation played out this fateful July morning, the two captains who usually commanded these steamboats were not at their posts. Thirty-six-yearold captain and owner Isaac Smith was not on board the *Armenia* at all. Captain and minority owner John Tallman, although present on the *Henry Clay*, was unable to command. Fate had stepped in and removed both captains from their designated duties. Instead, Mr. Bishop was on board the *Armenia* and Captain Collyer was on the *Henry Clay*.[17]

With or without a captain on duty, the boats were prepared for the Wednesday morning departure. The docks remained busy and noisy as ticket agents for the *Henry Clay* tried heartily to dissuade passengers from taking the rival boat. Jessup, the *Henry Clay*'s clerk was occupied selling his tickets as Collyer watched the hundreds of passengers walking up the gangplank. Among them was Adam Murray, who paid the fifty cents per passenger fare and boarded with his wife and their year-old son, John.[18]

Young Henrietta Traux, with her four-year-old little girl, Mary, boarded with the anticipation that her husband would be waiting at the docks in New York City to meet her later in the day. She had written a letter to him earlier about her planned trip home on Wednesday. The little family had previously lived in Schenectady, and the young wife stayed behind to sell the old furniture. That being done, she was on her way to rejoin her husband in their new home in Brooklyn. Also planning to meet her husband in New York City was Mrs. John W. Simons traveling with her two small children and their young nurse, Elizabeth Shanckey.[19]

John Dike, Esq had his niece, the somewhat frail Maria Hawthorne, with him. Returning from a trip to the spa at the Columbian Hotel in Saratoga Springs, they planned to travel back to Massachusetts to visit her brother, the writer Nathaniel Hawthorne. The pair of travelers decided to take the *Henry Clay* down the river to enjoy the scenery, rather than travel by train or overland by carriage.[20]

At the time, overland travel was comparatively less comfortable than what the steamboat had to offer. Trips by land over bumpy and often muddy roads could be a trying and dirty affair. They provided an exhausting mode of transportation that was at times a necessity. To reach the docks this morning, several passengers had arrived by horse-drawn stagecoach from the upriver city of Troy. One colorful character to step off of the stagecoach was self-described as "a citizen of the world"who had learned from life by embracing several careers and traveling about the country.[21]

This was Lloyd Minturn of Burlington, Vermont. He had previous business interests in New York City related to "cotton presses"and his adventures had taken him to places like Charleston and Savannah, up north to Rhode Island, and also to the west coast in California, where he was employed as an auctioneer. Upon learning the fast steamboat *Reindeer* was not running, Minturn decided to board the *Henry Clay* "believing her to be the better boat."[22]

As Minturn walked up the gangplank, there was much discussion around the docks. The crews were talking among themselves about a possible race. The *Armenia* and the *Henry Clay* were known racers, and both were fairly new boats.

As the talk continued, the crews became more excited. They moved more quickly with every word spoken. Perhaps it was just talk, talk that made the time pass by, talk that made their mundane jobs more interesting, or perhaps the talk was real and they were hoping to race.[23]

This talk was cause for some passengers to change their minds. Mr. John E. Cubbage of Hoboken, New Jersey, was on the docks when he heard the noisy chatter. He had first planned to take the *Armenia*, but upon noticing some excitement among the members of the crew and hearing talk on the docks about a race between the two boats, he rethought his decision. For his choice, Cubbage pondered not the faster, the more likely winning boat, but the stronger, safer boat. He chose the *Henry Clay*.[24]

The boarding of the boats was complete. Edward was there too, having arrived earlier than most passengers. He would spend his day on the *Henry Clay*, but not as a paying traveler whose day would be filled with plans of arrivals, appointments, and family reunions. For Edward, this Wednesday was a workday, and he set to his assigned duties standing at his post looking high above the bow of the famous *Henry Clay*. It was about 7:00 A.M. and the *Henry Clay* cast off. It was he, Edward Hubbard, who would guide the massive boat away from the docks into the channels of the Hudson River. He was the pilot.[25]

As the boat began its 150- mile journey, hundreds of passengers moved about the decks finding places to sit. Some decided to stand along the side rails to enjoy the scenic views of the Hudson. James Gilson, a postmaster from Clinton County, strolled to the barbershop for a shave. The "citizen of the world," Lloyd Minturn,

The Hudson River near Catskill with the Catskill Mountains to the west.

proceeded forward on the main deck and stayed there for most of the trip. At the bar, Mr. Way, from Wellsville, Ohio, decidedly settled into his spot. He chatted with the barkeeper, Mr. Eagan, who offered him a wager that the *Henry Clay* would arrive in New York City twenty minutes before the *Armenia*.[26]

The summer day was clear and warm with scarcely a cloud in the sky to block the hot sun. The two steamboats passed miles of bucolic countryside. Forests of willows and ash trees served as a backdrop to the river valley's scenery. They passed marshes along the shoreline with islands and sand bars visible in the waters. Other boats dotted the waterways, some with sails, scurrying to their own destinations, while the two steamboats headed south.[27]

On deck, John R. Harris was conversing with Thomas Collyer when Harris questioned, "I thought the *Henry Clay* was a fast boat." Looking about, pointing out landmarks, Collier dryly replied to him, "We are not going very fast." Then Harris responded, "The *Armenia* will probably pass us." Collyer casually added, "She won't pass us, I guess."[28]

Both boats cruised along in full sight of each other. The *Henry Clay* made a landing at Coxsackie, and then continued to travel toward its next stop at Hudson. It was about 9:00 A.M. when the *Henry Clay* arrived there first. The *Armenia* did not make a landing but sped past and down into the western channel to take the lead position heading toward the next landing at Catskill.[29]

Quickly the *Henry Clay*'s crew whisked their new fares at Hudson on board. The impatient crew hurried on board Charles Goodrich, a manufacturer from Stockbridge, Massachusetts, elderly Stephen Allen, a former mayor of New York City, and attorney Isaac Dayton. The new passengers made their way around the decks of the steamboat to find suitable seating. Goodrich found himself a seat on the promenade deck. Dayton proceeded to the aft of the boat where he would remain for most of the trip. The distinguished Allen would occupy himself by speaking with various passengers during the day.[30]

This stop took merely three to four minutes before the *Henry Clay* was on its way down the east channel of the river in chase of its rival, the *Armenia*. For several miles along the east side of the river, both steamboats would pass what was known as "Millionaire's Row." In those days, it spanned as far south as Hyde Park and was named for all the mansions and estates that lined that side of the river. For steamboat passengers, the quiet, serene beauty of the landscape and the view of numerous lovely homes were interrupted only by the roaring of the steamboat's engine. Such reminders of industrial age machinery were enhanced as one looked to the west across the river to see the river businesses like cement plants, brickyards, and ice cutting operations. It was a stark contrast to the elegant estates on the east shore.[31]

Nearing Catskill, the *Henry Clay* headed west toward the landing. Passengers may glimpse a view of the Catskill Mountains, rising over three thousand feet above the Hudson Valley. Nestled before it, by the river's west shore, was Catskill, a settlement about thirty miles south of Albany and itself a fairly sizeable place by the late 1840s. The town counted about three thousand citizens and four hundred homes. It had all the trappings of a significant river town for its time: a courthouse, banks, a jail, churches, and of course, its steamboat dock.[32]

Perched up in the mountains, two thousand feet above was the majestic grand dame of hotels, the Catskill Mountain House. The Greek revival hotel had its humble beginnings a quarter century before. Over the years, it was transformed into a splendid hotel attracting many a holiday seeker wishing to view the purple-blue mists of the Catskill Mountains and enjoy the clear mountain air during the summer months.[33]

Earlier, several of its guests had departed the hotel and journeyed the twelve miles by stagecoach to the steamboat landing, where the *Armenia* had already arrived. Among the group was E. M. Livermore, the son of the Honorable Isaac Livermore of Boston, accompanied by his wife and her sister. They boarded the waiting *Armenia*; the *Henry Clay* had not yet arrived.[34]

After the *Henry Clay* reached Catskill Landing, ticket agents and runners frantically tried to hurry the unsuspecting passengers on board. Paying his twenty-five cent fare to New York City, Samuel W. D. Cook of Durham, in Greene County, came on board. His daughter and son-in-law, Mr. and Mrs. William M. Ray of Cincinnati, and their young son and daughter were with him. Mr. Cook knew Captain Tallman and asked a member of the crew if he would get a chance to see him. Cook was informed of Tallman's illness, so the anticipated meeting would not happen.[35]

Jacob J. Speed, a lawyer from Baltimore, boarded the steamboat in the company of Mrs. Ann Hill and her sister Eliza Smith. Mrs. Hill, the widow of David Hill, was very prominent in Philadelphia society. J. J. Speed had been traveling about New York for some time. After a stay at the Irving House in New York City a few days before, he departed for Ithaca. On this day, he was returning back to New York City.[36]

Carrying a letter from her sister, Emeline E. Milligan boarded at Catskill with her mother, Mrs. Hester Tomkins. They had spent several days at Catskill and were returning home to New York City. Emeline's husband was in the city and would be quite surprised at her early arrival home. Emeline had not written to him about her plans to leave Catskill sooner than expected to return home.[37]

With the boarding complete, the *Henry Clay* pushed off from the Catskill dock and sped full steam after the *Armenia*. Morale of the crew suddenly turned high. The elated crew went about its work as the steamboat departed from the docks with one crew-member defiantly remarking of the *Armenia*, "We beat her after all; we took on twenty two, she took only fifteen."[38]

The *Henry Clay* charged in hot pursuit as its recently overhauled powerful

Belknap & Cunningham boilers and engines did their work. The steamboat had been out for repairs for a few weeks early in the season for a broken shaft, but that appeared to not affect its current performance. John Germain, the engineer, kept the fires burning with the help of his assistant engineer Charles Merritt and the furnace crew. It was a difficult job requiring strength and endurance. The heat of the furnace fires coupled with the hot summer weather caused the engine room to become a sweltering box in which the crew toiled. The more fuel consumed, the more Lackawanna coal was fed into the furnace's hungry mouth by the coal blackened, sweating furnace crew.[39]

To prevent fires, the furnace bottom was built with two plates housing water between them. The crew stored fifteen to perhaps twenty buckets of water on the hurricane deck in case a fire flared up. Standard practice meant orders to the crew for cleaning out the spent ashes and hot cinders from the fuel box. Hot smoldering waste was shoveled onto sheets of iron located near the furnace. From there, the burning embers were dumped overboard through a nearby porthole into the river. The waters hissed back in response to the heated assault with smoky vapors that waves of cool water smacking the side of the steamboat's hull quickly erased.[40]

The engine room was an inferno of heat, much too hot for a passenger to venture near for too long. Only the curious few would occasionally stop to look in for a moment then quickly move away to the cooler surroundings on deck. Passenger John Cubbage, while roaming about the decks, felt some strong heat coming from the machinery room and smoke pipe. He also viewed pieces of coal spewing from the smoke pipe and landing in spots, drop by drop, onto the promenade deck. Intermittent showers of hot coals quickly forced several surprised passengers to move from their seats on the deck to avoid being hit by the falling embers.[41]

As the *Henry Clay* drew nearer to Clermont Manor on the east shore, these burning embers on deck served as a reminder of the day the British burned to the ground this patriot home of Chancellor Robert Livingston. Clermont was one of several established manors that, for good or bad, served to populate the lands along the Hudson River with Europeans for almost two centuries. A colonial society and feudal system were established providing a means of livelihood, however grand or meager, for the colonists. Manor lords became powerful and wealthy, sometimes even greedy, a quasinobility. Until the system finally broke up in the 1840s, the resident workers paid for the right to work the manor lands and labored to scarcely support their own families while making the manor lords richer. Hard work was a fact of life along the Hudson River, and just as the peasant workers had labored for decades before, so did the furnace crew on the *Henry Clay* to keep the fires going strong.[42]

On deck, a passenger named John Spencer had his ticket in hand and was readying himself to get off at Bristol Landing. However, to his surprise and annoyance, the *Henry Clay* bypassed Bristol completely and did not make the scheduled stop. Looking to shore, Spencer could see that the *Armenia* was at the landing. He was visibly annoyed that he chose to board the *Henry Clay* instead of the *Armenia*. Spencer decided that he would go all the way to New York City. His purpose—sue the company for missing the scheduled stop for which he had purchased a ticket.[43]

Skipping landings was normal for steamboat travel, especially if a race was involved. The *Henry Clay* passed ahead of the *Armenia*, although the bold move stranded passengers. Minturn noticed that "many drinks were taken at the bar, congratulatory of the success of the *Henry Clay*, by the hands onboard." Excitement among the crew ran high. Collyer walked back and forth to the pilothouse, intermittently returning to Harris and Ridder to talk.[44]

The crew of the *Armenia*, seeing their rival steam pass them, quickly took their steamboat away from the Bristol dock. The two steamboats sped toward Tivoli and then downriver, each alternating the lead. For some time they traveled side-by-side. The *Henry Clay*, in the east channel moved closer and closer to the *Armenia* in the west channel. The crews of each boat jockeyed to be the first to arrive at Kingston Landing.[45]

The *Armenia* held the advantage because it was traveling in the west channel and therefore was closer to the landing. Adding to the scene was a slower moving sloop sailing nearby. The *Henry Clay* moved farther east past the sloop. Then, without a moment's notice, the *Henry Clay* quickly maneuvered west, heading toward Kingston Landing. Samuel Cook, a passenger on the *Henry Clay*, noticed a man come from the wheelhouse with a fender in his hands. When the order was given, the man threw it over the side to protect the ship's hull.[46]

Fears of impending disaster spread among the passengers of the *Henry Clay*. Many had become frightened about the speed at which the *Henry Clay* was traveling. Women withdrew to inside rooms and salons to avoid watching what they perceived as something disastrous. The *Henry Clay*'s engines worked hard as the boat pushed farther to the west toward the landing. The *Henry Clay* moved perilously close to the *Armenia* and cut across its path. Impact! The passengers on the hurricane deck of the *Henry Clay* were ordered to move to the "larboard side" of the boat.[47]

Hysteria broke out on the *Henry Clay*. Some women cried, others fainted. Husbands tried to calm their wives and children. Anxious passengers paced about. Several became angry and vented their antagonism toward the officers. Adam Murray approached the ship's clerk, Jessup, saying the women were frightened. Jessup replied that "every officer on board valued his life as much as any gentleman or lady on board." Jessup also commented that he "wished people would mind their own business."[48]

Isaac McDaniels, who had boarded at Albany with his wife and daughter, had been at the wheelhouse and clearly saw the *Henry Clay* crowd the *Armenia* in the middle of the river. He aired his protest to the person that he thought was the captain, but who actually may have been Jessup. Getting no satisfaction, McDaniels "proposed to call an indignation meeting on board, and publish him in the New York papers for jeopardizing the lives of so many passengers."[49]

Several men, including McDaniels, banded together to confront the ship's crew. Members of the crew immediately rebuffed their statements of concern and insisted that the boat was under full control and in no danger. Minturn, while at the bar, commented that the collision of the two boats was "rascally." The barkeeper responded with, "Damn her, let her keep out of our way then."[50]

Thomas Collyer quickly milled about attempting to calm passengers' jittered nerves. He believed that the boat was in no danger and that the *Henry Clay* was not running at excessive or dangerous speeds. Also, Collyer acted as if the authority on the boat was in his hands. Lloyd Minturn witnessed that Collyer "took more charge of the boat than any other person."[51]

One gentleman caught Collyer's arm and excitedly said, "This should be stopped, Sir." John Gourlie, a passenger who had boarded at Albany, added his own annoyed comment, "This is an outrageous business." Collyer's reply was repeatedly, "There is no danger." Collyer's remarks, and that of the crew, who echoed the same indifferent response, appeased few of the concerned travelers. One Canadian gentleman angrily made a suggestion to "throw the captain overboard, if he did not cease racing."[52]

Collyer, a seasoned river boatman, had seen it all. He was accustomed to the speed of the steamboats, competitive racing, near collisions, or whatever incidents may occur on the river. He was hardened to river life. Skittish passengers saw it differently. The variance in opinions made it unclear what really had happened and what actual danger was presented to the passengers. Some said the *Henry Clay* had moved westward in front of the *Armenia* purposely to arrive at Kingston Landing first. Others said it was necessary to avoid the suction resulting from the proximity to the *Armenia*. Many passengers believed that the two boats collided or that the *Armenia* was pushed aground and brought to a complete stop. Later, there were reports that the officers of the *Armenia* saw damage done to the guard.[53]

Following the encounter before Kingston Landing, the two steamboats went their separate ways. The *Armenia* had blown off steam and fell back. The *Henry Clay* steamed past the *Armenia* toward Kingston Landing to pick up waiting travelers. Kinston Landing was one of three options for boarding a steamboat from Kingston. Rondout Landing was the bigger and more popular landing, especially for night boats. But its location on Rondout Creek made it too cumbersome for the day boats wishing to keep up their speed, especially if a race was involved.

**The *Henry Clay* traveled south after leaving Poughkeepsie.
The view of the river is south from Poughkeepsie.**

There was a ferry available for carrying passengers across the river to Rhinecliff for boarding a steamboat from there. Or there was a primitive dock at Kingston Landing. This landing was not reliable because the access road crossed a swamp. However, the weather was favorable, making it possible for passengers to board at Kingston Landing. Among them was Mrs. Anthony (Mary Ann) Robinson who was with her daughter Isabella.[54]

The *Henry Clay* was on its way downriver when the *Armenia* arrived at Kingston Landing. The collision rattled the nerves of many of the passengers on both steamboats. Disembarking the *Armenia* at Kingston Landing were E. M. Livermore and his party. A month before, Livermore had been traveling on the *Reindeer* when it too had a scrape with the *Henry Clay*. The Livermore's "went ashore at Kingston, crossed to Rhinebeck, and after waiting there an hour and three quarters, took the cars for New York."[55]

Meanwhile, still ahead of the rival boat and still keeping a strong steam, the *Henry Clay* pressed forward. About two or three miles above Hyde Park, the *Henry Clay* passed by the steamboat *Alida* as she was heading north. The *Alida* was an opposition boat too and previously had raced the *Henry Clay*. That morning, the *Alida* left New York City at 7:00 A.M. heading to Albany. Here, about halfway in their respective trips, the two rivals met, but passed each other by as both were traveling in opposite directions.[56]

The next stop for the *Henry Clay* was Poughkeepsie, a village on the east side of the river. Here, the furnace crew changed shifts, the true halfway point for the day's trip to New York City. Among the passengers that boarded at Poughkeepsie were Isaac D. Sands of New York, his wife, and two children. Sixteen-year-old

Phoebe Ann Jordan was making the trip to New York City with her aunt and uncle, Mr. and Mrs. Jacob Schoonmaker. Among those leaving the steamboat was Mrs. John Simons, who had boarded with her children and nurse at Albany. She sent her two small children in the care of their nurse to continue on the *Henry Clay* to meet up with the children's father in New York City.[57]

Poughkeepsie, perched on a hill above the river edge, was a large industrious community with stores, manufacturing, schools, newspapers, and other businesses available to accommodate its ten thousand residents. Here, the steamboat easily picked up about one hundred additional passengers; no question that this stop was a prize for passenger fare. The *Henry Clay* hastily departed Poughkeepsie and soon moved into the waters of Newburgh Bay.[58]

**The Hudson Highlands tower over each side of the Hudson
as the river narrows south of the expansive Newburgh Bay.**

As the steamboat traveled west across the river toward Newburg Landing, it approached a vast expanse of water that widened to more than a mile and extended eight miles north to south. The mountains of the Hudson Highlands were to the south on each side of the river. To the west was Newburgh, spreading uphill from the wharf area and home to six thousand residents. The view from the steamboat was a spectacular sight with the expansive panorama of water and sky set amidst the sprawling hills and vast lands of the Mid-Hudson region.[59]

By the time the *Henry Clay* docked at Newburgh, it was successful in putting ten minutes between it and the *Armenia*. There was much flurry at Newburgh Landing and ticket agents were running along with tales of the day's events. Excited cheers could be heard from the crew. Some cheered in chorus, "Harry of the West." This nickname referred to the great American statesman, Henry Clay, for whom the steamboat was named. Sadly, the nation had recently mourned his death; he had died the month before.[60]

It was after noon when stately Andrew Jackson Downing, a distinguished landscape architect and the editor of the *Horticulturist* magazine stepped on board. With him was his wife Caroline, her mother, Mrs. Peter DeWint of Fishkill, a family friend, Mrs. Matilda Wadsworth, and Frank and Mary C. DeWint. The Downings were traveling to Newport, Rhode Island. Downing had projects there, the "Marine Villa" and the Daniel Parish Residence.[61]

No matter how grand these villas, Downing's real prize was something much larger. Two years before, he had received an appointment to design the landscaping for the grounds between the White House and the Capital buildings in Washington D.C. The project also included the grounds of the Smithsonian Institution. Downing had been at work planning those designs for the prestigious national project.[62]

Among the other passengers that boarded at Newburgh were the district attorney of Lancaster County, Pennsylvania, John L. Thompson, along with his wife, three children, and their nurse. They had arrived at Newburgh earlier on the new steamboat *Francis Skiddy*. Local farmer George Crist watched his brother, the attorney Abraham Crist, Esq. from Brooklyn board the *Henry Clay*. He was traveling with Mr. and Mrs. L. G. Spring. Elmore Thompson, a merchant from New York City, came on board with his wife, three-month-old daughter, Jennie B. and their servant Eliza. When James F. DePeyster boarded, he met up with John Gourlie, who had been on the boat since Albany.[63]

At Newburgh Landing, the *Henry Clay* easily picked up another eighty or more passengers. So popular was the boat that the ticket agents were able to sell fares for one shilling. However, by this stop, the *Henry Clay* was becoming crowded. Passengers had the option of waiting for the *Armenia*, which was a bargain at this point, as the *Armenia*, which lagged behind the *Henry Clay*, could sell its tickets for just sixpence.[64]

Some passengers on the boat's deck could see a woman standing in the pilothouse of the *Henry Clay*. She was the second pilot's wife, Mrs. Elmendorf, who was accompanying her husband on the trip to New York City. It was common in the day that wives or even entire families of boatmen travel along on the river. Also common, passengers were allowed to visit the pilothouse . Today, they could watch Edward Hubbard at the ship's wheel as he turned the *Henry Clay* from Newburgh and headed south on the river. The huge steamship soon passed by the village where Hubbard and his wife made their home.[65]

Near West Point, the Hudson River narrowed into a channel just fourteen hundred feet across. The Hudson Highlands appeared even higher from such a close vantage point. Below was the river's mud bottom, reaching to depths of two hundred feet. The steamboat kept up its speed through this ominous section of high hills and deep waters without any rival boat in sight. Dwarfed by the mountains protruding upward from each side of the river, it steamed through the turbulent waters between Constitution Island and West Point. This length was known as the "World's End,"a deep valley with water churning in the shadows of the dark mountains of granite.[66]

Emerging from the turbulence of the "World's End," the afternoon sun warmed the decks of the *Henry Clay*. A strong southerly breeze came up and, in action with the tides, created rough water under the steamboat that would last for the remainder of this trip.[67]

Standing one hundred eighty feet above the Hudson at Buttermilk Falls was Cozzens' Hotel. Below, at the river's edge was its landing, where passengers waited for the *Henry Clay* to stop. The crew hurried the passengers on board once again. Professor Jacob W. Bailey, a former graduate and now an instructor at the West Point Military Academy, boarded with his wife, Maria, their daughter, Maria W., and their nine-year-old son, "Whitty." Young sixteen-year-old Maria, who they affectionately called, "Kitty," had been feeling poorly. Her parents thought that some time spent in saltwater air might help to improve her health, so they were off to visit friends on Long Island. Boarding also were two sisters, Harriet T. Kinsley with her sister Eliza and Dr. Phineas Wells, a Brooklyn physician.[68]

As was custom for these Albany to New York runs, dinner was served in the interior dining room in early afternoon. After taking the earlier seating for the meal, Doctor Wells retreated to the aft of the promenade deck for the remainder of the trip. He watched in surprise as hot embers dropped from the smokestacks and fell through or burned holes in the awning. When the crew moved the awning to shade passengers from the afternoon sun, pieces of hot coal began to fall about. Drop by drop , one or two at a time, or several at once, fell onto the deck, smacking onto chairs, the waiting passengers, and luggage. The tiny hot meteors scattered, "making a noise like peas" as they hit their targets. By this time, there were perhaps five hundred passengers on board, occupying almost

Meteorological Table from *The Eagle* (Poughkeepsie), Saturday, 31 July 1852

The July weather was hot with temperatures reaching into the eighties by 28 July 1852.

METEOROLOGICAL TABLE, by Mercer & Co. 267 Main street.			
1852.	6 A.M.	12 P.M.	3 P.M.	6 P.M.
July 26th.	74 deg.	74 deg.	74 deg.	75 deg.
" 27th.	69 "	78 "	84 "	79 "
" 28th.	67 "	80 "	85 "	82 "
" 29th.	70 "	85 "	90 "	86 "

**After Yonkers, the *Henry Clay* traveled south toward
New York City with the Palisades to the west.**

every available chair in the lounges and on deck. Men used newspapers or tilted
the stools to whisk off the coals from the few remaining empty seats that were
available.[69]

The *Henry Clay* was far ahead of the *Armenia*, keeping a distance of about
three or four miles between them. If there was racing that day, it had evidently
finished by this time. Stacy Bancroft, who had boarded at Albany with his wife,
believed that the racing had ceased by the time of the dinner service. What caused
the *Armenia* to fall back? Perhaps the *Armenia*'s crew or Mr. Bishop had tired of
the pacing. Two days before, Mr. Bishop had agreed not to race the *Armenia* and
perhaps he decided to allow the *Henry Clay* the lead to avoid any further con-
frontations like the one that occurred near Kingston. Mr. Bishop was not an owner
of the *Armenia*, simply a subscriber. Perhaps he did not want to risk further damage to a boat of which he did not have a monetary interest. Maybe he did not want
to risk passenger safety. As a businessman, it would not bode well for him in the
headlines if he damaged either the boat or his passengers for the sake of a frivo-
lous race. Or was it something else?[70]

What drove Collyer of the *Henry Clay*? Collyer was in effect the commander
for the day's run, although it could be speculated that Jessup also may have had
some authority on board. Collyer was the builder of the *Henry Clay* and a majority owner. He too had agreed not to race, but perhaps he had some other plan,
especially since the *Armenia* sped out into the lead earlier in the trip. Collyer had
a connection with the *Armenia*, having built the boat in 1847, but then selling her
in 1849. Perhaps he harbored some resentment or anger about the sale. Perhaps
he needed to prove to himself or to others that the *Henry Clay* was the better of
the two boats. Perhaps he wanted to win the race or set a new speed record to
prove his *Henry Clay* was superior. Collyer was accustomed to both racing and

speed. He may have believed the events of the day were nothing unusual. After all, everything that happened thus far was normal for riverboat travel.[71]

As the passengers enjoyed the midday meal service, the *Henry Clay* steamed forward, ensuring its lead far ahead of the *Armenia*. By this time, the heat of the summer day was at its hottest. Meteorological information reported the 3:00 P.M. temperature that afternoon reached eighty-five degrees. Coupled with the heat generated from the *Henry Clay's* boiler, the wood surrounding the engine room had become hot. Lloyd Minturn was at the pilothouse after dinner and then left the nearby area because "the heat was very uncomfortable."[72]

John Thompson strolled about on deck for a smoke after dining with his family, when he noticed the deck was straining, perhaps groaning under pressure of some sort. The engine was working hard, heaving from the strain of over seven hours of relentless work. While passing the engine room, he commented to the engineer, "I suppose you have a good head of steam on" and somewhat forebodingly remarked, "I hope you will not blow us all out of the water." The engineer, John Germain, became rather cross from this unsolicited remark and replied, "I care as much for my own life as anybody." Thompson turned and prayerfully responded, "I trust in God you do." He then walked away to return to his family waiting near the ladies' cabin, while the crew continued to keep the *Henry Clay* running strong.[73]

The *Henry Clay* left the Hudson Highlands behind as it steamed through the widened river at Peekskill Bay. The steamboat followed the bend to the southwest and through the narrowed section at Verplanck Point. Reaching the Hudson's widest expanse at Haverstraw Bay, a three-mile width, the steamboat passed Van Cortlandt Manor, whose lands had belonged to one of the grand manors of the Hudson Valley's feudal history. The Van Cortlandt Manor House at Croton-on-Hudson is a reminder of the eighty-six-thousand- acre estate that the patriot Van Cortlandt family had owned.[74]

Passengers were close enough to see the solid rock formations of the Palisades come into full view on the New Jersey side of the river. Native Americans called the Palisades "Weehawken," meaning "rows of trees." Its trap rock made a home to quarries since the time of the Dutch. Icehouses along the shores indicated the river's thriving ice business and illicit memory of the cold of a Hudson River valley winter in such contrast to the summer heat on the boat this summer afternoon.[75]

Steaming into the Tappan Zee, the *Henry Clay* passed Tarrytown, where the river widened to two miles across. The steamboat followed along the Palisades for the remainder of the day's journey, but traveled down the middle of the river to avoid the shallow water at the river edges. Still the *Henry Clay* journeyed alone, as the *Armenia* was far behind.[76]

After finishing his dinner, the Honorable Stephen Allen retired to the hurricane deck where he sat with several gentlemen in polite conversation. The delicate Maria Hawthorne returned to her room to read *Pilgrim's Progress,* while her uncle remained on deck. Isaac McDaniels had gone with his little girl to have her nap, while his wife stayed in the ladies' saloon. Isaac Dayton was conversing with Mr. Crist. Those on board, satisfied by a midday meal were looking forward to their arrival at New York City, only sixteen miles downriver. Their thoughts went to home, family reunions, business exchanges, and evening plans.[77]

The *Henry Clay* steamed toward Riverdale, two and a half miles south of Yonkers. The furnace crew was hard at work, with each spade full of the black Pennsylvania fuel that was fed into the hard worked furnace. One of the crew members climbed up the ladder from the furnace room to the deck to cool off, while the other, Joseph Prarie, descended the ladder to the furnace room. It was shortly before 3:00 P.M.[78]

On deck, during the last few minutes of the day's journey, passengers by the side rails enjoyed the view of the Palisades on the west shore. Or, like John Gourlie sitting with his feet resting through the guardrails, they enjoyed the sight of the lovely estates and mansions that lined the river's east shore. The blue granite, gothic-style home of famed Shakespearean actor Edwin Forrest came into view high on a hill of the east shore.[79]

For the day's journey, it was a time of relative calm and anticipation for the travelers who occupied themselves in quiet whispers of chatter, a calmness to be broken suddenly by one simple word that rose loudly above the voices of intimate conversation. That word was

"FIRE!"[80]

Chapter 3

Fire at Riverdale

ON THE *HENRY CLAY*, John Thompson had completed his walk by the engine room and returned to his wife and two children situated near the ladies' cabin. He had no idea what was happening behind him. The children's nurse was attending the baby in the cabin. As Thompson looked upon his wife and children, the young nurse's eyes caught something in a distance. Unexpectedly, she exclaimed, "My God the boat is on fire!"[1]

Confusion, cries, and screams for help replaced the relaxed quiet atmosphere that was present only a few moments before. Passengers and crew alike frantically began moving amid chaos. Since the fire's origin was in the center of the boat people scurried away from the blazes to somewhere safe. Above the sounds of the hectic scene could be heard a loud order directed to the passengers, "Go aft." Listening, hundreds of passengers pushed each other and crowded their way to the stern section of the burning steamboat to where they believed they would be out of harm's way. Among them were John Thompson and his family.[2]

The smoke and ensuing flames roared from the engine room, where the fire hungrily consumed everything that surrounded it. Dry wood burned like tinder while the fires leaped up to reach the canvas canopies over deck. As the flaming fury rose upward, the crew and Captain Tallman grabbed buckets of water and threw them onto the unremitting flames. Lloyd Minturn, who was a man always prepared for adventure soon joined in the line for passing the buckets of water to curb the fire. Too soon the water was gone; the fire's rage won.[3]

Passenger George Conner, who had boarded at Albany with his wife, was on deck and purposely ignored the orders to move to the back of the boat. He had the plan in his mind to search for his wife who was on a lower deck. He found her by a saloon, and as the pair attempted to go forward, they were pushed back by a man ordering them to go aft. Again, Conner disregarded the commands of the crew-member and instead led his wife forward in the opposite direction. The dense smoke had traveled from the engine room and was spreading its heavy gray thickness rapidly over the deck floor toward the sides of the boat, making visibility more difficult. That did not stop Conner. He purposely took his wife directly into the thick black smoke where they vanished from sight.[4]

The fire in the midsection was raging and burning so intensely that no one could pass from one end of the boat to the other without risking injury or even death. There was no means to get word to either end of the threatened steamboat, and those on board had no idea what was happening beyond the wall of fire and smoke between them. People, desperate to find their family members, were trapped on either side of the fire.[5]

Mothers and children sitting in the ladies' saloon were separated from hus-bands and fathers who, after dinner, had gone to browse around the other parts of the boat. The blaze of flame prevented passengers on the promenade deck from reaching those in the rooms below. Families were separated without knowing the location or fate of their loved ones. They could only see the fierce flames burning up the center of the boat, bellowing a dark, black smoke that quickly crawled its way across the floor of the decks. With the fire came a heat so intense that the already hot summer temperatures were elevated to a point that could be likened only to that of hell.[6]

Thick gray and black smoke blinded passengers from seeing more than a few inches or feet around them. It stifled the air as those desperately trying to breathe gasped and choked. Some attempted to call for "the boats" with what little breath they had left. There may have been one or two safety boats on board. The fire con-tinually intensified as hundreds of helpless passengers became trapped on the stern of the flaming steamboat. They were forced to find a means of escape for themselves and their loved ones.[7]

Professor Bailey of West Point with his wife, daughter, and son "were sitting all to-gether just in front of the door of the ladies cabin." He had been talking to A. J. Downing and noticed nothing unusual when the cry of fire was heard. Bai-ley attended to his family and he could see Downing doing the same with his. At first, Bailey told his group to remain where they were because he believed the steamship would be taken to shore. "Be calm and I can save you all!" he exclaimed to his family.[8]

As the fires grew closer and more intense, Bailey decided he must take his family and the two young Kinsley sisters, who had been in his charge, somewhere else. Their choices were few. He instructed the group to climb through windows of the saloon onto the guards at the side of the boat, moving them a few extra feet away from the roaring fire. Bailey instructed them to hang onto the bolted down chairs as tight as they could to brace themselves for when the boat struck shore. Mrs. Bailey asked him, "Why don't they send us boats?" to which Bailey replied, "They will come soon, keep hold of your chairs and don't jump yet." The Bailey family group held on and waited.[9]

In the pilothouse, Edward Hubbard turned the wheel hard to direct the burning steamship at a ninety-degree angle and head her toward shore. The fire-engulfed boat was whisked from midriver directly to the east shore, a distance of perhaps a mile and far enough to feel like an eternity for those trapped in the inferno on board. It was too long for some who jumped overboard, ignoring the plea of John Harris who stood by the guard saying, "We would be very soon ashore." Thick gray smoke rose up from the burning decks leaving a signal of distress written across the sun drenched blue sky.[10]

As for Edward Hubbard, the pilot, "He kept on his course" as the flames closed in around him. He gripped his hands on the ship's wheel, keeping the steamboat on its final journey straight to shore. During his life he was known to be a kind person. His life had changed with the death of his first wife, Sarah, but somehow it had been renewed with his second marriage. Would he soon meet his departed loved ones in the eternity and leave his children fatherless?[11]

It took up to six minutes for the *Henry Clay* to travel the distance from midriver to reach the shore. The dying steamship smashed directly, bow first, onto the beach, its racking hull crashing onto the sand and plowing toward the grounds of the estate of Russell Smith. The steamboat slid across thirty feet of beachfront, digging into the shoreline, like a knife through butter. The fateful journey of the *Henry Clay* ended as the boat stopped just short of ripping up the railroad tracks.[12]

Fire and smoke blazed up from the burning midsection as the boat's front half rested on shore. One of the officers tried to scuttle the steamboat, possibly to get water into the hull to extinguish the flames. Several passengers and crew were thrown forward onto the sand as the boat jolted to a stop. Fate had looked kindly on those at the bow, like George Edwards who later stated, "I was pretty much one of the first ashore." The second pilot Elmendorf and his wife were also among those who jumped off safely. Once on solid ground, the crew and passengers threw luggage from the decks onto the beach, seemingly unaware of the tragedy unfolding behind the curtain of smoke on board.[13]

Just before the boat had hit shore, John Cubbage tried to help young Henrietta Traux and her small daughter to the guard from the ladies' saloon. His plan was to get them to the promenade deck where he thought it would be the best place for an escape from the burning boat. As he reached to pull the child up to him the boat struck the beach. The harsh jolt threw Cubbage backward several yards and separated him from the two he had hoped to rescue. As he scrambled to his feet and made his way forward, he realized that the mother and child were no longer there.[14]

The boat was so long that the stern did not reach the beach or shallow water. Instead, the back of the boat jutted far out into the river. Fires continued to blaze at the midsection, and hundreds of passengers on the stern decks had no way to jump safely to shore. They were trapped by a wall of fire that blocked them from going to the bow and to safety. Below them were the unknown depths of the river made rough by the southerly breeze and tides. For John Thompson, like so many others, he had obeyed the crew's first order to "Go aft." In so doing, he and his family were cut off from the shore, from the front of the boat, and from any reasonable escape route. [15]

Choosing the water of the river to a death by fire, many terrified passengers jumped overboard into twenty-foot depths, not knowing what fate would hold for them. They plunged one by one, some clutching their children and spouses, others in groups, and over each other's head in no particular order. Chaos ruled the scene as screaming victims both on board, some with clothes and bodies burning, and those drowning in the waters below, struggled to survive, as others around them perished.[16]

In the ensuing commotion, John Thompson heard his ten-year-old daughter Mary plea, "Help me father or we shall drown." Their nurse's clothes had caught

"Destruction of the Steamer Henry Clay, by Fire, on the Hudson River,"
by Elwin M. Eldredge, wood engraving by Shapin.
The Mariners' Museum, Newport News, Virginia

on fire. As the fire came upon him and the smoke thickened around his body, Thompson no longer could see his wife, his daughter Mary, or his son John. He surmised that his family had already jumped overboard, so he followed and jumped into the dark waters to search for them.[17]

Through the blackened smoke Thompson was able to locate his wife as she struggled to keep from drowning. He reached for her, but in her terrified state of mind, she frantically grabbed her husband around his neck. As Thompson coaxed his wife to adjust her grip to keep them both from going underwater, in an instant she was gone. At the same time, other women who were also struggling in the water saw him and also grabbed and clutched to him, their only thread of hope for survival. The struggle and additional weight upon him drew Thompson underwater with them, and they all quickly sank into the depths.[18]

As the terrified women gripped him for their salvation, Thompson struggled to free himself, and returned to the surface. He searched but could not find his wife again. The struggle had made him exhausted. Thompson began to give up and readied himself to die not knowing the whereabouts of his dear wife. Suddenly, a sailor grabbed him by the hair and brought him the distance to shore.[19]

Still on board the fire engulfed boat, George Conner who had defied those orders to go aft was battling the thickening black smoke that made it impossible for him to see anything before him. Leading his wife, he felt his way through the door near the saloon and up the dark stairs both totally inundated with a heavy blanket of black smoke. Feeling along the walls with his hands, walking blindly, Conner stumbled his way to the upper deck, keeping his frightened wife close to his own body and leading her with him. They reached the front of the boat where he helped her get to the main deck. From there they were able to jump safely to shore.[20]

Also on deck, was Professor Bailey who said to his family, "Wait till I give you orders, and then jump." Time had run out; the flames were getting closer, so close that Bailey was burned on the nose. His son "Whitty," frightened by all the turmoil, had jumped into the water. Bailey helplessly watched as his son struggled in the choppy waters and was washed away. The distraught father, convinced he lost his son, woefully sobbed, "There goes poor 'Whitty.' "[21]

All the remaining Bailey family members jumped into deep water about midway along the boat. For a few moments it appeared Bailey would be able to save his wife and daughter. With himself in between, Bailey held up his daughter and wife by their arms, keeping their heads above water. Using only his feet he began to swim. Air had collected in their clothing that provided some buoyancy, while Bailey desperately attempted to help them to safety.[22]

Seeing ropes hanging on the side of the steamboat Bailey tried to hand one to his daughter. She said, "I have got it." His wife reached for another. Luck turned against him as a woman grabbed Bailey around his neck. He let go of his wife and daughter so that they would not be drawn underwater with him. By the time he could free himself from the unknown woman's clutches and resurface, the boat and surrounding area were engulfed in flames and smoke. Bailey "was blinded and scorched by a mass of flame and smoke which was now pouring down. . ." and was unable to find his wife and daughter.[23]

Bailey struggled to swim and avoid the flames. He fought exhaustion by swimming on his back until he came across a plank on which he could support himself. A blinding, dark and thick smoke, through which he could see nothing, surrounded him, and he knew, "not a [v]estige of hope remained for my dearest treasures." Suddenly, he spotted the tip of a pole being extended to him through the black fog. Bailey called out that he lost sight of his wife and children. But the rescuer, a teamster named Peter Herring, who had come by the disaster site to offer his assistance, replied, "You must save yourself." Herring proceeded to pull Bailey toward the wharf to safety.[24]

Many of the poor souls who jumped overboard found themselves drowning in the waters with nothing but fire and smoke around them. In desperation, they grabbed for whatever they could to keep their heads above water and away from death's ugly hand. Many tried grasping others, in tight clenches, thrashing about, bringing themselves and would-be rescuers underwater to drown. Others held onto scraps of wood or deck chairs or took hold, if only by their fingertips, to whatever wood trim, railing, or ropes that were not already afire.

Young "Whitty" Bailey spent some time sinking and then returning to the surface of the water. He came across a chair floating in the water and took the opportunity to grab onto it. This proved to be of no assistance to him, as the current of the water worked against his small body and drove him back to the stern of the boat farther from shore. Wanting to get to safety, the young boy realized his desperate predicament and released his grip, to let go of the only thing keeping him afloat.[25]

That decision left him thrashing about in the water. He was burned on his head, face, and hands from the falling cinders. Struggling to breathe and to keep from drowning, "Whitty" next grabbed onto the coat of a man who was clutching the boat's rudder. "Whitty" held on for several minutes until, through the smoke and flames, there appeared some men reaching toward him from a boat. "Whitty" saw them and gasped, "For God's sake, save me!" He was then plucked from the water and brought to shore. His only memory of that short boat ride to shore was watching "the cruel flame eating its way through the words 'Henry Clay' on the paddle box." A pair of servant girls had found "Whitty" soaking wet, dazed, and confused.The girls delivered him to the home of Mr. Nevins. There, the young boy was given care and a comfortable place to sleep.[26]

When the fire broke out, Elmore Thompson, along with his wife, baby girl, and servant girl were sitting in the ladies' saloon. Seeing the flames coming from everywhere, Thompson cut a settee free to support his wife and child in the water. In the commotion, he next saw his wife clinging to the side of the boat. Thompson was able to push her into the wheel where they both held on tight.[27]

Unexpectedly, the wheel turned and pushed their bodies and faces down under the water. Coming back to the surface, they saw boards being pushed toward them. They took hold and floated themselves to safety with the knowledge that their young child and servant girl were both missing.[28]

Also from the saloon was Mrs. Sands, who had waited with her nine-year-old daughter while her husband, holding their baby, was elsewhere on the boat. As the smoke and fumes overtook the mother and daughter, they found themselves unable to wait any longer for his return. They jumped overboard into the unknown waters below. The two were close enough to the hull to grasp onto the braces of the boat. Two men clung to Mrs. Sands' skirts as she struggled to keep her hold on the boat.[29]

The task drained her strength and finally her hands slid down from the wet wood. She descended far below the water line, weighted down by the two men who then disappeared into the depths. The loss of the extra weight gave her enough lightness so she could struggle her way to the surface of the water. Mrs. Sands reached out for a wooden plank and was drawn ashore. Rescuers in a small boat saved her daughter from drowning, but her husband and baby were missing.[30]

On the flaming aft deck, a terrified woman stood, not knowing what choice would save her endangered life. Should she stay and hope for rescue or jump into the deep waters below? A man by the name of Edwards, seeing her, called to her and asked, "Will you go with me into the water and run the risk of being drowned, or will you be burned to death?" The woman made her choice. The two jumped into the waters below; they both survived.[31]

In the shallow water's edge, ragged and wet, perhaps burned and injured, the survivors of the deadly disaster either walked or were carried to shore. Among them was a despondent and burned Professor Bailey who walked alone on the beach, lamenting that his entire family was gone. Approaching a nearby railroad car, he requested that the passengers report that he had survived but that his wife, son, and daughter had been lost. He continued to wander about in a daze until he heard of a young boy with the name of Bailey who was sent to a house about a half-mile below the wreckage. Bailey could not bring himself to believe that the boy was his son. He had seen his "Whitty" drown. Bailey proceeded to the Nevins' home for at least some rest. There, he did find his son "snug and warm in bed." It was a bittersweet reunion as Bailey had found his son, but lost his wife and daughter. Knowing his son was safe and secure, Bailey changed to dry clothing and went back to the wreckage site to search for the rest of his family.[32]

The aged Honorable Stephen Allen, who had at one time been the mayor of

New York City and was also a former state senator, was understandably excited after the fire broke out. He asked passenger James F. DePeyster, "What are we to do?" DePeyster spoke to him and tried to reassure him. Afterward, like many others escaping the burning boat, Allen jumped overboard into the waters below after the boat was grounded. Mr. Jewett of Poughkeepsie threw the elderly genteel man a rope, but, the next moment, he was gone.[33]

DePeyster was one of several men traveling individually on the *Henry Clay* who made their way to safety once the boat had run aground. He clutched a loose bench and dashed to the bow of the boat. At the first clearing of smoke, he jumped to shore. Another passenger, John Gourlie also jumped, first down to the main deck from the hurricane deck, and then to shore.[34]

Dr. Phineas P. Wells was in the aft section when the fire started. He ran forward to the bow through the burning midsection while accompanying four women. He guided them along as the wind forced smoke and flames into their faces. As the little group made their dark and treacherous journey, the flames seared burns onto the arms of the women. In some manner, the group managed to find their way through the blinding thickness of smoke and fire down to the main deck and to safety on shore.[35]

Unfortunately for Isaac Dayton, he could not swim. He believed his only hope for survival was to hold onto the stools that he had thrown into the water. When he jumped, he missed his mark, missed the stools, and sank down into fifteen feet of water. The ebbing of the tide mixing with the southerly breezes created rough water, making it even more difficult for him. He could see two rescue boats nearby, and luckily a third boat came to his rescue. So exhausted from his struggle to survive, Dayton did not have the thought or strength to thank his rescuers.[36]

Others, unable to rescue their loved ones, had to simply save themselves. Mr. Hillman of Troy had been in the front of the boat, and his sister at the rear, at the time the fire broke out. He witnessed the confusion near the engine room but being hard of hearing, a few moments passed before he realized there was a fire on board. He attempted to go back to find his sister but the flames coming from the engine room in the middle of the boat made it impossible for him to pass. Attempts to reach his beloved sister made futile, he had no choice but to jump overboard.[37]

Stacy Bancroft, on the steamboat since Albany, found his wife on deck during the fire and instructed her to jump into the water after him. When he jumped overboard, several women jumped over him. He quickly recovered, but the smoke reduced visibility so much that he could no longer find his wife. He had no choice but to swim to shore without her.[38]

Isaac McDaniels, who had been below deck looking after his daughter while she slept, was unable to reach his wife after the fire broke out. He was forced to leave the burning boat in order to save his daughter's life. Holding his little girl, he jumped from the hurricane deck as the boat slammed onto shore. He had not seen his wife since she was in the ladies' saloon and did not know of her whereabouts.[39]

When McDaniels reached shore, he noticed Jessup, the ship's clerk, on the beach. McDaniels, earlier in the day, had endeavored the crew to slow the boat's speed, but was told there was "no danger." A few hours later, he was wet and had survived but did not know his wife's fate. He walked over to Jessup and sarcastically questioned to the ship's clerk: "Is there any danger now?"[40]

Barely a brief moment passed before those who initially arrived safely on shore realized the true severity of the situation for those left onboard or struggling in the water. The ensuing tragedy forced ordinary people to perform heroic acts. Once on shore, survivors and crew ran to a nearby fence and ripped off boards that could be extended out to people struggling in the water. Among the many who offered assistance was Mr. Way from Wellsville, Ohio, who swam to shore, gathered some wood, and returned to hold up his wife and two other women in the water until the rescue boats could pull them out. John Gourlie stood on the beach and assisted the children and women to shore. He brought medicine back to the beach from Russell Smith's house.[41]

Captain Alexander Cunningham, from Newburgh, also assisted in the rescues. Cunningham was the captain of the *Catherine F. Hale*, but on the day of the fire, he was simply a passenger aboard the *Henry Clay*. He was standing in the waters helping bring people ashore when he saw a small boat belonging to a schooner manned with four rescuers. When three of the four decided otherwise and went to shore, Cunningham jumped in to help with rescues. From the yawl he and other rescuers snatched as many as they could from death.[42]

Lloyd Minturn jumped into action on board to save several lives. He caught women and children from the deck above him who were thrown down to him. Once the forward deck was cleared he removed his coat and jumped into the water to assist further. He rescued two children and a woman, bringing them to safety, though he was burned on the arm. He later recalled, "Soon after striking, the water around the stern was literally covered with men, women and children."[43]

Owen Lynch was mentioned in the newspapers, "gratefully remembered by many survivors, as the fortunate instrument of their preservation." The newspaper added, "he did his work manfully and well." Stacy Bancroft was one of the people that Lynch had rescued.[44]

Mr. Radford, one of the owners of the *Henry Clay*, had been on board the *George Washington*, traveling upriver. Upon hearing the news that the *Henry Clay* was burning, he boarded a small boat to reach the nightmarish scene and offer his help. Collyer, also an owner of the *Henry Clay*, had safely reached shore from the burning boat. He pushed out several pieces of boards into the water to assist sur-

New-York Daily Tribune,
6 August 1852.

Lloyd Minturn testified
that he had assisted several
people to safety. In this
notice, Maria Dunn
expressed her thanks.

A Card from a Survivor.
NEW-YORK, Monday, Aug. 2, 1852.
To the Editors of The N. Y. Tribune:
May I beg you will allow me, through
your columns, to express my heartfelt thanks, which
illness, brought on by exposure in the water, has until
now prevented, to Mr. Loyd Minton, I believe of this
City, for his noble conduct in saving me, and my baby,
from a dreadful death, at the burning of the Henry
Clay; and let him be assured, that the prayers of the
widow and the fatherless will ever attend him.
MARIA DUNN, S. Louis.

vivors. Captain Tallman, who was still very ill, had remained in the water to help the victims.[45]

Was it destiny or simple chance? Here the three owners, Collyer, Tallman, and Radford, were each brought into the ravaged waters at Riverdale to witness the final moments of their steamship the *Henry Clay* and many of those unfortunate passengers who had chosen to board her.

The three owners assisted in the deadly waters, as did other members of the *Henry Clay*'s crew. A fireman on board the burning boat escaped the raging flames of the engine room, making his way through a hatch, although his clothes were set on fire. On his way to jumping overboard, he took a woman with him and brought her to safety. The fireman continued his efforts to save others and stories came to light about other officers also making rescues. Wells "saw a young man, whom I suppose was the clerk of the boat. He had his coat off; was in the water, and rendering assistance to the passengers." The second pilot Elmendorf, and the engineer Germain, were both seen in the water. Joseph Prarie, a fireman, was pushing out boards. He later said, "I could not swim, and so I did the best I could." One witness "saw Mr. Hubbard at the water, shoving out boards." Another witness, George Edwards, "saw the pilot, he was assisting to rescue the passengers from the water."[46]

The fires of the *Henry Clay* clouded the bright summer sky with thick gray smoke, sending its signal of distress into the distance. Crews of several boats, including the captain of the *James Madison* and captains of a schooner and a brig and some towboats all came in to help in the rescue. Hewlett Lake was piloting towing barges downriver about a half-mile or so behind the *Henry Clay*. He saw the boat turn to shore and surmised there might be a fire on board. Lake and some of his crew members jumped to action and took a small boat to assist in the rescue. The same held true for Captain Verrell, of the schooner *Advance*, who took some crew members in a small boat to help in the rescue. One of his successes was Isaac Dayton.[47]

The *Armenia*, which had been trailing the *Henry Clay* by a few miles, rushed in and sent its small boats to rescue. The *Armenia* crew dutifully worked in the rescue operations and carried survivors to their boat. Polhemus, the pilot of the *Armenia*, saw one of his crew, Peter Bishop, jump into the water and pull a drowning victim to shore. Polhemus docked the *Armenia* nearby and waited for any rescued survivors, some of them burned, to be brought on board for transport to New York City for medical help.[48]

Pulled from the waters too was an exhausted Captain Tallman. His trip to New York City would end, not as the proud commander of his steamship *Henry Clay*, but as a sick and weakened survivor of perhaps the worst steamboat tragedy to occur on the Hudson River, and one that had occurred on his

LETTER FROM CAPTAIN VERREL.
RONDOUT, Ulster Co., N. Y., Saturday, July 31, 1852.
To the Editors of The N. Y. Tribune:

Observing in your paper of yesterday that Mr. Isaac Dayton is desirous of ascertaining the persons who rescued him from the water, I take the liberty of writing to you, with a request that you will let him know that the vessel referred to was the schooner Advance, whereof I am master. So soon as I observed the flame and smoke issuing from the Henry Clay, I immediately manned my small boat with four of the crew, and dispatched her to the burning boat, while I, with the assistance of a small boy—all that were left on board—steered the vessel as near as I considered safe to the wreck, in the hopes of picking up some who might be floating out into the river.

It is a matter of heartfelt satisfaction to me and my crew that we were the instruments, in the hands of Providence, in saving the lives of between thirty and forty of our fellow creatures, and we only regret that it was not in our power to have been more active in rescuing human life, in this most awful calamity, which is now casting a gloom over so many firesides.

I expect to be here for one week, with my vessel, after which I will sail to the eastward with a cargo of coal.   Very respectfully, yours,   JOHN VERREL,
Captain of the schooner Advance.

New-York Daily Tribune, Tuesday, 3 August 1852.
Isaac Dayton did not know who his rescuers were in order to thank them.

Captain Verrel posted a notice in the *New-York Daily Tribune* to notify Dayton that he was rescued by the crew of the *Advance*.

watch. As a final insult to his career, his trip would finish aboard the *Armenia*, the rival steamboat. He believed only a handful of victims had died; he was unaware of the true severity of the disaster. In another irony, a wet Collyer boarded the new adversary to the steamboat industry, the railroad, for his trip to New York City. Collyer too, mistakenly believed that "not over ten persons have perished by drowning."[49]

The air was filled with smoke, fires, and the screaming of frightened passengers. The waters of the Hudson River became an ocean of debris, struggling victims, and the dead. Bobbing in the waters were the black trunks, boxes, and luggage of those on board that day. "Hats, shawls, fragments of dresses" and other possessions without their rightful owners floated along the top of the water, the remnants of lost souls. Overshadowing the tragic scene was the doomed vessel burning to its death with a roar of smoke and fire that reached to the mid-afternoon skies like a monster reclaiming its rightly place on the seas.[50]

A New York City bound train stopped near where the *Henry Clay*'s hull burned on shore. Mr. Livermore and his party, who had departed the *Armenia* at Kingston Landing, were on board that train. From their position on the train, they witnessed their worst fears of the day materialize as the *Henry Clay* burned.[51]

As if this horror was not enough, witnesses to the disaster saw a small child standing on the deck of the doomed burning steamboat. The child was alone, about five years old, having lost or been separated from his or her family. The blazing inferno, not satisfied with the victims it had already taken, surrounded the child, with burning flames, moving closer and closer until it overtook one of the littlest victims, engulfing the child with deadly fire. The Livermores and others watched helplessly as the fire burned the very life away from the innocent little child. [52]

Boarding Livermore's train were women who had traveled with him from the Catskill Mountain House earlier that day. They had been passengers on the *Henry Clay* and survived the fires by bravely running from the back of the boat through the flames and smoke of the midsection to the front where they could jump to safety. One woman sustained some burns on her wrist but it was a small price to pay for the safety of her life. She was among several survivors that would be boarded onto the train for transport to New York City. She was a lucky one. Others had burned to death on the boat as their flesh melted from the extreme heat. Some badly burned or injured victims, who had survived the wreck, would die on the train or later succumb in the city.[53]

The Hudson River Railroad, a great competitor to the steamboat industry, willingly served as a haven for the ravaged victims of the steamboat wreck. Railroad cars provided the resting place for weary or injured survivors as they were transported to New York City by rail. Throughout the ordeal, and in the days that followed, the railroad was there. Each of its trains stopped by the disaster site in the following days, by order of its board of directors. Southbound trains would stop to pick up coffins with the dead at the disaster site for transport to New York City. Northbound trains did the same for transport to Albany.[54]

The railroad company's former president James Boorman had been on the steamboat with his daughter. They both were rescued but the railroad company may have also lost one of its own. The Honorable Stephen Allen, a director of the Hudson River Railroad, was reported missing.[55]

Assemblyman Russell Smith, on whose property rested the massive burning wreckage of the *Henry Clay*, along with his wife and servants, lent the privilege of their wealth to good use. That day, the Smith house became an emergency hospital for the victims. Personally getting involved in the tragedy, they cared for the injured and frightened. The horror they witnessed inside their own home was reaffirmed with a simple glance outside on their riverfront. Their coachman Robert Sherman, their gardener Clement King, and King's son all assisted in the rescue. In a similar manner, William G. Ackerman, the owner of the nearby dock opened his house to the injured, giving care and even clothing to those in need.[56]

Miss Jeannette McAdams, a resident of Yonkers walked about the shore giving any assistance she could to the survivors. Going a step further, she carefully and respectfully arranged the remains of the deceased females that were brought to rest on the shore. Professor Bailey, in a letter he sent to a friend wrote about her. Evidently he did not know her name, but he was grateful: "Enough to say I found my wife that evening, & poor Kitty next morning, both unburned & unbruised–and thanks to an angel of a woman who took upon herself the last sad duties, I had the inexpressible comfort of fixing in my memory as the last picture of my departed ones, looks of calm, placid repose-I would not I think be selfish enough to recall them to the trials of this world, if it were in my power—they are saved from many a pang, & their agony must have been the briefest possible, if they were conscious of it at all."[57]

Many of the dead victims washed to shore or floated in the waters as if a part of all the debris. They floated amid the remnants of the burned boat, loose equipment, furniture, and baggage. The crews of several boats found the remains of victims over a wide area. The crew of the steamer *New Haven* had "picked up the body of a young female and left it at the first wharf below Hastings." The crew of a sloop picked up another female body.[58]

Human nature can be cruel, and many of the victims became victims twice at the hands of villainous thieves. Reports were made that crews from several boats were there for one reason—not to search and rescue, but to take advantage of the situation and rob the valuables still clinging to their dead owners, or to pilfer through the luggage of the *Henry Clay* passengers. It became necessary to post guards to prevent such happenings. Russell Smith's coachman, Robert Sherman, thwarted robberies by wayward sailors by pushing them overboard. He took charge of their small boat and used it to rescue survivors, one of whom was Mrs. Jewett.[59]

By late afternoon, the newspapers and the coroner William Lawrence began their tallies: lists of the survivors, of the dead, of the identified, of the missing, and of the baggage and belongings left behind. At the disaster site, Lawrence, who was the coroner for Westchester County was already at work, wasting no time with his investigation. On the afternoon of the disaster he had assembled a twelve member jury:

G. F. Coddington, Foreman	Lewis Costegan	Walter Doran
James F. Valentine	William Knight Jr.	John H. Williams
G. B. Rockewell	J. H. Post	Thomas Towndrow
Edward Le Fort	W. G. Ackerman	Henry Coats[60]

At Riverdale, an evening darkness that shrouded much of the disaster scene replaced the shadows of the afternoon sun. Floating in the dark waters were the remains of more lost souls, several of which slowly drifted down toward New York City, their journey to be completed in death. The silence of the evening was doubly so after the chaos witnessed on the river a mere few hours before.

About fourteen miles downriver in New York City, the remnants of the day had been scattered. Victims were cared for. Lost luggage and belongings were piled up at steamboat offices. Coffins were readied for shipment to the disaster site. Several hotels provided accommodations for the survivors.[61]

Night came and the darkening skies shrouded the emotions of the day, casting a sleepy shadow over the once lively city. As the shadows grew darker, only the spire of the Old Trinity Church stood tall above the quiet, sending its message of peace and hope, until it too was blanketed by the night.[62]

The day had ended in silence, the silence of those lost. For the survivors, there was a place to sleep, but that sleep would be elusive. For them, the dark hours of the night were shrouded in shock and grief, disbelief and

OUTRAGE.

ASTOR HOUSE.
Mr. and Mrs. Van Dyck, Philadelphia.
Mr. and Mrs. Merrill,   do.
Mrs. Woodward,   do.
John C. Carpenter,   do.
MERCHANTS' HOTEL.
James Craig, W. H. Shelmire, G. M. Grier.
Mrs. Romaine, and 2 children, Brooklyn,
Miss Austin, and sister, the latter lost, Brooklyn.
PACIFIC HOTEL.
James Brewster, 2 daughters.
PATTEN'S HOTEL.
Annna M. Wilson, Norfolk, Va.
A. Foreman,   do.
N. Foreman,   do.
J. G. Martin,   do.
Miss M. Wilson, was slightly injured.
LOVEJOY'S HOTEL.
J. R. Harris, Bellows Falls.
W. R. Williams, do.
AMERICAN HOTEL.
Captain S. Dean, lady and daughter, Pittsburg, Pa.
Crpt. C. W. Batchelor, lady and s'v't., Pittsburg, Pa.
G. W. Manning, Pittsburg, Pa.
P. A. Spring, Cincinnati, Ohio.
IRVING HOUSE.
E. Cooper, Memphis, Tenn.
Joseph Pierce, Cambridge, Mass.
Wm. A. Irvin, Pittsburg, Pa.
J. Farrow, Montreal, Canada.
James Henry, Baltimore, Md.
John W. Whiting and lady, New-Orleans.
John Steele, Albany.
[Mr. Steele is an aged man, and come within an ace of losing his life. He was in the water nearly half an hour, and when rescued, was nearly exhausted.]
HOWARD HOTEL.
J. I. Thompson, child, and servant, Lancaster, Pa.
T. Y. Mills, Columbus, Ohio.
[Mr. Mills was instrumental in saving twenty lives.]

New-York Daily Times, 29 July 1852.
The newspapers composed several lists, one of which was of those given accommodations at New York City hotels after the disaster.

Chapter 4

Meeting at the Astor

"TERRIBLE CATASTROPHE!" "DREADFUL CALAMITY on the HUDSON RIVER" and "TERRIBLE STEAMBOAT CALAMITY" read the next morning's headlines. The morning newspapers wasted no time in telling the story of the disaster. Details were offered, some of which proved to be incorrect, on the specifics of the disaster. The press thrived on the news, hungry for the scoop. Newspaper correspondents gathered information from eyewitnesses and pieced together the story for printing. Eager readers picked up the newspapers to learn the horrid details. For some it was their only way to learn the fate of their loved ones.[1]

The The New York Herald described it as "a disaster that has thrown the city into consternations, and carried sadness and desolation to hundreds of families." Already appearing in the morning papers were details of the injured, the missing, and the dead.[2]

For the survivors, it was still too soon to piece together the remnants of their lives. Adam Murray had survived the tragedy. His dead child had already been found, while his wife was listed as missing. The same sad story would repeat itself over and over with others. Mr. Bancroft survived, his wife had drowned; her body was recovered. The wife of John L. Thompson and two of his children were lost. Among the names mentioned as missing were the elderly Stephen Allen and prestigious Abraham Crist.[3]

The early sunlight brought no end to the shock and grief. Relatives soberly made their way to the *Henry Clay*, its hull still smoldering on the beach. They had hopes of finding their loved ones alive. They feared the worst of having to identify the remains of their dead. At the same time, a meeting was scheduled to take place at the Astor House in New York City. An announcement had been printed in the morning papers urging survivors to attend:

MEETING OF THE PASSENGERS

The male sufferers who escaped from the Henry Clay, which was burned this afternoon on the North River, are requested to meet at the Astor House, on Thursday, (this day) at eleven o'clock, A.M. It is hoped that none will fail to attend this meeting punctually.[4]

By mid-morning, a group of men congregated at the Astor House. Several were survivors of the disaster. Others were just interested parties, all waiting for the meeting to begin. They conversed in small groups here and there about the hotel's rooms and corridors to discuss the tragedy that had beset their lives. Lloyd Minturn, Isaac Dayton, Edward Cooper, Mr. Way, John Cubbage, and John Gourlie, all survivors, were among the many in attendance. Gradually, the groups of men moved into the gentlemen's parlor, graciously arranged for by Astor employees Mr. Coleman and Mr. Stetson. The congregation of men settled themselves and prepared for the meeting that was called to order at the specified time of 11:00 A.M.[5]

The first order of business was the selection of the chairman, Theodore Romeyn, Esq. a resident of New York City. He was not a passenger on the *Henry Clay*, but "those with whom he was closely connected had been just saved." He was fortunate that his family members who were on the *Henry Clay* had survived. "He did not know how many, then present, had cause to mourn for friends mutilated or destroyed." After some consoling words, he came straight to the point at the meeting.[6]

Theodore Romeyn believed that " the criminal carelessness of some person or persons who are at present unknown to us," caused the catastrophe. A single voice from the crowd called out "I think rather the criminal recklessness." Romeyn replied to the comment with further accusations without naming names: "Yes criminal and wicked recklessness on the part of those intrusted with the care of lives, and unmindful of that trust, desired to accomplish an object of no earthly consequence to any one but themselves, and by that criminality have brought mourning and desolation on many."[7]

Chairman Romeyn impressed upon the gathered group that it was the duty of those present to use whatever legal means available to make sure such a disaster never happened again. He stated that this meeting held a higher priority above that of any monetary satisfaction: "You, gentlemen, are called to take action in this matter, and I am sure you feel as I do, that there is a duty incumbent upon each one, above the mere recovery of property, or the vindication of a claim for dollars and cents, to protect the public by taking advantage of all the opportunities allowed by the laws of the land to prevent a recurrence of another such calamity."[8]

The chairman said the owners and officers of the steamship must be held accountable for the loss of life and property the *Henry Clay* disaster caused. Romeyn and a personal friend, attorney Mr. Lovell, both benevolently offered their legal services free of charge, as "a labor of love," to bring, "the perpetrators of this deed to justice, for the sake of guarding the public against a recurrence of the catastrophe which have rendered traveling so unsafe." Applause sounded throughout the room.[9]

A Mr. Berg of New York City, who had been a passenger on the *Henry Clay*, and E. O. Perrine, Esq. the attorneygeneral of Tennessee were both named as secretary for the meeting. The purpose of the meeting had been identified, the offices defined, and the duty of those present assigned: to find those responsible for the catastrophe and bring them to answer. Romeyn added, "we could not do this as citizens—it must be done by judicial process."[10]

The next order of business was for the drafting of resolutions in accordance with the defined purpose of the meeting. Mr. Van Dyck from Philadelphia proposed that a five-man committee should be organized for the purpose of drafting the resolutions and, "also with a view to embody some suggestions as to the proper course of conduct to be pursued." The motion was swiftly carried.[11]

Chairman Romeyn appointed the members including three men from New York City, Mr. E. S. Phillips, Captain Barnard, and John H. Gourlie. Also in this committee were Captain Dean from Pittsburgh and Mr. Van Dyck. The five-man group left to convene their own meeting to come up with appropriate resolutions.[12]

Meanwhile, Mr. Bergh severely criticized the officers of the *Henry Clay* regarding their behavior. He, as a surviving passenger, had witnessed the countless women and children trapped on the aft part of the steamboat. He was skeptical that any judgment would be made against the officers, due partly to politics. He suggested that the battle must be fought in the press and added, "The indignant voice of the public is our only hope to make a remedy." Bergh asked the press to find and publish the names of steamboats and their officers or owners who practice reckless acts while transporting passengers. It was his hope that steamboat travelers would learn of the dangers to which they were exposed. Applause broke out in the audience at this suggestion.[13]

Mr. E. O. Perrine "denounced in severe terms the criminal negligence of the officers of the boats." He "invoked the aid of the public voice, to prevent the constant recurrence of such scenes." Perrine also agreed with Bergh's suggestion of calling on the press to help with their cause.[14]

Those remaining in the general meeting began to recount their own experiences on the *Henry Clay*. Others imparted the details of the trip downriver including the suspected race, the mid-stream collision near Kingston, and the skipped stops. A passenger remarked, "she did not stop until a collision took place." Mr. Ramsey, who was on the *Armenia* said, "So far as the officers of the *Armenia* are concerned I wish to mention that before the fire took place, it became the subject of conversation on board the *Armenia*, that the *Henry Clay* had raised too much steam, and at the time of the collision she began to fire up very much." Another man dared praise the officers of the *Armenia*, but Captain Barnard was quick to point out that they were just as guilty.[15]

Mr. Ridder mentioned that he too was a passenger on the *Henry Clay* and had traveled on the Hudson River for forty years. He retold his experiences of the prior day while mentioning that owner Collyer, "had done everything to alleviate the calamity." In conflicting newspaper articles, it was reported that Ridder placed the blame on the officers for the disaster.[16]

Ridder described how he saved his own daughter, finding her practically suffocating from the smoke on board the burning steamboat. The intense fire prevented him from going by the gangway, so he jumped in the water with her and brought her to shore that way. Ridder said he then aided other women to safety. He made a point to say that there were not enough buckets of water or firemen on board.[17]

More stories surfaced at the Astor House meeting, fueling the escalating emotions and anger. Captain Barnard said he heard from a man in the meeting that the "*Henry Clay* took fire about a week ago, and that the flames were extinguished with the utmost difficulty." He also added that he heard from a passenger that the crew was "feeding with tar." Livermore told the group that a month before, he was traveling on the *Reindeer* when "the *Henry Clay* then ran into her as maliciously and heedlessly as she did into the *Armenia* yesterday." He added that three weeks ago his cousin had been on the *Henry Clay* when "she took fire on that day, but the flames were extinguished readily."[18]

The tension at the meeting was such that it was difficult to separate fact from fiction. Gourlie added the "evidence should be given before the Coroner at Westchester and the matter would then assume an official shape."[19]

The Chairman Romeyn suggested that there should be a list of surviving passengers, at least those present at the meeting. With that suggestion, the participants quickly set to recording the names.[20]

Chairman Romeyn informed those gathered that he was in receipt of a letter from one survivor who had lost his wife and child. The writer was unable to attend the meeting but forwarded his letter to the Astor House group to be read at the meeting.[21]

By the time Isaac McDaniels' letter was read, the Resolutions Committee returned and presented their proposal to the members of the meeting.[22]

There was a great cry of descent from one particular gentleman in the audi-

Names of Survivors.

J. H. Gourlie, N. 1 Hanover-street.
J. Isaac Bayton, No. 319 West Twenty-fourth-street.
Mrs. T. Romeyn and daughter, New-York.
Miss Doty, Rochester.
J. R. Harris, Bellows Falls.
Wm. R. Williams, Bellows Falls.
L. Meyers, Fishkill Landing.
J. W. Ostrander, No. 356 West Eighteenth-street
Pierson A. Spinning, Cincinnati, Ohio.
N. F. Ott, Monson.
S. H. Shelmyer, Philadelphia.
Henry Lawrence, No. 718 Broadway.
J. H. Longbottom, No. 93 John-street, New-York.
Capt. C. W. Batcheldor, lady and servant, Pittsburg.
Capt. Samuel Dean, lady and daughter, Pittsburg.
J. W. Mullen and lady, Pittsburg.
B. Way and lady, Melville, Ohio.
James H Kelly, No. 125 Navy-street, Brooklyn.
J. G. Corler, No 54 Wall-street.
A. Shepherd, Melville, Ohio.
Thomas H. Phelps, Sciptoville.
Thos. A. Phelps, Sciptoville.
Miss Phelps, Sciptoville.
Edward Cooper, Memphis, Tennessee.
Geo. F. Connor, No. 65 Pearl-street, Albany.
Wm R. Irvin, Pittsburg.
Joseph Locket, Brooklyn.
Francis Carpenter, Webster, Massachusetts.
Samuel M. Beck, New-York.
W. B. Prescott and Lady, Holmesville, Louisiana.
J. W. Prescott, Alexandria, Louisiana.
Miss M. M. Tucker, Milledgeville, Georgia.
Mrs. H. Livingston, Brooklyn.
Miss M. Livingston, Brooklyn.
J. H. Randolph, Ibberville, Louisiana.
Marcus Bosbom, Rock Island, Illinois.
James M. McGregor, No. 179 Forsyth-street, N. Y.
L. Minturn, New-York.
G. W. Greer, Philadelphia.
E. R. Cubbago, Philadelphia.
Isaac Dayton, New-York.
Capt. Geo. F Barnard, No. 370 Broadway.
Capt. Samuel Dean, Pittsburg.

New-York Daily Times, Friday, 30 July 1852.
The survivors who attended the Astor House meeting on the morning after the disaster recorded their name on this list, which was then published in the newspapers.

ence. He said the two boats had not been racing. The group learned that this man was not a passenger from the *Henry Clay*. He simply believed the *Henry Clay* was a far superior boat. Several in the crowd yelled back at him, "You are sent here to interrupt the meeting, and make it appear unharmonious! You were not on board and know nothing of the matter! Turn him out! Turn him out!" The man finally edged toward the door and discreetly left.[23]

Some discussion followed among the participants, especially about a section in the resolutions concerning the claim that the crew of the *Henry Clay* used flammable substances in the furnace. The wording was changed to say that they did not "learn" of the flammable substance, but "heard" of it. The change in wording avoided any unsubstantiated claims. There was some dissent and concern that the stories heard may not be reliable as fact. Finally, the members unanimously passed the resolutions.[24]

The press was called upon to spread the story, which was done with great success. The accusations were quickly printed and spread among the various newspapers. One comment printed in the *New-York Daily Tribune* stated, "The running ashore is generally deemed to have been badly done. The bank was shelving, and if the pilot had run diagonally upon the sand, many lives might have been saved, as the wind was blowing off shore, and would have kept the flames in the most advantageous position."[25]

The next day, the *New-York Daily Times* commented, "We are assured that while the *Henry Clay* was running at the height of her speed, below Sing Sing, she was carrying an unusual pressure of steam. . . ."[26]

The following week, on August 4, 1852, *The New York Herald* printed, "We learn that on Monday an engineer went down as a witness for the prosecution, to examine the machinery before it was disturbed, and on looking into the flue, he found it completely choked with pieces of coal, so that in case of a strong fire the flame must have been thrown back, and consequently spread around the wood work. This shows a state of neglect highly culpable."[27]

IRVING HOUSE, NEW-YORK, July 29, 1852.

To the Survivors of the Henry Clay:

I see in the *Herald* a notice for a meeting of the passengers, to be held at the Astor House this day, at 11 o'clock. I regret I cannot be with you, to enter my protest in the management of said boat.

I stood at the wheel-house, above Kingston (I think it was), when the *Armenia* came alongside. I then thought the manager of the *Clay* was to blame in crowding the *Armenia* so near the shore. I immediately went to the man whom I supposed to be the captain, and protested against the boat racing. I also went two other times to him, and importuned him against such conduct. All the answer I could get was, " *No danger.*"

I had a wife and little daughter aboard, 7 years of age ; left my wife in the Ladies' Saloon, and took my little daughter below for her to get a little sleep. She fell asleep immediately. I laid down by her, and about half an hour after, I heard an uncommon noise above. I went to the cabin door, and saw smoke. I returned to my daughter, took her in my arms, and carried her on deck. It was with difficulty I opened the cabin door. I saw flames and volumes of smoke around the chimney. I handed my little girl to a gentleman on the hurricane-deck I then thought of looking for my wife. All was in commotion ; my little girl crying. "Don't leave me, Pa !" I climbed up the hurricane-deck, took her in my arms, carried her on the windward side of the smoke-pipe, and climbed out out on the timber that held the canvas upon the bow of the boat, held my daughter in my arms until the boat struck ; handed my daughter to a gentleman in the bow of the boat, commenced the throwing of baggage ; jumped down myself, caught my little daughter in my arms, and dropped her some twenty to thirty feet over the bow into a gentleman's arms, and then jumped down myself, took my daughter in a farm-house near by ; since which time I have seen nothing of my wife. I suppose she perished in the flames or found a watery grave. I left Yonkers at sundown last night, to telegraph and write my friends, and return there to find the remains of my wife this morning. This is the reason I cannot be with you. I think there was gross mismanagement by the Captain of the boat, and so enter my protest.

ISAAC McDANIELS, Rutland, Vt.

New-York Daily Times, Friday, 30 July 1852.
Isaac McDaniels was unable to attend the Astor House meeting. He sent this letter to be read to those attending.

For days after the disaster the newspapers continued to give an accounting of the survivors, the missing, and the dead. Bits of information, anything that could

RESOLUTIONS.

1. To express our heartfelt thanks in this public manner to an all-wise Providence for *our* preservation, and that of *our* families, amid the scenes of so much danger and death—whilst so many, each of whose lives were of much value, have met, under the most painful circumstances, an untimely end.

2. To express our deepest sympathies for those who were lost, and for their families in their distress.

3. To express our disapprobation in the most unqualified terms of the apparent recklessness of human life, in the system of racing practised by steamboats generally.

4. To adopt such measures as will secure us from pecuniary loss, and if possible to bring the offenders to punishment, and to protect the traveling public from such like occurrences, so far as our influence and action may extend.

Whereas, This meeting is credibly informed by one of the passengers that he assisted in extinguishing a fire on board previous to the disaster at Yonkers,

Resolved, That in any investigation which may be made into the cause of this calamity, inquiry should be particularly directed as to whether the steamboat had not been on fire during a previous, if not the greater portion of the passage from Albany, and whether, after the fire had been broken out, the boat was headed towards the shore as speedily as the circumstances permitted and called for, and with such skill and discretion as a prompt regard for the safety of the passengers demanded.

Resolved, That this Committee have seen in the *Herald* a statement, on the part of Capt. TALLMAN, that the boats were not racing—this the Committee do most unqualifiedly deny. The Committee, who were on board, witnessed that the *Henry Clay* and the *Armenia* had been racing from the moment of their leaving Albany until the time of the disaster.

Resolved, That inasmuch as many of the sufferers and members of this meeting are non-residents of this City, that they respectfully request the public authorities to see that this matter is the subject of the strictest scrutiny.

It is recommended that all parties who have suffered loss, present their claims, duly attested, to counsel in the matter, in order that he may proceed to the recovery of the same; and also that we request counsel to consult with the District Attorney as to the propriety of pressing a criminal suit against the officers and owners; and that all parties who know anything of the facts in reference to the cause of the accident, make them known without delay to counsel.

Resolved, That we learn with deep regret that tar, or some such inflammable ingredient, was freely used to make steam while racing with the *Armenia*; and that the safety-valve was actually tied down during this reprehensible race.

be found on the disaster were printed. Letters and statements from passengers and from officers from both steamboats were regularly included in the daily presentations. Editorials were largely caustic against the officers of the *Henry Clay*.

Such newspaper reports easily turned public sentiment against the officers and owners of the *Henry Clay*. What Gourlie had suggested during the meeting at the Astor House had already commenced at Riverdale. Witnesses were called to tell their stories to Coroner Lawrence at the

INQUEST.

Facing page: *New-York Daily Times*, 30 July 1852.
The attendees of the Astor House meeting approved these resolutions
with respect to the *Henry Clay* disaster.

Chapter 5

The Living and the Dead

ON THE DAY FOLLOWING THE DISASTER, the morning sun slowly lifted the night's shadows from the smoldering hull of the *Henry Clay*. All through the past night, the tidal waters could not erase the charred evidence left on the beach at Riverdale. Evidence proving the disaster was all too real. This was not a dream from which one awakens to take a deep breath and realize the world is the same. This was a terrible nightmare for the living. The world was not the same. For the survivors, their world had become different in less than thirty brief minutes the day before on the *Henry Clay*.

The realization set a pall over the dawning summer day. Fire and death were in the air. Survivors arriving at the disaster site were forced to relive the memories of the inferno, rendered helpless to save their loved ones from a death by either drowning or fire. To remember was too painful; to forget was impossible.

Hundreds of observers stood on the beach, staring at the horrific scene, watching as grappling teams searched the waters for more victims. They watched as more dead were found and carried to shore, solemnly laid out on the beach, side by side. They watched as the bodies were covered with leafy branches for temporary protection from the now scorching summer sun. They saw the dead with water-soaked clothing, hair snarled and matted, bodies injured and burned, bearing a demeanor far different from what they once carried in ordinary lives. Many of the victims suffered such a disfigurement that recognition was nearly impossible. That being the case, their possessions, the clothing and jewelry upon them, would become the only means of identification. Some of the lost would never be found or identified at all.[1]

New-York Daily Tribune,
29 July 1852.

**Little J.B.M.H.—one of
the younger victims
of the tragedy.**

One of the saddest yet most lovely pictures of this scene of death, was the body of a beautiful little girl about 2 years old, with the face of a cherub, laying on a rough plank smiling in the cold embrace of death. Her body had not been recognized, she was dressed in light pink, her short sleeves looped up with coral beads, with gold clasps, on which were the initials J. B. M. H. A more angelic picture we never beheld.

The morbid state of affairs at the scene was quickly and thoroughly covered in the press. The very morning after the disaster, the New York City newspapers described the events of the previous day and included the sad specifics about victims and families. A particularly somber item illustrating the depth of the tragedy appeared in the *New-York Daily Tribune* the day after the disaster. It was quickly reprinted in other papers.[2]

The tiny body lay amidst a littered beach lined with the other unfortunate victims of the *Henry Clay*. The only hints to her true identity were the initials J. B. M. H. on her dress. Who was this little cherub, the innocent victim of such a monstrous tragedy? Who were all the others whose remains rested on the shore with her?

Twenty-three bodies had been recovered on the day of the disaster, and a handful of survivors already testified before Coroner Lawrence. As each testimony progressed, piece by little piece of information about the tragedy was revealed. Always within the testimony a revelation about what was once a life—perhaps a description of the hair, an age, the name of a husband, wife, or child, an occupation. There was something gleaned that reinforced the fact that these victims were once very real and alive before the yesterday that took their life away. Each of the witnesses had their own story to tell, yet each story shared a common theme. They each had lost a loved one in the disaster.[3]

Elizabeth Hillman, age sixty-eight, had been on board the *Henry Clay* to travel to New York City to attend to business including the draft of her last will and testament. It was a task she did not live to fulfill. She was identified by her brother, Jacob Hillman, who had been on the steamboat with her. He testified, "finding that I could render my sister no assistance I jumped overboard and succeeded in reaching the shore; sometime afterward, I found my sister ashore, dead."[4]

Stoddard Colby of Montpelier, Vermont, who identified his thirty-two year-old wife, Harriet, followed Hillman's testimony. Colby testified that she had been in the ladies' cabin because the racing upset her. It was the last he saw of her. A mention of her death appeared in the *New-York Daily Tribune*: "Mrs. Colby, of

Montpelier, left four children to mourn the loss of a mother." She was buried in the Proctor Cemetery in Vermont.[5]

The third survivor to testify on that fateful afternoon was Stacy B. Bancroft who identified his fifty-five year-old wife, Amelia. They had been married for seventeen years. "I thought the boat was racing with another called the *Armenia*, until we reached a place where I understood to be Kingston; after leaving there I thought the racing ceased." He included in his testimony, "I do not know of any impropriety or carelessness on the part of the officers of the boat."[6]

However, the press and several witnesses to the disaster disagreed with him. Editorials and interviews occupied the pages of newspapers for days as the inquest continued. Included among the many such printed articles was a very caustic statement written by a

STATEMENT BY A PASSENGER.

I, with many others, have just been witnesses to one of the most awful scenes, the direct result of that reckless disregard of life and limb which you, as a public journalist, have frequent occasion to record.

I was a passenger on board the *Henry Clay* yesterday, on her way to New-York, when she suddenly took fire, and was run upon shore, whereby a great number of human beings, of all ages, sexes and conditions, were instantly hurried into eternity! I could feebly, it is true, give you some of the horrid details of this dreadful scene as I witnessed them—of husbands, wives, parents, and children quickly separated from one another by a dreadful death, when least expecting it ; but all such particulars you will learn through other channels ; therefore it is not my present purpose to dwell upon them.

My object is to request you, as the proprietor of a powerful and widely circulating journal, to call the attention of the authorities, if they can spare time from their absorbing occupation of President-making, to the important truth, that the lives of hundreds, I may say thousands, are daily jeopardized by the accursed practice of racing upon the Hudson River.

It is a fit time now to bring this subject before the community, while the lifeless bodies of so many victims are yet above ground, to lend their ghastly evidence against this atrocious evil. I left town yesterday in the *Francis Skiddy*, which runs to Albany ; and so determined were the managers of her to beat the *Alida*, which started at the same time, that the cylinder and surrounding machinery became so hot, that, after starting and getting out into the river, it was found necessary to "lay by" and cool it before the steam could be properly condensed. After an hour and a half's labor in throwing water upon it, we again got under way ; but whether any calamity such as I have called your notice to, happened her ere she reached her place of destination, I am unable to say, as I landed previously. It was reserved for my return trip to behold the practical working of what was earlier in the day foreshadowed—the destruction of many valuable lives, when in the enjoyment of health and happiness, to gratify the accursed fancy of a Captain and proprietors. This boat and the *Armenia* had been racing all day, I am told by some of the passengers, and they several times ran into each other, by crossing before the bows of one another, after the manner of our Broadway omnibuses.

Will you not, sir, lend your voice to suppress this monstrous wrong done the unsuspecting travellers, by holding up to public scorn the boats which race? If you will, you may doubtless prevent many similar scenes, such as I have been obliged to behold.   A PASSENGER.

Above: *New-York Daily Times*, Friday, 30 July 1852.
Statement of a passenger of the *Henry Clay.*

Facing page, top: *New-York Daily Times*, Friday, 30 July 1852.
Statement of Captain Tallman of the *Henry Clay* explaining his version.

Bottom: *New-York Daily Times*, Saturday, 31 July 1852.
Card from the owners of the *Henry Clay* stating there was no racing.

STATEMENT OF CAPT. TALLMAN, OF THE HENRY CLAY.

It was about 3 o'clock in the afternoon when the alarm of fire was given. He was lying down in his state-room at the time, having been quite unwell, and under the care of a physician for two days past. As soon as the alarm of fire was made, he jumped out of bed and found that the boat was on fire in front of the boiler; and finding the flames could not be extinguished, he ordered the pilot to steer the boat ashore, which was accordingly done, and the passengers on the forward part of the boat jumped on the sand bank, while those on the after part of the boat were compelled to get ashore the best way they could, by leaping into the water. At the time the fire broke out there must have been near four hundred passengers on board. The boat was not racing, and he thinks the fire was caused by the hot cinders falling from the furnace, and permitted to collect, instead of being raked up.

Capt. TALLMAN came to the City in the *Armenia*, and says that when he left he saw ten females dead on the shore and one child, which he has reason to believe was all who lost their lives. He did not think any of the males suffered in the calamity. But it will be seen from the sad details that Capt. TALLMAN is unfortunately mistaken in the number of lives lost.

The owners of the *Henry Clay* have issued the following Card:

To THE PUBLIC —We ask at your hands a suspension of opinion for a few days, during which time we promise to satisfy all reasonable men that there was no racing between the *Henry Clay* and *Armenia*, at the time of the late accident, or on that day, and will prove an *agreement* entered into between the owners of the two boats previous to starting, that no trial of their speed should be made, while running together, and furthermore we will prove to the public beyond all doubt, that the *Clay* was running at her regular speed and no faster, and neither at the time of the accident, nor at any previous time during the day, did she carry as much steam as was allowed by her certificate, or as she has carried previously with perfect safety, and that every thing was done by both officers and crew that men could do to save the lives of the passengers.   W. RADFORD.
   [Signed]   THOS. COLLYER.
Dated New York, July 31, 1852.   J. F. TALLMAN.

The following are the names of the officers and hands on board the *Henry Clay*, who expressed their willingness to give testimony in relation to this sad tragedy, when called on:

J. T. Tallman, Captain;   John Germain, Engineer;
Edward Hurlbert, Pilot;   Jas. Edwards, Second Pilot;
Chas. Merritt, 2d Engineer; —— Lasher,
Jas. Donohoe,   John J. Brooks, Firemen.

---

passenger who survived the *Henry Clay* disaster. The statement was written on the day following the fire.[7]

The steamboat owners and officers wasted no time in taking the opportunity to get their side of the story in print as well. A statement from Captain Tallman appeared in the newspapers the same day.[8]

Tallman was one of three owners of the *Henry Clay*. A day after his statement appeared, the three owners, together, took upon themselves to issue their own statement in the press for their defense.[9]

While the battle of the written word was waged in the newspapers, the official inquest was conducted at the disaster site. Hardly a pleasant situation, Coroner Lawrence had first held the inquest on the beach. Suspicion aroused that unsavory characters may attempt to rob from the remains of the victims, so the coroner ordered guards. Later, the bodies were transferred from the beach and moved to a building at the steamboat dock at Yonkers Station for safekeeping, again under the watch of guards. The inquest proceeded in an adjacent room for a short time until successive hot summer days caused an odor to permeate from the room of the dead, through the walls, into the witness room. Conditions became intolerable, and once again the inquest was moved, this time to a room at the railroad station.[10]

During the entire process Constable Nodine was in charge of the recovered bodies. He first was stationed on the beach to accept the remains of those brought to shore and organized the dead for the identification process. Also present was District Attorney Wells and former district attorney William Scrugham, who advised Coroner Lawrence.[11]

The witnesses at the inquest came forth to identify their dead and tell their stories. Often the saddened survivors or family members were overcome with emotion as they told the details of their lost loved one's life and tragic death. The task at times was gruesome as the witnesses were led to where the victims lay in state, first on the beach under leafy branches and then in pine boxes in an unfinished room at the steamboat docks. The lifeless bodies of the victims lay baking from a summer heat that intensified as each hour of the day passed.[12]

Once the identification was made, the witnesses watched as their dead were placed in coffins. For the poor, a simple wooden box was sufficient. For the wealthy and those of means, arrangements were made for metallic or splendid wood coffins, perhaps a mahogany with fine craftsmanship. In either case, the railroad transported the rich and the poor alike to destinations north or south on the rail lines. In death, class status made no distinction.[13]

Professor Bailey testified at length about the trip and recounted the story of the loss of his forty- year-old wife and sixteen-year-old daughter who were both named Maria. He identified their bodies and stated, "they died by drowning, undoubtedly in consequence of the accident yesterday." At the news of the disaster, several West Point officers and friends traveled to Yonkers to assist Professor Bailey. The gift of their generosity could not alter the facts of his loss.[14]

Samuel Cook of Durham, New York, said that when the fire started a crew member told him, "Don't be frightened—it is all out." Shortly thereafter, Cook witnessed the uncontrollable flare-up of the fires and said with resignation to his family members, "We shall all perish." His daughter pleaded, "Father, you can swim, you better save yourself." He thought for a quick moment, took hold of his young grandson, and brought him to shore. He was unable to save the others. Cook came to the inquest to identify the bodies of his daughter, Abby, thirty years old, her husband William M. Ray, thirty-five years old, and their six-year-old daughter, all residents of Cincinnati.[15]

The tides and current, perhaps with assistance from the wind, dispersed several bodies away from the disaster site. Six miles north of where the last vestiges of the *Henry Clay* lay, the body of Mrs. McDaniels was discovered near Hastings. Her husband, Isaac, identified his thirty-six- year-old wife, who had drowned, "I recognize the body of my wife, Lucy B. McDaniels, by her dress and jewelry which is marked." McDaniels testified about the events leading up to the fires and explained how he was able to save his daughter. He ended his testimony with the statement, "I never saw my wife after I left her in the ladies' saloon until I found her body here."[16]

Adam Murray came to identify his wife. During the fire he had found her and they jumped overboard, while he tightly held onto his baby son. The waters were crowded with debris and struggling survivors. Murray testified, "I recognize the body of my wife among the dead before me; deceased was about 30 years old, born in Edinburgh, Scotland; I have no doubt as to her identity; she was drowned from the Henry Clay." Murray continued his testimony and explained how he lost his son: "the child is named John, aged one year and 14 days old; when I leaped off the boat I had the child in my arms, but in the struggle I lost it."[17]

Throughout the days, witness after witness came forth to tell their stories of the supposed racing, the fire, and whatever details they knew of the last moments of their deceased loved ones' lives. For some, the truth was incomprehensible, knowing that their loved ones may have burned to death, drowned, or both.

John Chatillon testified that he lost his wife Margarete, age twenty six, and brother-in-law George Thielman. He identified their remains and said, "the two appear to be drowned." When the jury asked if he had lost anyone else, the question overwhelmed the man and he was unable to hold back his tears. "I also had two children on board who were lost; their names were Catherine and Helena— one three years old, and the other fourteen months." Chatillon was later recalled to identify little Katarina, while his daughter Helena was placed on the list of the missing.[18]

The identification of the children was the most heartrending of moments at the inquest. These little children, who had their lives ahead of them, snatched away too soon by the cruel hand of fate—a death by fire and water.

A father, John W. Simons of New York City, was present to identify the remains of one of his sons. He had discovered the little boy himself. The father lamented, "two of my sons and a nurse were on board the *Henry Clay*. . .all of them were lost; one of them, which I found, is three and a half years, and the missing one is two and a half years old. . .the child found is named John H. Simons; . . . I have not the least doubt as to the identity of the deceased. . .I am of the opinion the little creature was burned to death." His son, Howard H. Simons, was identified later at the inquest presided under Coroner Ives, held at the Hudson River Railroad in New York City.[19]

Who was little "J. B. M. H." whose body was described earlier in newspapers? Susan Marsden, a resident of New York City, sworn in her testimony that the little angel of a girl was her niece: "I have seen the body of an infant, named Johanna Hanford, aged 17 months, and recognize it as the child of the late Cyrus Hanford; the mother of the child was on the boat with the babe, and has not been found; they were coming from Newburg. . . ."[20]

The child's name was placed on the list of the dead as Johanna B. M. Hanford. Her parents had been married just a year or two when her father died eight months ago. Now the infant child was also dead and her young widowed mother was listed as missing. Later, Susan Marsden identified the child's mother as Joan B. M. Hanford who was only twenty-two years old.[21]

Death by drowning tragically haunted the Hanford family. "About three years ago, Mr. Handford's father died suddenly while traveling on one of our northern lakes; subsequently, Mrs. Handford's father and a brother were drowned together—and still subsequently, an uncle and nephew were drowned together." In an uncanny twist of fate, little J.B.M.H. and her mother shared the same unfortunate end as that of their close family members.[22]

Another survivor, Matthew Crannell of Albany had been on the steamboat with his wife and son. He came to identify his little boy: "I had a son on board of the Henry Clay. . . he was thirteen months old . . .my child was drowned from the Clay." The day before Crannell gave this testimony, the *Daily Albany Argus* printed the following statement confirming the truth: "Mr. M. Crannell and lady, of this city, who took passage on the Clay, were saved—their child was lost."[23]

Theodore Wing identified the son of Isaac D. Sands who had been placed on the missing list. Mrs. Sands sent Wing to make the identification of her little boy. Wing gave this testimony: "I recognize the body of the babe alluded to; it is nine months old today, the child is male and belongs to Isaac D. Sands of No. 86 Stanton Street, New York; the father of said child was also on board the Henry Clay and was lost, his body has not been recovered; I wish to take the child, by the authority of its mother; she sent me for it, and I have no doubt of its identity."[24]

Younger than the Sands' baby was the daughter of Elmore Thompson. He testified that he and his wife survived the disaster, but regarding their baby, Jennie, "she appears to have been drowned. . .she was 3 months and 26 days old; she was born in New York and was a passenger by the *Clay*."[25]

Perhaps the youngest recorded victim was six-week-old Eugene Thompson. His father John Thompson was called several times during the inquest to identify those lost from his family. One of the many multiple tragedies, this district attorney of Lancaster County in Pennsylvania lost his wife, his ten-year-old daughter Mary, and baby Eugene.[26]

Family members and friends who had not been on the steamboat also provided testimony. Some had awaited the arrival of the *Henry Clay* at the steamboat docks in New York City and others had recently bid their goodbye at some other upriver landing, never thinking that a catastrophic calamity would take their loved ones from them. Word of the disaster quickly traveled upriver to numerous Hudson River towns, where the information was printed in the local newspapers.

Selah J. Jordan, a farmer by occupation in Jordanville, and also justice of the peace, learned of the steamboat tragedy through the newspaper reports. He came to New York to identify the body of his oldest daughter, Phoebe Ann Jordan. Being "deeply affected" during his testimony, Jordan said, "her death appears to have been caused by drowning." His daughter had been traveling with her aunt and uncle who also perished with her.[27]

Jordan identified his brother-in-law Jacob S. Schoonmaker, a merchant, also from Jordanville. The Schoonmakers were evidently quite prosperous, as six hundred dollars were found on Jacob's body. The Schoonmakers had been on a trip to New York City to purchase merchandise. Mrs. Schoonmaker was listed as missing.[28]

A favorite son of Newburgh, thirty-six-year-old landscape architect Andrew Jackson Downing was among the lost. He had been seen in the ladies' cabin attending to his family when the fire was discovered. Later, he was seen assisting young Mrs. Wadsworth in the water. This was the last sight of him alive. Two others in the Downing traveling group also perished that day. His mother-in-law Mrs. Caroline DeWint was listed as missing, and Mrs. Wadsworth had drowned. The newspapers reported the circumstances of Downing's death by writing: "He was dragged down by a lady who was under his charge, clinging to him in the water." Speculation was that the woman was Mrs. Wadsworth.[29]

Calvert Vaux, a friend of A. J. Downing, made the identification of his mentor, stating, "I am the partner of deceased in business. . . .I have no doubt of the identity; deceased was drowned from the *Henry Clay*."[30]

The delicate Maria Louisa Hawthorne, sister of Nathaniel Hawthorne, also had perished by drowning. Her uncle John Dike had been in another part of the boat and was able to save himself. Before returning to Salem, Dike gave a description of Maria, including her clothing and jewelry, to one of the jurors. Edward LeFort, the juror, made the identification after boatmen had recovered Maria's body from the water.[31]

Robert Manning, a nurseryman from Salem, Massachusetts, and Maria Hawthorne's cousin traveled down to the inquest. He also confirmed her identification by the clothing and possessions. He recognized a pin with a "Rachel Forrester" marking and a handkerchief monogrammed with the letter "H" in a pocket of her clothing. Maria's body was placed in a metallic coffin for transport back to Salem.[32]

Anthony Robinson, a porter and cider manufacturer from New York City, identified his wife Mary Ann and daughter Isabella. The news was particularly unnerving as he explained, "I have seen the bodies, and fully recognize them; my wife spoke after she got on shore but died in fifteen minutes after."[33]

Attorneys John Thompson and Isaac Dayton survived the disaster. However, there were others of the same profession who were not so fortunate.

Abraham Crist died a hero. He was a strong swimmer, and brought his traveling companions, Mr. and Mrs. Spring, safely to shore. Crist then returned to harm's way to offer further assistance, but an unknown victim's clutch drew him underwater.[34]

The identification of Abraham Crist was made by his brother David Crist, a farmer from Walden, New York. David Crist testified, "he was a lawyer, having his office in New York, and residing in Brooklyn; his age was about 49; he leaves a wife and 5 children; the body I have seen here is his; the cause of death appears to be drowning; his body was found in the stern of the Henry Clay. . . ." George Weller, Crist's brother-in-law also confirmed the identity. Being well-to-do, Crist's remains were placed in a mahogany coffin and removed for transport.[35]

Undoubtedly, people were looking for the Honorable Stephen Allen after friends had posted a one hundred dollar reward. His body was found in the water near the Forrest property, about a mile north of the disaster site.[36]

The gold watch still on Allen's body was stopped at 3:26. Perhaps the water or an impact forced it to cease its ticking, but the watch confirmed the undeniable facts. It took only a half hour for this fateful event to snuff out dozens of lives, including Stephen Allen's. Among the other possessions found on him were gold eyeglasses, some keys, jewelry, and personal papers.[37]

Allen's son-in-law A. Reade of Troy confirmed the identity and testified, "I have no doubt as to his identity; the cause of death appears to have been drowning." There had been speculation that Mrs. Allen was lost as well, but Reade confirmed, "no person was in company with Mr. Allen, as he left Mrs. Quincy, his daughter, at Lebanon."[38]

The body of fifty-year-old Jacob J. Speed, Esq., a successful attorney from Baltimore, was found downriver from the wreck. Walter Harding confirmed Speed's identity and testified, "He appears to have been drowned, and to have received a wound on the head." Daniel Darcy and William. J. Ackerman also confirmed Speed's identification by the clothing, the appearance of his body, and two handkerchiefs found on his remains.[39]

Throughout the days after the disaster, the search in the waters of the Hudson River continued. Each day, the work crews laboriously searched for the bodies of the missing. Initially, the crews employed cannons, firing onto the beach to shake any victims free that may have been below the surface of the water. Those that floated to the surface of the waters and near shore, either as a result of chance or the cannon fire, were readily recovered.[40]

Onlookers and relatives who gathered had become more anxious as time passed and speculated that a number of bodies must be buried underneath the wreckage. However, getting to them presented a huge problem, as the steamboat was a tangled mass of burned debris. A *New York Herald* reporter wrote: "The wreck of the Henry Clay has gone almost entirely to pieces. The smoke pipe is lying in the water, and the wooden portions of her hull are floating about in charred fragments. Her timbers appear to have been very slight, and in their dry condition the flames must have ravaged them as though they were wicker work. She is completely burnt on the inside, down to the kelson. Nothing remains but the mere floor, the machinery and the smashed paddle wheels, which are immoveable, by reason of the weighty machinery attached to them."[41]

Partially submerged, the *Henry Clay's* boilers were visible underneath the water. The problem at hand for the crew was a lack of further means of recovery. Larger equipment was needed. For that reason, several gentlemen who had friends or relatives still missing from the disaster implored the coroner by letter to hire a derrick.[42]

A derrick did arrive and was positioned on Ackerman's Dock. William G. Ackerman lent more than his dock to the rescue operations. He was a juror on the inquest panel and had accompanied many of the bodies as they were brought to shore. Due to his close involvement, he testified several times regarding the identity of various victims. Ackerman continually showed true compassion as the *New-York Daily Times* noted: "Wm. G. Ackerman, owner of the dock of that name, has shown the utmost kindness and attention toward the unfortunate sufferers, and the afflicted friends of the deceased. His personal exertions from the first moment have been un-ceasing. Not only have the sick and wounded been tended with the greatest care, but his house has been hospitably thrown open to all who were called to the scene of the calamity. Even his wearing apparel has not been reserved, but was liberally distributed among those needing it."[43]

The derrick, E. K. Collins, which Bishop of the East River owned, made the recovery scene more curious for spectators. Hundreds passed by the disaster site on foot or in railroad cars to watch the recovery operations. The derrick ripped apart and moved the tangled and burned skeleton and machinery of the *Henry Clay* as the search for more victims continued.[44]

For days, people had speculated that the body of

> JULY 30, 1852—2 o'clock P. M.
>
> *To the Coroner of Westchester County:*
>
> Sir: Inasmuch as no derrick, or apparatus for raising the machinery, &c., from the bodies under it, has to this time arrived, we, the undersigned, parties who have relations and friends missing, and supposed and known to be lost by the burning of the *Henry Clay*, urgently request you to forthwith employ means to raise the machinery, &c., from the bodies, now known to be under the same. (Signed.)
>
> Elmore Thompson, John C. Hart, John C. Acheson, Rev Abijah Green, Geo. Holberton, N. H. Van Wagner, Jas. Mackel, S. Hart, H. C. Arnold, Peter Mitt, Edw. W. Leggett, Henry Stevens.
>
> The CORONER was understood to say that a derrick had had been sent for, (to New-York) at 2 o'clock; and he promised to give the matter his attention.

New-York Daily Times, **Saturday, 31 July 1852. Several survivors and families were growing impatient with recovery operations. A group requested that Coroner Lawrence engage additional machinery to assist in the recovery.**

Isaac Sands was pinned underwater near the wheelhouse. His gold watch had previously washed up on the shore. By using the derrick to move parts of the massive wreckage, the crew found and recovered Sands' lifeless body. Daniel Sands, his father, identified his remains: "I recognize the body of my son, Isaac D. Sands here. The body was found this afternoon under a part of a wheel of the *Henry Clay*; he appears to have been drowned. . . his wife and daughter were saved, his son Sylvester, 11 months was drowned and body recovered; Mr. Sands was 33 years old. . .he was a carman in New York." The deceased and his baby son were buried in a Hicksite Friends' Cemetery in Dutchess County, New York.[45]

As each day passed, from weekday to weekend, the inquest identifications methodically continued. On Sunday morning, Reverend Abijah Green of West Point was called with regards to twenty-one-year-old Miss Harriet T. Kinsley: "I am a minister of the gospel; I used to be pastor of the Highland Church, which Miss Kinsley attended; knew her well in life; and recognized her by a description of the articles of her dress and jewelry. . .her death appears to have been caused by drowning. . . ."[46]

Harriet's thirteen-year-old sister Eliza, who also died in the disaster, had been identified at Manhattanville. Other cities throughout the area were drawn into the tragedy as the bodies of victims washed downriver and were recovered or washed up on the shores within that city's jurisdiction. In Manhattanville, William Rowley, an aged house servant of the Kinsley family, tearfully attested to Eliza's identification: "have been in the Kinsley family for eighteen year past, was not on board the Henry Clay, drove Miss Kinsley, her sister and brother to the boat at Cozzens' Dock; Miss Kinsley and her sister went on board; the brother did not go. . .I know the body by the dress and a purse and by the name-Eliza Kinsley-upon the handkerchief." To add to the horror, her clothing and personal property were the means in which she was identified, and not her natural features.[47]

Unfortunately, this held true for most of the other women recovered south of Riverdale near Manhattanville and Tubby Hook. Four hot summer days coupled with deterioration by water made the bodies unrecognizable. Their remains were taken to the Twelfth Ward Police Sub-Station where Coroner Ives held an inquest.[48]

Caroline DeWint's body was also at Manhattanville. John Allen Smith her brother, and James Mackin a friend of the family from Fishkill Landing made the identification. Again, facial features were not used for identification. Rather, jewelry and the overall appearance were used to identify the victims. The unforgiving waters had washed away any resemblance of Mrs. DeWint's former presence.[49]

Smith testified, "I was not on board the *Henry Clay*; the deceased here present is my sister, and is known to me to have been on board the *Clay*, and to have been drowned on board of her near Yonkers; the body was found at Tubby Hook, and brought to this Station house; I recognize it by the general appearance, and by jewelry upon her person." Caroline DeWint was the mother-in-law of A. J. Downing, another victim of the disaster. She was the wife of John Peter DeWint, a wealthy landowner and businessman of Fishkill.[50]

The body of Elizabeth Thompson was also at Manhattanville. Charles Boughter made the identification along with J. Franklin Reigart, who confirmed, "the body was discovered on the beach near this place, I recognize the peculiar light colored hair, white eyebrows, and the height of person; Mrs. Thompson was a neighbor of mine; she was short in stature; I am positive as to her identity."[51]

Emeline Milligan, also recovered at Tubby Hook, was recognized by her husband, John. He had no idea she was traveling home that day and read her name on the list of the dead. The letter his wife was carrying from her sister aided in the identification. Milligan testified to Coroner Ives, "this was the letter found on her person." He also added that Emeline's mother, Hester Tompkins, was missing.[52]

Because several bodies had been washed down the Hudson River, towns across the river in New Jersey became the site of other inquests. At Hoboken, under Justice Samuel Browning, Catherine Ann (Demarest) Schoonmaker, wife of Jacob S. Schoonmaker was identified by Ann Marie Thompson. The bodies of Mr. Schoonmaker and their niece Phoebe Ann Jordan had been recovered several days before and were identified earlier. The verdict judgment on her death was deemed, "death by drowning occasioned by the burning of the steamer *Henry Clay*."[53]

The Fort Lee, New Jersey, inquest under Coroner Theodore V. Ayres issued a judgment far more to the point. The jury did not mince words regarding the death of Matilda A. Fennell. Although her death was ruled as death by drowning, the jury concluded that she "came to her death by the misconduct and culpable carelessness of the officers and conductors of said steamer, in racing."[54]

At Manhattanville, New York, Peter Traux was present to give his testimony. The day of the disaster, he had planned to meet his family at the steamboat docks in New York City to take them to their new home. Instead, he was called to make the identifications. He told the coroner that his wife had written to him "to meet her at New York." He continued, "I identify the body by the dress." Traux recognized his child, "Know this to be the body of my child." As a father, the intensity of his emotions became clear as he claimed his little girl: "I recognize the body of my child by the face, hair and dress; should know it among a hundred, or a thousand." The mother and child were later buried in the Episcopal burying ground in Yonkers.[55]

There were additional burials in Yonkers, that of the eight unidentified victims. Coroner Lawrence kept meticulous records regarding the remains of the unknown victims. He logged the personal articles found on each body and put them into safe keeping so that they could be used for future identification. Each of the unknown victims was placed in a coffin and marked with a number that corresponded with the description and belongings.[56]

For the record, the coroner held inquest for the bodies numbered 1, 2, 3, 4 and 5 and later for three other unrecognized women. The verdict for all was death by drowning. The coroner also provided a description of each to the newspapers in the hopes someone may come forward.[57]

There were two separate funerals for the unrecognized victims. The first funeral took place on Friday July 30, the second two days later. The first included a church service at the Reformed Dutch Church with a procession to the burial place. The second funeral progressed directly to the plot from the railroad depot.[58]

The coroner instructed Mr. Scrugham, his advisor, to place a public notification in the newspapers before each funeral: "As it has become impossible to longer retain the bodies of those lost from the *Henry Clay*, on the 28th, the funeral of such as have been recovered

New-York Daily Times,
2 August 1852.

**Description of the
unrecognized appearing
in the newspaper.**

Description of Bodies Unrecognized.

The following is an accurate and complete description of the bodies recovered, but not identified:

1. A woman, dressed in black, between 50 and 60 years of age, hair originally dark brown, turning grey; black gaiter boots, prunella, no tips; white cotton stockings; jet buttons on dress, open in front, with frill. Supposed to be Mrs. Hill, of Philadelphia, by Mr. Henry C. Arnold, of New-York. Mrs. Hill was in company with Mr. Speed, and left Peekskill with her sister.

2. Boy, 20 or 22 years old, apparently Irish. Check cotton shirt, figured neck tie with colored ends, brogans. In his pocket were too keys, one having a brass chain attached a comb, a clean check shirt, and a cotton-stamped pocket handkerchief, and a pipe; also a slip of paper with the direction, "JAMES DONNAHIES, No. 60 Laight-street, N. Y."

3 German woman, dark brown hair, gold ear-rings, brown merino dress, calf-skin brogans and worsted stockings. A card found in her pocket from Donelan's Hotel, No. 37 Dean-street, Albany; blue colored, round tin snuff box, comb and pocket knife, and a few cents.

4. German laborer; thick whiskers extending round under his chin; some grey hair, brown frock coat, heavy boots, and blue overalls, in front of which was a cross, stamped underneath "GLAUBER HOFFE." In his pocket was a card of a jeweler residing in Rivington-street, New-York.

5. An old lady, apparently German, hair turning grey— blue figured dress, black gaiter boots tipped with patent leather, and white cotton stockings.

6. A female, apparently about 18 years of age; has not been identified. See testimony of JOHN ARCHER for a full description.

7. A woman, supposed to be BRIDGET BRODERICK, aged about 30 years; black hair, light figured dress; on her neck was a string of white glass beads, a white paste breast pin, set with seven stones, one large gold ear ring, (crescent shape,) one trunk or closet key attached to a ribbon, one large plain gold wedding ring, one pair white kid, and one pair of cotton gloves; one cotton purse, steel slides and tassels, containing 52 cents in specie, and a card of a window shade-store at Nos. 175 and 177 William-street, New-York, in the style of a $100 bill; also, a certificate in the following words:
"BRIDGET BRODERICK leaves with our full consent, in order to be married; we having no ill will toward her whatever, sincerely wishing that, in the contemplated change, she may better her condition.
(Signed)   C. H. PALMER,
                      W. P. PALMER,
JULY 4, 1852,   No. 41 Irving-place."

8. A woman, with a black and white speckled muslin de laine dress, black open-worked straw hat, a dark leather pocket-book, containing two $5 bills on the Marine Bank of Baltimore, $9 in dollar gold pieces, one half-dollar piece, three slips cut from newspapers—one from the *Evening Bulletin*, being a notice of the History of England, in verses; another slip, containing a piece of poetry styled "The Welcome," by THOMAS DAVIS; also, another piece of poetry, styled "The Satisfied," and the "Prisoner's Song," from the German of UHLAND; one diamond ring; and in her pocket was one pair of black kid gloves.

For description of two other unrecognized bodies, lying at Bellevue Dead-House, see *Inquest at Manhattanville.*

Description of Unrecognized Bodies:

The following is a full description of the two bodies still unrecognized, found at Manhattanville, and now lying at Bellevue Dead-House for identification:

1. Body of a woman, apparently 35 or 40 years old; calico dress, with two rows of buttons down the breast, interlaced with black cord; black mits upon the hands; white stockings and gaiters; height about 5 feet 6 inches. On the fingers were found two gold rings, one plain and the other quite richly chased; the latter with the following initials engraved inside: "J. M to E. E. T.;" also, a gold pencil-case, with double slide; brown silk bead-purse, containing $1 in silver and a large trunk-key; gold brooch-pin, set with a cluster of small brilliants, artificial.

2. Body of a female child, apparently 3 or 4 years old; long dark-brown hair; short white dress; white stockings and high morocco shoes; one stocking tied with a strip of calico as a garter.

These bodies will remain for inspection at the Dead-House, as long as it is possible to preserve them.

———•———

New-York Daily Times, 2 August 1852.
The coroner posted a list of eight bodies that had not been identified. Two more bodies found at Manhattanville were listed separately.

and not recognized will take place this afternoon, at 6 o'clock, from the house on the new Steamboat Dock. The bodies will be interred in the Cemetery of St. John's Church, Yonkers, the Vestry having given a lot for that purpose. Citizens are invited to attend. WM. W. SCRUGHAM. By authority of the Coroner." The second funeral announcement was somewhat more abbreviated. [59]

For each funeral, the jury members served as pallbearers for the solemn ceremony. A line, two by two, was formed to pay last respects to the unknown victims as the procession headed toward the Reformed Dutch Church for the first funeral service. At the second graveside service, people noted that William Radford, an owner of the *Henry Clay*, was among the group of mourners.[60]

Ominously, during the first funeral, the darkened evening sky was filled with rumblings of thunder and crashes of lightning. While the village bell tolled in the distance, a cart slowly transported the coffins up the steep hill to the donated plot in Saint John's Cemetery. Reverend Seward of the Presbyterian Church, Reverend Cook of the Episcopal Church, and Reverend D. H. Miller of the Baptist Church shared their prayers at the two services. Reverend Seward pronounced the words that committed the unknown victims to their final resting place. As the mourners stood silently, he prayed, "Here, amid the shades of evening and beneath a dark and frowning sky, we commit the bodies of these strangers to the ground.

'Earth to earth—ashes to ashes—dust to dust.' "[61]

Chapter 6

Remembrance

THE REPORTED TOTAL of lost was listed at seventy lives. There were undoubtedly more. All perished in one terrible disaster on a sunny summer day on the Hudson River. While the unknown victims were committed to their eternal rest in Yonkers, the other victims were also remembered. Remembered for the life they had led; remembered by those who remained behind.

The weeks and months that followed were filled with darkness and sadness, emptiness and loss. Always present, a deep aching for the loved ones who would never walk the earth again, never smile, never laugh, never love. With the darkness of mourning, came only time for remembering—that was all that was left.

In 1852, Nathaniel Hawthorne and his wife Sophia moved to Concord, Massachusetts, into the first house that they had ever owned. Hawthorne was working on writing the campaign biography of Franklin Pierce, and in his free time the young author passed the lazy July days walking about his country grounds, especially the hillside which he had grown to love. The previous owners, the Alcotts, had called the place "Hillside," but Hawthorne quickly chose a new name for his own home, "Wayside." It was the year of their tenth wedding anniversary, and the couple joyfully awaited the arrival of Nathaniel's dear sister **Maria Louisa Hawthorne**, who was coming for a visit.[1]

Louisa, as she often did, delayed her visit to her brother for a few weeks. She had written to him from Salem on the first of July, "I must put off coming to you till next week. I am glad you like your house, and that you seem at last to be settled." The following week offered another diversion for Maria Louisa as she was off to Saratoga with her uncle for a two-week stay at an upstate New York spa. Upon her return, she once again planned to visit her brother, who provided her

LIST OF THE DEAD.

We have carefully revised and corrected the list of names of the dead, and the following statement may be relied upon as accurate—including all that have been found and recognized up to last night

1. Miss Elizabeth Hillman, aged 68. A maiden lady.
2. Mrs. Harriet E. Colby, of Montpelier, Vt., aged 32.
3. Mrs. Matilda A. Fennell, of New-Hanover County, N. C.
5 and 6. Sarah Denison and Miss Mary Cooper, of West Farms, Westchester County.
7. John K. Simons, son of John W. Simons, of No. 67 Eldridge-street, New-York ; and
8. Elizabeth Shanckey, his nurse.
9. George K. Marcher, of No. 345 Broadway, New-York.
10. Joan B. M. Hanford, aged 17 months, daughter of the late Cyrus Hanford, No. 215 West Twentieth-street, New-York.
11. Mary Ann Robinson, wife of Anthony Robinson, of No. 69 Perry-street, New-York.
12. Isabella, their infant daughter.
13. Matthew Crannell, aged 13 months, son of Matthew Crannell, of No. 150 Hudson-street, Albany.
14. John Hosier, of 214 Wooster-street, New-York.
15. Mrs. Maria Bailey, wife of Prof. Jacob W. Bailey, of West Point.
16. Maria Bailey, daughter of the above.
17. Mary Thompson, and
18. Eugene Thompson daughter and infant son of John L. Thompson, of Lancaster County, Penn.
19. W. M. Ray, of Cincinnati, Ohio.
20. Abby Ann Ray, wife, and
21. Caroline Ray, daughter of the above.
22. Margaret Chattilon, wife of John Chattilon, No. 184 Cherry-street, New-York.
23. George Thielman, of Poughkeepsie, brother of the above.
24. Katarina Chattilon, aged 3 years, daughter of the above.
25. R. A. Sands, aged 9 months, son of Isaac D. Sands, Stanton-street, New-York, carman.
26. Charlotte Johnson, (colored,) of Poughkeepsie.
27. Jane Murray, aged 30, wife of Adam Murray, of Chicago.
28. John Murray, aged 1 year and a few days, son of the above.
29. Christopher Benjamin Hill, aged 15, (colored,) servant in the cook's galley, on board.
30. G. F. Whitlock, No. 96 Allen-street, New-York.
31. Mrs. Whitlock, wife of the above.
32. Mrs. Julia Hey, Newburg, N. Y.

33. Elizabeth Pearsall, aged 15, step-daughter to D. Tillou, of South Brooklyn.
34. A. J. Downing, aged 37, merchant, Fishkill.
35. Miss Adeline M. Holmes, No. 96 Allen-street, New-York.
36. Mrs. Emily Bartlett, wife of Professor Bartlett, of the Collegiate Institute, Poughkeepsie.
37. Mrs. Matilda Wadsworth, of Fishkill, widow, aged 26.
38. Abraham Crist, Esq., counsellor-at-law, of New-York City and Brooklyn.
39. J. J. Speed, Esq., of Baltimore, Md., counsellor-at-law.
40. J. S. Schoonmaker, of Jordansville, Ulster County, merchant.
41. Phœbe Ann Jordan, of the same place, his neice.
42. Elizabeth McNally, domestic servant, New-York, aged 27.
43. Hon. Stephen Allen, ex-Mayor of New-York City.
44. Howard H. Simons, infant son of John W. Simons, of New-York, aged 2½ years.
45. Mrs. Johanna Hanford, widow of Cyrus Hanford, of No. 215 West Twentieth-street, New-York.
46. Mrs. Thompson, wife of John L. Thompson, District Attorney, Lancaster County, Penn.
47. Isaac D. Sands, carman, of Stanton-street, New-York.
48. Mrs. Isaac McDaniels, of Rutland, Vt
49. Henrietta Truax, of Schenectady, 19 years of age, wife of Peter Truax, of Brooklyn.
50. Mary Frances Cecilia Truax, about five years old, daughter of the above.
51. Jeanie B. Thompson, infant daughter of Mr. Elmore Thompson, No. 181 Henry-street, New-York.
52. Mrs. Anna B. Marcher, of East Chester, aged 60.
53. Miss H. W. Moore, aged 45, of Oxford, Miss.
54. Miss Maria L. Hawthorne, (sister of Nathaniel Hawthorne, the author,) of Salem, Mass.
55. Caroline A. Dewint, aged 58 years, of Newburg, New-York.
56. Miss Eliza Kinsley, aged 13, of West Point.
57. Miss Harriet T. Kinsley, aged 18, of West Point.
58. Miss Thielman, No. 84 Cherry-street, New-York.
59. Mrs. Catherine Ann Schoonmaker, Jordanville, Ulster Co., N. Y., (wife of J. S. Schoonmaker.)
60. Miss Elizabeth D. Ledyard.

Add 10 bodies yet unrecognized, and we have an aggregate of SEVENTY LIVES known to be lost, the bodies being already recovered. It is quite certain that more remains under the wreck. Efforts will be resumed to-day for their recovery.

New-York Daily Times, 2 August 1852.
Various lists were compiled of the dead. This one lists sixty known and ten unrecognized. Other reports noted higher numbers in the days following the disaster.

New-York Daily Times,
4 August 1852.
This list added more names to the known victims list. There was also a #63. She was Mrs. Ann Hill who was buried in Yonkers.

The Dead.

The following bodies having been recognized by the friends, we append the names to the list of the Dead :

61. Mrs. EMELINE E. MILLIGAN, wife of JOHN MILLIGAN, of New-York.
62. Miss HOLMES, of No. 96 Allen-street, New-York—aunt to Mrs. G. F. WHITLOCK, lost.

with train schedules. Unbeknownst to him, Maria Louisa did not board a train on July 28, but instead boarded the steamboat *Henry Clay* at Albany.[2]

In the early morning hours of July 30 , Hawthorne's dear and trusted friend William Pike arrived at "Wayside" to deliver the dreadful news, "Your sister Louisa is dead!" The words quickly erased the bright morning atmosphere and cloaked it with darkness. Hawthorne stood as if in a trance brought upon by shock of the news. The words he heard from his dear friend were incomprehensible. His wife Sophia, also stunned by the words, began to ask questions as if not understanding what Pike had said. Pike answered each of her inquiries with "She was drowned!" and continued, "On the Hudson, in the *Henry Clay*!"[3]

Unable to say one word, Nathaniel silently left the room. He preferred to be alone in his study and then to walk solitarily along the hillside of his beloved home at "Wayside." His young son, Julian, would later reminisce that his father had "an expression of darkness and suffering on his face such as his children had never seen there before."[4]

Overcome with grief, Nathaniel Hawthorne was unable to bring himself to go to New York and allowed his cousin Robert Manning and his uncle John Dike to handle affairs at the disaster site. After Maria Louisa's remains were recovered, Manning made the identification. Arrangements were made for a funeral in Salem on the morning of August 3rd. Hawthorne arrived too late to attend because the letter sent notifying him of the funeral arrangements had not arrived in time. He missed his sister's funeral by a few hours. She was already buried in the Howard Street Cemetery near the grave of her beloved mother who died just three years before.[5]

Nathaniel Hawthorne, when he purchased his home, had planned that Maria Louisa would possibly come to live with his family. He knew Maria Louisa loved his children, and they in turn had loved their special aunt. Now these plans were gone, gone with the death of Maria Louisa. There were only the memories left of her to cherish. For Nathaniel and Sophia there was also the grief. Their son young Julian could not hold back his tears. For their daughter Una, there was a memento to cherish. She was given the damaged broach that had been affixed to Maria Louisa's dress when she was lost.[6]

Images of the circumstances of Maria Louisa's death whirled in the minds of family members. Nathaniel's wife Sophia, in a letter to her mother, anguished, "I have not the courage to ask whether she was burnt before she was drowned."[7]

After the funeral, Nathaniel returned to Concord and immersed himself in his work and in his thoughts. Unable to truly express his feelings about his grief, he absorbed himself in his biographical writings about Franklin Pierce.[8]

On August 2, 1852, at the Stuyvesant Institute in New York City, the monthly meeting of the New York Horticultural Society was called to order. At the meeting for those who had not heard, the members were informed, "the death of Mr.

A. J. Downing, the eminent Horticulturist, was announced in feeling terms, and appropriate tributes to his memory were expressed by Mr. Meade and other members of the Society."[9]

Andrew Jackson Downing, born to humble beginnings, grew up in Newburgh where the majestic beauty of the Hudson River and the Hudson River valley surrounded him. In 1838, he married Caroline DeWint of Fishkill, the daughter of Mr. and Mrs. John Peter DeWint. The Downings made their home in Newburgh.[10]

By the early 1850s, many of A. J. Downing's dreams had come to fruition. He had already written several successful books and had been the editor of *Horticulturist* magazine for many years. In 1850, he had been appointed to design the grounds of the nation's capital and the Smithsonian Institution. In the same year, he set to paper a design for "Springside," an estate in Poughkeepsie for the businessman Matthew Vassar. "Springside" was nearly finished, but Downing did not live to see its total completion.[11]

The *Washington Republic* printed the following acknowledgement upon his death, commenting also about his unfinished projects in the Washington D.C. area.[12]

> **The Washington *Republic*, speaking of the death of Mr. A. J. DOWNING, says:**
>
> " Among the passengers destroyed by the recent catastrophe on board of the steamer *Henry Clay*, on the Hudson River, was Mr. A. J. DOWNING, of New-York, editor of the *Horticulturist*, and extensively and favorably known as a rural architect. To him was intrusted by the President the duty of marking out and generally beautifying the public grounds lying south of the canal, and the Lafayette, Franklin and other squares in this city. With the work, as far as it has progressed, the utmost satisfaction has been expressed; and those who take an interest in city improvements have looked forward with anxiety to the consummation of the well-matured plans of the distinguished artist, under his own immediate superintendence."

New-York Daily Times, 4 August 1852
One of the many obituary notices for Andrew Jackson Downing.

Downing owned a successful architecture firm in Newburgh and, following his death, a notice appeared in the *Newburgh Telegraph* on August 5, 1852, informing the public that the business of A. J. Downing would pass to his partner Calvert Vaux. Vaux was an English architect who had come to the United States to specifically work with Downing. He now had the responsibility to complete Downing's unfinished work.[13]

Downing had supported the idea of spacious parks within the limits of large cities. He was particularly supportive of a grand park in the center of New York City. It was a dream unfulfilled for him, as were his plans for the Washington Mall and the Smithsonian Institution. However, for Downing there would be a remembrance. The American Pomological Society arranged for a large marble urn, designed by Calvert Vaux, to be placed in the gardens at the Smithsonian Institution to honor the well-respected architect. An inscription on the statue is a tribute to Downing's inspiration to others:

"The taste of an individual, as well as that of a nation, will be in direct proportion to the profound sensibility with which he perceives the beautiful in natural scenery. Open wide, therefore, the doors of your libraries and the picture galleries all ye true republicans! Build halls where knowledge shall be freely diffused among men, and not shut up within the narrow walls of narrower institutions. Plant spacious parks in your cities, and unclose their gates as wide as the gates of morning to the whole people."[14]

Downing was buried in Old Town Cemetery in Newburgh. Directly across the Hudson River, in what today is Beacon, there stands a church named Saint Luke's. In 1852, it was known as Saint Anna's. In the old church burying ground is the grave of a Matilda Wadsworth.[15]

Mystery surrounded **Matilda Wadsworth**, a young widow from New Orleans. She had been visiting her uncle Dr. Rumsey in Fishkill, New York, before the *Henry Clay* disaster. She was an acquaintance of the Downing family and was traveling with them on the *Henry Clay* when she tragically lost her life. Strangely, her body did not have any inquest records according to any reports in newspapers. A short obituary appeared in the *Newburgh Telegraph* on August 5, 1852: "Mrs. Wadsworth was a resident of New Orleans, and a niece of Dr. Rumsey of Fishkill, where she had been visiting for her health."[16]

There is a Matilda Wadsworth buried in Saint Luke's Churchyard. However, true confirmation of her identity still is elusive as there are no church records of her death. Was this the mysterious Mrs. Wadsworth from the *Henry Clay*? An old printed record of the church's gravestones indicated that the Matilda Wadsworth buried there was the daughter of William and Anna Caverly Boyer. The records indicated her date of death as July 1852. Buried in the same churchyard was a James Sykes Rumsey, whose wife was named Harriet Caverly. Could this be the Uncle Rumsey that Matilda had visited? [17]

For Matilda Wadsworth, her death proved just as mysterious as her life. She was reported to have died clinging to A. J. Downing. Now, with the wide expanse of the Newburgh Bay between them, the Hudson River that took their lives together now keeps them eternally apart in death.[18]

It was noted in the *New-York Daily Times* that **Mrs. Caroline DeWint** "resided at the village of Fishkill, and was a lady of large fortune, being the owner of a vast amount of property in that vicinity. Deceased was an estimable lady, kind, humane, and benevolent, and was the only surviving niece of Hon. John Quincy Adams."[19]

Caroline came from both patriotic and politically prestigious stock. She was the grand-

The following obituary notice of Mrs. DE WINT, from the Fishkill *Standard*, is a worthy tribute to the memory of that lady:

"In the death of Mrs. DE WINT our community is called to mourn one of its brightest ornaments, the family circle a head, whose warm affections and endearing cares had secured for her the most devoted attachment, while the Church is called to part, also, with an esteemed and consistent member. Accomplished, affable, and hospitable, her heart seemed bent on doing good to her fellow-creatures, while her chief delight was to secure the happiness of those about her. Unassuming in her manners, she secured the friendship of all who knew her, and her name will long be cherished in our midst, with emotions of the most grateful remembrance."

The Eagle (Poughkeepsie), 7 August 1852.
Obituary notice for Caroline DeWint,
the wife of John Peter DeWint.

daughter of John Adams, the second president of the United States. Caroline was just eighteen years old when she lost her mother, Abigail "Nabby" in 1813. The following year, young Caroline married a friend of her brother's. Her new husband was John Peter DeWint, a stable and hard working young man of independent means. The couple moved to his family estate in Fishkill, New York, where they raised their own family for the following four decades until her own untimely death on the *Henry Clay*.[20]

Upon Caroline DeWint's death, the *Fishkill Standard* printed her obituary in tribute. Mrs. DeWint left her husband John Peter and her children to mourn. For her daughter, also named Caroline, the sadness was doubled. The younger Caroline lost not only her mother Mrs. Caroline DeWint in the tragedy, she also lost her husband Andrew Jackson Downing.[21]

Words spoken before the Brooklyn Supreme Court expressed the loss of another in the *Henry Clay* tragedy, that of **Abraham Crist, Esq.**: "At this bar, Mr. Crist was always recognized as a leader." Mr. Van Cott stood before the court to request an early adjournment in respect for Crist. Van Cott went on to expound the skills and virtues of his associate saying among other things, "Mr. Crist was destined to rise to a very high distinction in his profession."[22]

Eloquently, the speaker continued, saying that Crist's death was due to his heroism: "He was a man of extraordinary nerve; always cool, collected and energetic, and of all the men I ever knew, fitted to confront a sudden and terrible

DEATH OF A. CRIST, ESQ.—In the Supreme Court, Saturday, special term, forenoon, Mr. Robert H. Morris alluded to the death of Mr. C., (one of the sufferers in the Henry Clay,) an eminent member of the Bar, and moved, out of respect to his memory, that the Court adjourn. The motion was seconded by Mr. Shepard, who, with Mr. Gould, offered remarks, which were responded to by Judge Edwards, and the Court adjourned. After the adjournment of the Court, the members of the Bar present called Mr. Robert H. Morris to the chair, when addresses were delivered by Mr Brewster and others, and measures adopted in relation to testifying respect to the memory of the deceased.

New-York Daily Tribune,
Monday, 2 August 1852.
Death notice for attorney Abraham Crist.

emergency; and withal an expert swimmer. . . . Instead of escaping at once he remained to counsel, encourage and aid others. . .he was carried to the bottom by the desperation of those who clutched him in their death-struggle between the boat and the shore. He thus perished, filled with the noble thought of saving others. . . ."[23]

Abraham Crist had been a resident of Montgomery, New York, for several years, but most recently resided in Newburgh. He, with his wife and children, were visiting some relatives in the Montgomery area at the time he took the *Henry Clay* back to the city. His family had remained behind. At his death he left a grieving wife and five children.[24]

Found in **Stephen Allen**'s possession at the time of his death was a paper with the words, "keep good company or none." The short phrase was a testament to a man who had been known for his respectable life and service to community and country. Born in 1767, he grew up to young manhood during the American Revolution while he apprenticed with a sail maker to learn a trade. By the time he reached his twenties, he was in business for himself.[25]

His public career began as a council member in 1817, and four years later, he served as mayor of New York City for three terms beginning in 1821 to 1823. In 1824, he worked as a commissioner to study the prison conditions in New York City and Auburn, New York. His study resulted in the acquisition of land at Sing Sing for the construction of a new state prison. Later, he served in the state senate, and in 1833, he became one of several water commissioners to bring a clean water supply to the city. [26]

Allen held many positions during his life, including president of the Tradesman's Bank and president of the Mechanics' Society. He was a director of the Mechanic's Bank and also a director of the Hudson River Railroad Company. His years of public service included that of trustee of the House of Refuge and a commissioner for the Introduction of the Croton Water.[27]

The *New-York Daily Times* posted a fitting memorial of Stephen Allen from *The Journal of Commerce,* which described him as "truly one of nature's noblemen-generous, patriotic, upright, honorable true. . .had lived to a good old age, and filled up a life of eminent usefulness and honor. . . ."[28]

Allen was eighty-five years old at the time of his death, a death by drowning hardly a fitting end to such a prestigious personality. His funeral served to make tribute to such a devoted American and consummate gentleman. The service was the appropriate gesture for one who led an illustrious life of public service. Reverend Thomas H. Skinner Jr. performed the funeral ceremony at the Mercer Street Presbyterian Church in New York City and spoke of the years of service Mr. Allen gave to his community.[29]

The minister provided an example of Allen's generosity with an incident occurring during Allen's tenure as sub-treasurer during the presidency of Martin Van Buren:

"Mr. Allen had two clerks, whose salaries he thought were too limited for the duties they were called upon to perform; he therefore, in order to remunerate them, divided his own salary between them. . . ."[30]

New-York Daily Tribune,
**30 July 1852.
One of several obituary notices regarding Stephen Allen.**

The Evening Post gives the following notice of Mr. ALLEN:

Among those who perished in the destruction of the steamer Henry Clay was one of the most useful and highly valued citizens of New-York, Stephen Allen. Mr. Allen began life as a sail maker, and laid the foundation of his fortune in that business. He had few advantages of early education, but was endowed with a strong understanding, and a mind of such activity that he found no difficulty in accomplishing himself with the requisite information for all the important posts which he filled in the course of his long life.

He was made, in 1809, President of the Mechanics' Society in this city, and this led to the establishment of the Mechanics' Bank, of which he was one of the founders and first directors. He held the post of Mayor of the city from the year 1821 to 1823 inclusive, and left the office with the reputation of having been one of the best chief magistrates the city ever had. He was most strict and impartial in the execution of the laws, never wavering in his duty, or yielding for a moment to the temptation of making himself popular by winking at their violation.

In 1826, he was made President of the Tradesmen's Bank. He was, whether before or after this we do not recollect, a member of the New-York Assembly, of which his good sense and his habits of careful investigation, and his incorruptible probity, made him a most valuable member. In 1829 we find him a member of the New-York Senate.

He took a very active part in the introduction of the Croton water into this City, was one of the first Water Commissioners, and assisted in forming and executing the plans by which that important enterprise was at length happily completed.

He took a great interest in the reform of our City Charter, and sat in the Convention which remodelled it some twenty years since, giving it a more popular character. In 1846, he was a member of the Convention which revised and amended the Constitution of the State, making those important changes which have since been adopted by other States, introducing an elective judiciary, pruning the Executive of its patronage, and imposing restraints on legislative prodigality.

In short, Mr. Allen was one of those to whom, for nearly half a century, the community looked when a public servant was wanted in whose clear, practical judgment and inflexible integrity it could place the utmost confidence. It was in acknowledgment of these qualities that he received from Mr. Van Buren the commission of Assistant Treasurer in New-York, immediately on the enactment of the Independent Treasury law.

Mr. Allen was a decided Democrat in his political opinions, and one of the early members of the Tammany Society. He was much occupied with the management of public institutions of various kinds, such as the House of Refuge, of which he was one of the Trustees, and in the success of which he took great interest.

He perished—was murdered, shall we say?—at the age of eighty four, when the infirmities of age had begun to creep over him. He had not, however, retired from active life, and held a place in the Board of Directors of the Hudson River Railroad at the time of his death.

J. J. Speed, Esq.

The Baltimore Clipper has the follow-ing particulars as to this lamented gentleman, who per-ished among the lost passengers of the *Henry Clay*:

Mr. Speed had lately been confined by a severe indispo-sition, and went to New-York for the benefit of his health. He was on his return; and, unfortunately, took passage in the ill-fated steamer. Mr. Speed represented the city of Annapolis in the House of Delegates of Ma-ryland, at the session of 1825, and was an active, intelli gent and useful member. He subsequently removed to Baltimore and practiced law with success. Some years ago he was a prominent candidate for nomination by the Whig Convention, as Governor of the State. In the monetary crisis through which our State has happily passed—and when apprehensions were entertained that the State debt would be re-pudiated, Mr. Speed stood conspicuous among those who insisted that the State's credit should be sustained, and her obligations be hon-orably fulfilled. In a series of letters he gave his opin-ions at large upon this important subject; and these letters were said to have revived confidence among the creditors of Maryland in Europe.

Above: *New-York Daily Tribune*,
Monday, 2 August 1852.
Below: *New-York Daily Tribune*, 31 July 1852.
Notices regarding the death of J. J. Speed, Esq.

[By Telegraph.]

The Death of J. J. Speed, of Baltimore, by the Henry Clay Catastrophe.

BALTIMORE, Friday, July 30, 1852.

The death of Mr. Speed by the catas-trophe on board the steamer Henry Clay, has caused great regret here. He was a prominent member of the bar, and enjoyed a highly lucrative practice. He took an influential part in the measures for restoring the credit of the State, and was generally recognized as an able and profound writer. Mr. Speed would have been the next Whig candidate for Governor.

Reverend G. D. Abbott followed the speech with prayers, after which the coffin was moved to the vestibule of the church. Onto their shoulders the six pall-bearers lifted the coffin "made of rosewood, orna-mented with silver beaded screws, and a plate bearing the usual inscription—the name and age of the deceased." The procession moved forward with the two reverends leading, then the pallbearers with the draped coffin.[31]

The procession of mourn-ers followed to the gravesite. Stephen Allen was buried in his family vault at the Second Street Cemetery in New York City. Today, the cemetery is also known as the New York City Marble Cemetery.[32]

The management at Irv-ing House in New York City had been holding letters for several days sent there to the attention of **Jacob J. Speed**. He was expected to return there after his trip to Ithaca, New York. But Speed's arrival at New York City would not come as planned.

He drowned and was found about a mile downstream from where the *Henry Clay* had burned. His identity had been confirmed; two handkerchiefs were found on his person with the mark "J. J. Speed."[33]

A successful attorney, Speed had political aspirations. His obituary from Bal-timore, placed in New York City newspapers explained.[34]

Upriver Hudson River towns were called to mourn several of its citizens as well. **Jacob Schoonmaker** was a prominent merchant from Jordanville. He and his wife were on the *Henry Clay* with their niece on the day of the fires. The three all lost their lives. The *New-York Daily Times* printed a statement on August 3, regarding Mrs. Schoonmaker, who was a longtime resident of New York City:

"Mrs. **Catherine Ann Schoonmaker**, whose body was found on the Jersey shore, was married about two months since, and was on her way for the first time since her removal from the City, to visit her relatives and friends, when she met with such a distressing death. She was an amiable, intelligent and active member of society, and was much esteemed by those acquainted with her. She was for seven or eight years Assistant Secretary of the Greenwich Sabbath School, in this City, corner of Bleecker and Amos-streets."[35]

Two days later the *Newburgh Telegraph* printed: "**Mr. And Mrs. Schoonmaker**, of Jordanville, had been married but a short time. Mr. S. was on his way to the city for the purpose of purchasing goods. He is represented to have filled a creditable position among the citizens of his place of residence-a man of good morals, honest and impartial in all his dealings. Mrs. S. was much esteemed for many virtues and her loss will be deeply felt in the social circle in which she moved and was respected."[36]

The Schoonmakers were buried in the Schoonmaker family burying ground to the west of Tuthill, New York.[37]

In the same *Newburgh Telegraph* a paragraph about the Schoonmaker's niece was also included:

"**Miss Phoebe Ann Jordan** was a daughter of S. T. Jordan, Esq. of Jordanville—a young lady of prepossessing personal appearance, of cultivated taste . . .a kind and obedient daughter and consoling friend . . . .From the statements made by those by whom her body was rescued it appears that when taken from the water her body gave evident signs that the vital spark had not yet fled and that had it been possible to obtain medical aid she might have been restored to life. Her loss is mourned by a wide circle of relations and acquaintances."[38]

She is buried in the Schoonmaker family burying ground along with her aunt and uncle, as well as her father who died two years later.[39]

The loss of the two sisters **Harriet and Eliza Kinsley** age twenty-one and thirteen respectively, was among several tragedies that haunted the Kinsley family. Their predeceased father was Zebina James Duncan (Z. J. D.) Kinsley who grew up on the Kinsley family lands adjacent to the West Point Military Academy along the Hudson River. On an 1844 map of West Point, the location of the Kinsley lands was indicated south of the military installation and north of Cozzen property.[40]

Z. J. D. Kinsley attended and graduated from West Point and for fifteen years served as an instructor there. He then left the military installation to begin his own academic institution in Highland Falls, New York, where he established the "Classical and Mathematical School."[41]

Tragedy for the family struck in 1836 when Z. J. D. Kinsley and his wife lost three children, Mary, Julia, and Joseph, ages nine, eight, and seven,, to scarlet fever. Z. J. D. Kinsley died in 1849 at only forty-eight years of age after a horse threw him to the ground. A year later his five-year-old daughter died; she was thrown from a carriage due to a runaway horse. Then in 1852, the *Henry Clay* disaster took his daughters Harriet and Eliza.[42]

One could only imagine the grief and pain Z. J. D. Kinsley's widow, Eliza, suffered. Only four months would pass after the deaths of Harriet and Eliza when, mysteriously, their mother, Eliza, was discovered sitting in a chair dead. As tragedy brought death one by one to this family, the burials took place in the Kinsley family plots. After Eliza's death, there remained one surviving son, Edward, who inherited the Kinsley family lands.[43]

The story of the Ray family is another multiple tragedy brought about by the *Henry Clay* catastrophe. Samuel Cook was on board with his daughter, her husband, and their two young children. Cook could only save one of them. He took his grandson to shore, unable to help the others. **William M. Ray, Abby Ann Ray, and Caroline Ray** all perished. The *Cincinnati Enquirer* of July 31, 1852, printed the following regarding the *Henry Clay* disaster:

"New York, July 30—William M. Ray, his wife and daughter aged about nine years, of Cincinnati, are among the bodies taken from the wreck of the *Henry Clay*. It is believed that many more bodies are still beneath the wreck, which cannot be reached. . . ."[44]

On August 1, the same newspaper noted the following statement taken from *The New York Herald*:

"Mr. W.F. Ray, wife and daughter of Cincinnati, Ohio drowned. Mr. S.W.D. Cook saved one of Mr. Ray's children, by swimming from the stern of the wreck to the shore."[45]

The little family is buried in Saint Paul's Lutheran Church Cemetery/Oak Hill Village Cemetery in the town of Durham and village of Oak Hill, New York.[46]

Another family to suffer many deaths was that of the John Thompson family of Lancaster, Pennsylvania. **Mrs. John L. Thompson, Mary Thompson, and Eugene Thompson** all lost their lives. On July 31, 1852, The *Saturday Express* of Lancaster, Pennsylvania, noted:

"Among the list of the lost we regret to record the names of Mrs. John L. Thompson, and her two children of this city. Mr. John L. Thompson, his nurse, and other child escaped. Mrs. T. was a most estimable lady, and her loss is deeply mourned, not only by her bereaved husband, but by a large circle of friends and acquaintances. . . ."[47]

On August 4, 1852, the *Examiner* and *Herald* of Lancaster, Pennsylvania, printed:

"This community was startled on last Wednesday evening, by the news of the terrible catastrophe on the North river, of which the wife and two children of our respected townsman, John L. Thompson, Esq., were among the victims. No event has occurred for a long time which created a deeper sensation. The deceased lady was highly esteemed by a large circle of friends, whose deepest sympathies are with the bereaved husband and father.

"The bodies of the two children were recovered on the day after the disaster, but that of the mother not until Saturday, it having floated several miles down the river. They were interred at Princeton, N.J. (Mrs. T.'s native place) on Monday afternoon. A committee of gentlemen from this city attended the funeral."[48]

The Thompson burials took place in Princeton Cemetery, an old burial ground founded in 1757 that houses the remains of several prestigious people, including President Grover Cleveland. After the loss of his wife and two children, life had changed for John L. Thompson and his one surviving child. By the following year, they had moved to Fairfield, Connecticut.[49]

Jacob Bailey of West Point and his sons grieved for their own loss, another double tragedy from the *Henry Clay*. Jacob's wife **Maria Bailey,** and their daughter **Maria,** who both lost their lives, were buried in the West Point Cemetery. A short time thereafter, Professor Bailey received a letter from Captain Henry Coppee, who had known Bailey from the days when Coppee was an army officer at West Point. In later years, Coppee became a professor at Lehigh University. In Coppee's letter of condolence to Bailey, he included the following delicate poem he had composed in memory of Bailey's wife and daughter:

I saw two flowers at morning,
The one was a full blown rose,
And it lay at rest, on a matronly breast
Its hue like the sunset close,
The other an opening rose bud,
As white as the sea-washed pearl,
And it graced, amid masses of dark
    brown hair
The head of a beautiful girl.
And the flowers were types of those
    lovely ones
That Mother and Daughter fair;
Sending abroad o'er lifes arid road,
A fragrance everywhere.

I saw two graves at even
'Mid the fading light of the day,
And there at the head of the cherished
    dead,
The morning flowers still lay.
And I said "O gentle flowers,
Are those beautiful ones beneath?
Can aught so bright and so lovely,
Feel the withering hand of death?"
"Not so ! Not so!" spake the flowers,
'Tis but dusk beneath this sod,
But the holy souls, on this sunset ray,
Went up to the bosom of God-"

H.C.[50]

The village bell tolled on a dark and ominous night as the bodies of the unidentified victims were laid to rest in Saint John's Cemetery in Yonkers. The plot was at a high point in the old cemetery and would be drenched with sunshine for the centuries to come. In the days that followed the disaster, family and friends came forward. They identified some of the unknown victims by the detailed descriptions that Coroner Lawrence had maintained.[51]

Bridget Broderick was known as unrecognized number 7. Her sister identified her. It was also reported that Joseph Jackson had been buried at the plot. His parents later identified him. [52]

Anne Hill and Eliza Smith were two other women identified. They were sisters traveling with J. J. Speed, and they shared the same fate in the *Henry Clay* disaster. The sisters also came to share the same burial plot. A short obituary appeared in the *Philadelphia Public Ledger*:

"Suddenly on the 28th ult. Mrs. ANNIE HILL, wife of the late David Hill, of the city of Philadelphia and daughter of the late Samuel Smith of the city of Baltimore.

"Suddenly, on the 28th ult. Miss ELIZA A. SMITH, daughter of Rebecca H. and the late Samuel Smith, of the city of Baltimore."[53]

Their families were fortunate to know of their fate. However, for three of the other unrecognized victims who were buried in the donated plot, their identities remain unknown for eternity.

After the burial of the unknown victims, local residents collected contributions to erect a marker for the gravesite. Local lore has it that wealthy Robert P. Getty went to Getty Square in Yonkers to pass a hat collecting donations. The "Odd Fellows," a local brotherhood, was credited with donating the monument. A small white marble column was set in place over the gravesite to mark the plot where the seven coffins were buried. The inscription on the column read:

"Here lie the bodies of Mrs. Ann Hill and her sister Miss Eliza A. Smith, both of [] Bridget Broderick, Wm. McCluskey and two women and one man whose names are unknown, all of whom were lost from the Henry Clay on the burning of that steamboat two and one-half miles below the village of Yonkers on her passage from Albany to New York, July 28, 1852."[54]

The words once inscribed on the white marble stone were worn away long ago. But the fragile column still stands today pointing to the heavens, marking the graves of these victims buried below—serving as a simple monument of

REMEMBRANCE.

Book 2: Retribution

Chapter 7

Truth Under Oath

IN WASHINGTON D.C., at the time, members of Congress had already been working on a revision of the Steamboat Act of 1838. The driving force for such legislation was the result of several deadly steamboat accidents occurring around the country over the course of many years. The *Henry Clay* disaster was one of the worst and perhaps the most severe in the history of the Hudson River. News of the fire, the great loss of life, and the public outrage to riverboat racing all endeavored the politicians to hasten their work on an appropriate bill.[1]

Back in New York, the numbers were clear. Death came for too many. From the inquest, the official count of the dead was seventy. In the following days and weeks, the numbers crept higher in varying newspaper reports. During the inquest testimony, Elmore Thompson said, "the boat appeared very full, in all directions, there was not a seat vacant in the ladies' saloon; the hurricane deck was also crowded, and no seats vacant; there were a great many on the forward main deck; all stools were full; all seats on the after deck were occupied; there must have been 400 persons on board; the boat was uncomfortably crowded." John Gourlie estimated three hundred fifty passengers on board, George P. Edwards, another passenger, believed the number was "between four and five hundred passengers," and John Thompson leaned toward the five hundred figure. It would never be known how many others, those who had no one to ask for them or account for them, were lost in the river on that tragic day.[2]

In the days that followed the disaster, the newspapers compiled and printed various lists of the dead, but a final, thorough, and accurate count would never come. There was no official record of the passengers who had boarded on the *Henry Clay* that eventful day. Whatever documents may have existed were burned in the fires. Bodies of victims were found up to six miles north of the disaster site and south to the Jersey shore. If any remains made their way past New York City and beyond, they could have been swept out to sea to fall into the abysmal depths of the Hudson Canyon.[3]

The loss to the families of victims was inestimable. Slowly, thoughts turned to the survivors and to a quest for justice. The *New-York Daily Times* issued a sympathetic statement on August 2, asking that the families of the victims be given financial help, as some "are cast destitute among us." The owners of the boat had thus far made no offers of assistance. The newspaper added in its statement: "The evidence adduced before the Westchester Jury must add to the weighty proof already accumulated against the officers of the racing boats."[4]

Theodore Romeyn, Esq., the chairman at the Astor House meeting issued his own statement: "Preliminary to a selection of any definite course of action against the owners of the Henry Clay, it is proper that we ascertain the actual facts, as they can be made to appear by the testimony of disinterested witnesses. This we are striving to do. It is our desire to do this in a spirit of impartiality, without favor or prejudice, and we wish to find reasons for removing our present impressions, which certainly are strongly against the officers and owners of the steamer." He also added that the testimony indicated that the boat had previously been on fire and there were inadequate precautions for passenger safety, such as adequate water buckets and small boats.[5]

The accusations flourished in the press as witness testimonies at the inquests added to the mountain of negative sentiments against the owners and officers of the *Henry Clay*. *The New York Herald* printed a caustic editorial, professing, "That the whole trip was a desperate race, does not now admit of the shadow of a doubt; and that the accident was caused by racing, is equally clear. And when the fire took place, there was no man in charge of the boat who showed the slightest ability or self-possession, in saving the lives of the passengers. With ordinary capacity in a commander, and even the ordinary means of escape, not a life might have been lost. The boat was not headed to the shore in the proper direction—the passengers were sent aft, instead of forward—there were no small boats, no buoys, not even a line, to rescue the devoted victims from death, though the stern of the unfortunate steamboat was actually on land; and one gentleman testified that he was for half an hour struggling in the water."[6]

The public demanded retribution. In response to the printed and verbal accusations, the owners of the *Henry Clay* hoped to have the opportunity to present their own side. They sent a letter to Coroner Lawrence a few days into the official inquest.[7]

McMahon was the legal counsel to the owners and wanted to question witnesses at the inquest. Counselor Scrugham, the advisor to Coroner Lawrence, was against allowing McMahon any participation at the inquest and was also against any of the owners being called to testify. He reasoned that there might be criminal charges pressed against the owners, and it would be inappropriate to allow their involvement at an inquest that

To the Coroner and Jury acting on the Inquest respecting the steamboat Henry Clay, at Yonkers:

GENTLEMEN—On behalf of the owners and officers of the steamboat Henry Clay, for the purpose of the investigation of the truth respecting this most lamentable occurrence, I would request that all of the hands of the boat, and the officers and owners, be called up and rigidly examined as to their knowledge of the facts concerning this disaster. There is a Mr. Harris, of Burlington, Vermont, who was a passenger on board of the boat, who will testify to what he knows concerning the matter. We will furnish the names of all the officers, for that purpose, if desired. We desire to conceal nothing.   D. McMAHON, JR., Of counsel for boat and owners.

New-York Daily Tribune, Tuesday, 3 August 1852. McMahon wanted the owners and officers, his clients, to have an opportunity to testify at the inquest at Yonkers.

may find them guilty. Lawrence heeded his advisor on both counts and called other witnesses to testify.[8]

On August 3, the official inquest testimony was nearing an end. Coroner Lawrence decided to question one owner of the *Henry Clay*. He called William Radford. In his testimony, Radford confirmed that Thomas Collyer built the *Henry Clay*. He also confirmed the ownership of the steamboat and that he was not on board the day of the disaster.[9]

Radford was asked to name the officers working on the boat that day. He testified, "A young man named Jessup acted in the capacity of Clerk, and in the absence of the Captain officiated as second Captain." Radford confirmed that the engineer on that day was John Germain and the first pilot was Edward Hubbard. Radford testified that he did not know the barkeeper or assistant engineer but mentioned, "James Elmendorf sometimes assisted the head pilot." He did not know the names or exact number of firemen on board but testified, "there were as many as four." Radford also indicated that there were two small boats located on the promenade deck and as many as twenty buckets of water were stored on the hurricane deck.[10]

The questioning turned to the operation of the boat's furnaces, and Radford used a drawing of the *Henry Clay* to illustrate several points. He described the furnace as having a water bottom, which was "a perfect security against fire." He explained that ashes and cinders were normally collected and then disposed of overboard. He did not know if it was normal practice to hold onto the cinders and ashes until the boat reached its final destination. Radford testified that the furnace used Lackawanna coal and added, "I am positive that tar, pitch or resin would have a tendency to slacken the fire; wood was used to kindle the fires; they never used wood on the trips, to my knowledge; but they could, however, use wood with as much safety as coal."[11]

Following the formal questioning, Radford was given the opportunity to make a statement. He explained he had an agreement with Bishop, Smith, and Collyer that there would be no racing that day. Radford indicated that the "Henry Clay was capable, of making, with the tide, in slack water, from twenty to twenty-two miles an hour; in figuring up the time from Albany to where she burned deducting the landings, her running was about sixteen to seventeen miles per hour. . . ."[12]

Radford then requested "to say to this jury something about the men we employed; the Engineer we hired, we paid him $1,000 per year, and considered one of the most competent in his profession; we also paid our Captain $1,000 per year; Mr. Hubbard we paid $60 per month, he being a pilot on this river for many years; all our men were of the best character, and we paid the highest wages on the river."[13]

Radford explained that he and Collyer asked the captain to have the engineer run the boat at "an easy gait, and steady, as the *Armenia* would stay behind him. . . ." He went on to say, "the boat had on board a certificate showing her boilers good for thirty five pounds of steam at any time; the boilers were new and strong. I have examined the boilers since, and as far as I am capable of judging, they are now in good order, even since the fire."[14]

His final statements concerned insurance. To confirm his confidence in the safety of the *Henry Clay*, Radford stated, "I had less insurance on the *Clay* than any other of my boats, believing her to be the safest boat against fire among them all. I never heard of her being on fire before, as report says she has been."[15]

Other witness testimony at the inquest indicated that there was much confusion as to what actually happened on the day of the disaster. Testimony differed greatly depending on where a witness had either stood or sat on the steamboat on the day of the fire. Some passengers were in sight or hearing distance from officers of the boat, while others were not in close proximity to any of the officers. Some passengers had retreated to cabins in lower levels and avoided seeing anything. However, through the course of the inquest, much of the eyewitness accounts the jury heard condemned the officers of the *Henry Clay*.

The inquest testimony indicated that there had been visible, intense conflict between the crews of the *Henry Clay* and the *Armenia*. Witnesses often used the word "strife" to describe that tension. Adam Murray testified, "I noticed at Albany that the agents were in great strife to get passengers for their respective boats." Elmore Thompson testified, "There did seem great strife, particularly on the dock; the runners were each recommending their boats as the fastest." [16]

How bad was this contention? Excitement among runners was nothing new on the Hudson River. Such behavior was part of everyday business. Lloyd Minturn's testimony put the runners' behavior into better perspective. Minturn was a well-traveled person, and he believed the discord he observed had far exceeded what he considered ordinary: "There was more excitement among the runners than I ever saw before." [17]

Was this the prelude to a race between the two steamboats? John Cubbage surmised just that: "I discovered the anxiety of each man belonging to the boat, and thought there must be a race of extraordinary interest."[18]

The tension, or as was stated, the strife, endured at least as far downriver as Newburgh Landing. John Thompson, who had been waiting at the Newburgh docks that day, testified that he "did not see the *Armenia* but heard by the ticket-sellers at Newburg, that there was great strife between the boats, and when they came in sight at Newburgh, they cheered for "Harry of the West," referring to the *Henry Clay*.[19]

Inquest testimony indicated that long before the *Henry Clay* reached Newburgh, there was what some believed to be a race with the *Armenia*. The race was suspected to have started either at Hudson or Catskill. Matthew Crannell Jr. testified that the two boats did not appear to be racing at the outset until after Hudson Landing, but, "they then appeared to run each other hard." "When we reached Catskill," Cubbage testified, "the excitement was intense among the officers and men of the *Clay*; I saw the officers continually examining the *Armenia* with the aid of a telescope; this was after leaving Catskill, when the *Armenia* was ahead; they were on the fore part near the wheel-house, and also on the promenade deck." He added, "I also heard the continual tapping of the pilot's bell; I think it was a bell to increase the steam, as I felt the boat shake after the ringing each time; I thought if it had been to trim the boat it would not have sounded so often and in such quick succession."[20]

Several inquest witnesses indicated that the crew of the *Henry Clay* was intent on racing. Samuel Cook, who had boarded at Catskill testified, "I heard the hands observe the *Clay* would make Kingston Point first. They appeared to be striving to get ahead of the Armenia." Isaac McDaniels noticed, "from all appearances, the men on the *Clay* were bent on beating the *Armenia* at any and all hazards; I mean the firemen; they would put wood in the boiler and look out the window to see if the Armenia had gained on us."[21]

Such behavior presented the appearance of a concerted effort to race on the part of the officers and crew. John Gourlie testified that during the race, Thomas Collyer "was going from the pilot house to the main deck, and back again, frequently." These actions were construed as his taking an active role in the command of the boat and the suspected racing. Cubbage "noticed how pleased the officers and men (that I saw) were that we had passed the *Armenia*." Lloyd Minturn noted, "the crew were excited, and many drinks were taken by the hands and others, congratulating the success of the *Clay*, in outracing the *Armenia*."[22]

However, other witnesses contradicted the testimony indicating a race. Two men, who each lost loved ones in the disaster, refuted the idea of any racing between the two boats. Jacob Bailey "had not noticed anything unusual in the speed of the vessel." John L. Thompson also "noticed nothing unusual in the speed of the boat. . . saw no indications that the boats had been racing." He "spoke to one of the hands, telling him I had heard there had been racing, and he replied that the *Henry Clay* never raced."[23]

The inquest jury spent some time inquiring about the collision that occurred north of Kingston. Witnesses detailed the events preceding the collision. Stoddard Colby testified that, "the boats while racing came together so as to touch." Cook noticed a man come out with a fender to throw over the guard during the collision, and Gourlie said there was an order given for passengers to move to the larboard side. Witness testimony indicated many passengers became fearful, but the officers responded to passenger complaints with the simple words, "There is no danger." For some of the passengers, the collision with the *Armenia* was no accident. Murray testified, "The *Clay* could have kept off; the *Armenia* was close to the shore and I do not think that she could have got nearer without great danger."[24]

After the *Henry Clay* passed by the *Armenia* to make Kingston Landing, several witnesses believed the racing appeared to have subsided. Stacy Bancroft testified that he believed the racing continued until Kingston, but, "after leaving there, I thought the racing ceased." Cook confirmed, "after we left Kingston Point the *Clay* was far ahead of the *Armenia* and I did not notice any further racing; all was quiet on board after leaving Kingston."[25]

While Cook believed it was quiet on board, other testimony indicated that the *Henry Clay* kept up a strong speed for the remainder of the trip. Whether the speed was excessive during the latter part of the trip was up for debate. Phineas Wells said that he had "traveled on steamboats at the speed of twenty-six miles an hour. I think the *Clay* was running from seventeen to twenty miles an hour. . . ." George Edwards testified that the *Henry Clay* "was running quite sharp to Stony Point. I have seen her run as fast before." Adam Murray noted that around 2:00 P.M., "The *Armenia* was at this time three or four miles behind, and the *Clay* did not appear to slacken her speed at any time. On the contrary, she was straining every nerve, and driving ahead rapidly."[26]

This strain may have caused extreme heat to emit from the steamboat's machinery. Cubbage had gone "up on the *Clay* the day before the calamity, and stood on the promenade deck, often near the pipes, the greater part of the day, and did not observe such intense heat there." That was the day before the disaster. However, on the next day, when the *Clay* was on its return trip from Albany to New York City, he noticed "the intense heat around the smokepipe and machinery." Minturn's testimony corroborated that "the heat of the machinery was intense, and, indeed, more so than I ever felt it before on any boat and I have traveled on them all over the world." He also mentioned "there was a knot of waiters on the forward deck and one of them remarked that he 'wanted to get well forward when the boiler burst.'"[27]

Phineas Wells and James DePeyster both testified to seeing cinders and pieces of coal emitted from the smoke pipe, and Matthew Crannell noticed a "considerable smell, like burning wood." Cubbage indicated in his testimony that at the time of the fire near Yonkers, there was a smell like he observed at Kingston, the smell of "burning wood."[28]

This smell of burning wood was the harbinger of death. The massive fire on the steamboat that erupted from the furnace room caused confusion and hysteria among the passengers. DePeyster testified, "I can only compare the scene to a bee hive; it was all confusion and excitement." At the same time, an order was given to "go aft." Minturn had testified that the barkeeper gave this order. This fateful order was one that changed the destiny of many passengers' lives. John Thompson testified, "I think at the time some one connected with the boat directed us to keep on the stern, as the fire was in the center of the boat." He later added, "That was the fatal mistake." Cook shared similar sentiment: "We could have all got on the forward deck." He continued, "in the space of a minute all communication was cut off from forward to aft."[29]

The "go aft" order was one of several circumstances that would, in the end, result in extensive loss of life. With hundreds trapped on the stern of the boat, there was little option for safety. The boat was burning up, but where were the small safety boats normally stored on board? Where were the water buckets to extinguish the blaze? Such were resources that should have been readily available on the boat for the safety and preservation of the passengers' lives.

According to several witnesses, there were neither. While Edwards saw the crew attempting to extinguish the flames with the pails of water, Minturn contradicted with, "I am confident there was no water in the buckets when the men commenced to use them." Wells testified that he looked for boats but found none, while Edwards testified that he "saw one boat. . .on the hurricane deck; did not see any attempt made to get out that boat." Bailey had the same impression; he testified that he "saw no effort to get out boats."[30]

When it became evident that the fire could not be extinguished, Minturn said that he "implored the pilot to head her for the shore; I told him the boat was "irretrievably on fire; and for God's sake to head her for the shore without delay." Edwards testified that he also told the pilot to go ashore but the pilot or second pilot commented that, "I did not know anything about it." Edwards, on his second attempt, saw another man go to the pilot and said, "he had better run her ashore." As the boat turned toward shore, Minturn, who had been on the forward part of the boat explained the scene from his vantage point: "the forward deck was densely crowded, and a breathless silence prevailed just before she struck."[31]

The handling of the steamboat became a contentious issue. Adam Murray was very critical, stating his opinion, "had the steamer been run on the shore broadside, there would have been nearly all the lives saved; it was not over five minutes after the fire was discovered by me before we felt the shock of striking the shore." The newspapers also presented negative opinions, one of which was printed in the *New-York Daily Times.*[32]

There were public outcries regarding the manner in which the boat was run aground, but the criticism of the actions of the officers and

MANAGEMENT OF THE HENRY CLAY.
To the Editor of The New-York Daily Times:

It seems the terrible loss of life by the burning of the *Griffith*, on Lake Erie, last year, occasioned by the temporary absence of the pilot from the wheel, whereby the vessel burned to the water's edge before she could be run ashore—has not made any impression on the pilot of the ill-fated steamer *Henry Clay*. Instead of putting the boat around towards the landing at Yonkers, or running her broadside on the shore, with lines ready, fore and aft, to fasten to trees, whereby every life could have been saved, as well as all baggage, he left his post, to find out the cause of the alarm, losing the most valuable time to save the lives of those intrusted to his care, as officer of the steamer. Where were the life-preservers? Where the life-boats, to run lines to the shore? Undoubtedly nowhere! We may well exclaim, How long will such conduct go unpunished?

Respectfully Yours,   J. C. S.

New-York Daily Times, **Friday, 30 July 1852.**
There was much criticism of the officers onboard the *Henry Clay*. This letter to the editor criticizes the pilot.

owners extended further. The speed of the boat and the condition of the machinery were criticized. The question of official authority on the boat was raised. Witnesses stated that no one was in authority at the time of the disaster. Testimony indicated that the clerk, James Jessup, had instructed passengers to remain calm and was acting like he was in charge, and the barkeeper gave the order to go aft. Tallman, although ill, made a few appearances on deck. Collyer, who was not an officer, but an owner of the steamboat, was walking about as if he had some authority.

Witness testimony indicated that before and during the race, Collyer had indeed taken an active role in the running of the steamboat. Cubbage testified that before Kingston, "I heard this officer say 'There's no danger;' I believe it was Mr. Collyer. I should have known him if I should see him again; I believed him to be an officer from the interest he took in the boat; he was giving orders, and very anxious to land the passengers in haste; at all the landings." Minturn testified, "during the race Mr. Collyer seemed considerably excited. . . he officiated as an officer. Mr. Collyer manifested his excitement by going to his friends, Mr. Harris, Mr. Ridder, and others, and talking with them in an excited manner about the *Armenia*, and then he would go back and forth to the pilot-house frequently."[33]

However, witness testimony indicated that at the time of the fire, there was no authority on the boat. This accusation resounded with comments such as those made by John Gourlie, who saw "nobody giving orders connected with the Clay;

Testimony of a Passenger on the Armenia.
To the Editor of The New-York Daily Times:

MISSIONARY ROOM, No. 150 Nassau-street, }
New-York, July 31, 1852. }

The late awful calamity attending the burning of the *Henry Clay* is largely occupying the public prints, and engaging very generally the public attention. I was on the *Armenia* from Albany to Newburg, and was a witness to what took place between those points ; and I am perfectly amazed at the statement in this morning's papers, from Messrs. RADFORD, COLLIN and TALLMAN, that there was no racing between the *Henry Clay* and *Armenia*, at the time of the late accident, or *on that day*. I have been on boats on the Ohio and Mississippi rivers, when it was *admitted* that they *were* racing ; but I have never witnessed anything that *appeared* to me so much *like* racing, or so much like a *desperate* struggle for victory, as was most manifest in the case of the two boats after they left Bristol landing till the *Clay* shoved the *Armenia* so near the shore that the latter boat slackened her speed, let off steam, and the boats separated. It *seemed* to me at that time, and before any accident occurred, that they were like two race-horses, to whom their riders were applying whip and spur, utterly regardless of everything but victory. And if it were not so, will those individuals explain why the *Armenia* did not land at Hudson, nor the *Clay* at Bristol ? Why the officers on either boat ordered the passengers to the side of the boat farthest from the other boat? Why about once in five minutes the pilot struck his bell twice, which *appeared* like calling for more steam, and the effect of which was like putting spur to a horse, and increased the comparative speed of the boats ? This was done several times, at intervals of about five minutes, and I felt alarmed, and said to my brother-in-law that we had better seek a safer place. Why in total disregard of the affrighted looks of passengers, and their expressed fears, were the boats brought so near, side by side, as almost to touch each other ? Why did the *Clay* run the *Armenia* in shore if there were no strife ? It *seemed* to me, and to many others, that the officers on both boats were utterly reckless of the comfort or safety of those who had taken passage with them.

That the officers of both boats were perfectly reckless in their conduct, and are justly chargeable with the awful calamity that followed, I, for one, have not the shadow of a doubt. Yours. &c.,

JAMES P. FISHER, Schenectady, N. Y.

I saw none of the officers until I got ashore; I believe if they had done their duty not a human soul would have been lost." In similar fashion, James DePeyster commented, "I have no question that if the officers of the boat had done their duty at the time of the alarm every passenger would have been saved. No officer gave any instruction; no boats; planks or anything else was done to aid the excited passengers; I saw no one connected with the *Clay* that appeared to aid or assist in saving the lives of the passengers, or to aid or counsel them; nor were they informed at any time of the danger the vessel was in."[34]

Minturn agreed in his detrimental testimony, "I saw none of the officers take any active part where I stood, or in my hearing; I saw none of them anywhere at the time." However, he added "in justice to Mr. Collyer, I would state that he was in the water and saved a large number of lives; he was the only man connected with the boat that I saw exert himself."[35]

New-York Daily Times,
2 August 1852
James Fisher was an *Armenia* passenger who left at Newburg. His letter details the racing and collision.

The Boston *Transcript* publishes the following letter, addressed to Hon. ISAAC LIVERMORE, of Boston, by his son, who was a passenger on the *Armenia*. Some incidents are mentioned which have not before transpired :

NEW-YORK, July 29, 1852.

MY DEAR FATHER : I hope never again to be obliged to witness what I saw yesterday afternoon. I left Catskill yesterday morning in the *Armenia*, which took the place of the *Reindeer*—the regular boat—while she is repairing. We were ahead, but having to stop at Bristol, the *Henry Clay*—opposition—overtook us, and we proceeded for several miles side by side, until finding that she could not pass us and make the landing at Kingston first, she bore down on us and crowded us in towards the shore, until we could go no further, and then she ran into us, staving in our works just forward of the wheelhouse. Our boat was stopped, and the *Clay* allowed to go on and land first at Kingston. My wife and her sister were so much alarmed that I went ashore at Kingston, crossed to Rhinebeck, and after waiting there an hour and three quarters, took the cars for New-York. When we were two miles this side of Yonkers, we found the *Clay* run bow first on the shore—her bow within six feet of the beach. The train was stopped, and all the assistance that could be rendered was afforded. The stern of the boat lay in deep water, and she was all on fire amidships and in the after part. The water was filled with women and children, clinging to stools and other floating objects, and the beach covered with the rescued and the drowned, and others whom they were trying to resuscitate—some with success, and others who were too far gone to survive. Women were uttering agonizing shrieks for lost children, husbands bewailing the loss of their wives, and rescued women and children, with their clothes drenched and torn, looking in vain for lost husbands and parents. One little boy, 5 years old, was too small to jump from the boat, over the railing, and he was seen to burn to death on board, without any means of rescuing him. The awful scene was one that could not fail to move the stoutest heart. We remained by the burning boat for an hour, and took on board as many sufferers as our train could accommodate, leaving the remainder to come in another train, which was due a few minutes after. Some died in the cars after we started, and there were others who, I think, cannot survive, whom we brought down. A family, consisting of a lady, her two daughters, and her sister, who had been staying at the Mountain House with us, and came down the mountain in our company, were on board. They were saved, after the boat struck, by rushing from the after part to the bow, *through the fire* and smoke. The lady's wrist was somewhat burned, but they received no other injury. I could not give you an idea of the horror of the scene in one letter, and will refer you to the papers for details.   E. M. L.

There were several other eyewitness accounts that indicated the officers were all in the water assisting in the rescue. However, that point did not appear to be strongly brought out at the inquest.

The newspaper reports about the inquest testimony and other eyewitness accounts fueled the anger of the public. Stories of the disaster were read with curiosity and outrage. Dr. Phineas Wells wrote of his experience as a passenger on the *Henry Clay*. Letters from Mr. E. Livermore and James Fisher, both passengers on the *Armenia*, also appeared in

New-York Daily Times, 2 August 1852. E. Livermore was a passenger on the *Armenia*. He wrote to his father about the *Henry Clay* disaster.

Facing page: *New-York Daily Times*, 30 July 1852. Dr. Wells was a passenger on the *Henry Clay*. He details his experiences in this letter.

LETTER FROM DR. WELLS.

The following letter, published in the *Commercial Advertiser* of last evening, furnishes the testimony of an intelligent eye-witness. The writer is a well known physician of Brooklyn :

I was a passenger on the ill-fated steamer *Henry Clay*, on the 28th inst. I took the boat at Cozzens landing, West Point ; I found on board a large company, variously estimated by passengers, from 400 to as high as 800 ; the last number I have no doubt was too large. The first, probably, is much nearer the truth. It was the general testimony of the passengers whom I found on board, that the *Henry Clay* had been racing with the *Armenia*, (not *America*, as erroneously stated in the *Herald*,) all the way from Albany ; that there had been a collision of the two boats ; that the officers of the *Henry-Clay* had been remonstrated with by the passengers for this racing as a dangerous proceeding, and that they were only told *there was no danger*. These facts I have knowledge of only from the statements of others, but they were confirmed by so many witnesses, that I have no doubt of their truth. Parties left the boat on account of these facts, before they reached Cozzens's, whom I afterwards met on the train which brought me from the fatal scene to New-York. I talked with them on the conduct of the officers of the boat, and they gave the above as their reasons for leaving and taking the cars. One party so left, and for such reasons, at Rhinebeck.

When I went on board I passed directly to the upper deck, where I noticed one fact which now seems to me to have had a fearful significance. The upper deck was literally covered with small fragments of anthracite coal in all directions which were not protected by the awning over head. A furled side awning was taken down from one side of the boat and carried to the other, the folds of which were filled with these pieces of coal. They fell in little showers every time the furnaces received a new supply of fuel, and the fragments were, some of them, nearly as large as peas, I should think. I examined some, and found they were entirely unmarked by the fire they had passed through, though it was such a fire as such a draft would keep up—a draft of sufficient power to blow such bodies through the furnace and chimney before the color could be dimmed.

After the boat was found to be on fire, I know no reason for censuring the conduct of the officers ; it was running nearly in the middle of the river, which might be a mile and a half wide at the place of the accident, if such a word may be employed to describe such an event ; the pilot turned her toward the shore immediately, and ran her bows on the beach with full force ; I was on the upper deck and at the stern of the boat.

The fire broke out in the vicinity of the chimney, which was about the junction of the forward and middle thirds. When the shore was reached, most of those on the lower deck were cut off from escape at the bows, by the fire filling the whole of the middle of the boat between decks. All on the upper deck I think escaped over the bows, there being a space on the right side of the boat, of perhaps two feet wide on the deck, where the fire was not yet burning when the last persons passed, who, I believe, were the writer of this and four ladies who had desired his protection. These were passed over the bows, and the writer followed, thankful to the merciful Providence to which he owed his preservation.

It was no part of my object in writing this account to attempt a description of the scene which the boat now presented, or to try to make others sensible of the agony of mind those suffered who were compelled to see it. Its miseries can never be told ; its horrors never be described.

It can be no relief to these to turn now upon the officers or owners with reproaches for their misdoings, which have had so sad an issue ; but is it too much to hope that in a Christian and civilized community these men will be held by the laws to the full measure of the responsibility of their deeds ? Not that their punishment can heal the desolated hearts and homes they have made, or soothe the anguish of which the memory of this scene is so full, by ministering to a spirit of revenge. This spirit I trust none will cherish. But if civilization has any value to men, its laws must protect their lives, and to this end, the laws of the land, in this case, should be most summarily administered.

The object of this communication was to state facts which I personally saw, and heard sufficiently testified to. But the most important one is yet to be stated—a fact which bears on the *owners* of the *Henry Clay* with fearful weight. I have said I stood on the stern of the upper deck when the fire broke out, and during the running of the boat ashore. While this was being effected, I looked about for the best means of safety for myself and the ladies who had appealed to me for protection ; I looked over both sides, where boats should have been suspended for the protection of lives in case of accident, but there *were no boats there*. When I had passed the ladies off over the bows, I turned and looked where small boats might have been, and where they are stowed or slung on some steamboats, but *there were none on this*. There were no small boats or other means of saving life on the *Henry Clay* except the poor help of floating settees and stools, which were thrown over in some numbers to those who were in the water.

The first boat which came to the help of the perishing was from a brig, at the time about three quarters of a mile distant ; the next from a tow-boat which was passing down the river ; the third was from the *Armenia*, the other racing boat, which did *not* pass by, as some of the morning papers state, but stopped and lowered her boat, and did good service in rescuing the drowning. A fourth boat came from a second tow, which came up before all the survivors were removed from the burning boat, to which they clung. *There was no small boat belonging to the Henry Clay* mixed in this scene, to the best of my knowledge and belief. My means for knowing if there had been I have stated. The remark has sometimes been made that human life is "trifled with" by men of steamboats and railroads, but let no man say this of the owners or officers of the *Henry Clay*. They have not trifled with the lives of their fellow-men. They have taken *them wantonly and wickedly*—and thus to take human life is not a "trifle."

The officers, that they might reach New-York City a few minutes before another boat, have sent unknown numbers of their fellow men to the bar of God, where they will meet them, and perhaps learn there that the scene of the 28th of July was made up of no "trifles." The owners, to save a few hundred dollars, have neglected to provide the means of safety in danger, suggested by the most common prudence, and the blood of these men, and women, and children, has fallen upon their skirts. To them this can be no "trifle." I pity those men ; from the bottom of my heart I pity them. The future to them can have no "trifles," if they be men.

And finally, when it is said the law knows no pity, may we not hope that it may be added, and does not "trifle" with such grave crimes as are involved in the calamity of yesterday ? The safety of the living demands this. The voice of every good man in the community must demand this. And there is a sense in which it may be said to be due to those whom this calamity has made to go mourning all the remnant of their lives, till their pains cease in their own graves. If they suffer, it should not be in vain ; others should have protection secured to them by the afflictions thus brought on those who have survived their friends and the horrors of this scene. That they may have this secured is the hope of

Yours, &c.,   P. P. WELLS,
No. 84 Clinton-st , Brooklyn, July 29, 1852.

the newspapers. The details from these eyewitnesses helped to arouse public opinion.[36]

Seven days had passed since the disaster. Lloyd Minturn's testimony served as a chronology of the day's events before and during the disaster. At the conclusion of his testimony, if no other witness could serve to affect those present, some of Minturn's last words could have moved even the most cold-blooded at heart. Minturn described one of the most horrific scenes of the entire tragedy.[37]

"I saw three little creatures burned to death on the promenade deck; the men of the boat threw off nothing; I think that if a hawser and lines had been thrown off, nearly all might have been saved; it could have been done in a minute; one of the children whom I saw enveloped in flames was standing in the coil of rope, with the flesh dropping from his body; there was ample time, to have made some arrangements to save life; had I been an officer of her, I know I could have accomplished something; I have traveled many years and I am free to say, there was no order or discipline on board the *Clay* at any time after she left Albany."[38]

Whether the timing of Minturn's testimony was perfectly planned or coincidence, the inquest came to a close. Coroner Lawrence and former district attorney Scrugham diligently imparted their guidance to the jury for determining a verdict. The section of the "Revised Statutes" was reviewed for the jury, as they were instructed to consider the evidence in accordance with the legal definition of murder.[39]

Deliberations began at 7:30 in the evening, and after twenty minutes the jury had arrived at their decision. However, there were necessary documents to be obtained, which delayed the releasing of the verdict until sometime after midnight.[40]

The inquest jury had decided. The owners and officers of the *Henry Clay* were found to be responsible for the deaths of so many lives on that fateful day, July 28, 1852. For those owners and officers, it was now clear that they would be put on trial for the crime.

The day had begun as any other on the Hudson River on July 28, 1852. Neither that day, nor the days to follow were anything ordinary. It ended in death and an accusation of:

MURDER.

Facing page: *New-York Daily Tribune*, 4 August 1852.
Verdict of the coroner's jury. There is a James Hubbard listed.
The name should have read James Elmendorf.

The Henry Clay Catastrophe!

THE VERDICT OF THE JURY.

Owing to the lateness of the hour at which our reporter arrived this morning, we are unable to give more than an abstract of the verdict of the Coroner's Jury, in relation to the Catastrophe of Henry Clay.

THE VERDICT.

The Jury find that on the 28th of July, 1852, the persons described as having been found dead at Yonkers were passengers on board the Henry Clay, that she took fire and was consumed, and that J. K. Simons, one of the persons, was burned to death, and that all the other persons, either by reason of the shock occasioned by the collision of the boat on the land, were thrown overboard, or that in order to save themselves from being burned, cast themselves overboard and were drowned in the Hudson River. That on the above-named day the Henry Clay left Albany, with passengers, about 7 o'clock in the morning; that Capt. John F. Tallman was Captain, and part owner; that Thomas Collyer was also one of the owners, James L. Jessup was clerk, Edward Hubbard was pilot, James Hubbard assistant pilot, John Germain was engineer, Charles Merritt assistant engineer; that a certain young man (whose name is unkown to the Jury, but) who was employed to tend the bar of the steamboat, and that these persons were on board at the time, and had each of them part of the charge of the said boat; and that for the purpose of excelling in speed a certain other steamboat called the Armenia, or for the purpose of increasing the speed of the Henry Clay, created an unusual and unsafe quantity of steam, and in so doing made excessive fires, and did not use ordinary prudence in the management of said fires; and, although often being remonstrated with by different passengers, did for a long time continue these excessive fires and in consequence thereof through their culpable negligence and criminal recklessness, the Henry Clay did, at 15 minutes after 3 o'clock, P. M., take fire, and all the deaths of the passengers afore described ensued;—so the jurors say, that the deaths of all the said persons, and of each of them, were the result of an act perpetrated by the said John F. Tallman, Thos. Collyer, James L. Jessup, James Ellmendorf, Edward Hubbard, John Germaine, and said barkeeper.

The act was imminently dangerous to others, and evinced a depraved mind, regardless of human life, although it was perpetrated without any premeditated design to effect the death of any particular individual.

Chapter 8

Indictment

AS SOON AS THE INQUEST JURY issued their verdict, the newspapers reported arrests of the owners and officers of the *Henry Clay*. Thomas Collyer, part owner of the *Henry Clay*, was reported to be the first arrested. In truth, he surrendered himself to authorities. Collyer was brought before the United States commissioner, George W. Morton, Esq. His defense attorney, Mr. Dennis McMahon Jr. was with him when the judge set the bond at ten thousand dollars, a large sum for that time.[1]

Newspaper reports also printed that the case would be heard in the United States Court, and as such, James Jessup, Edward Hubbard, and John Germain were brought before Commissioner Morton as well. The defendants were charged under federal law "with causing the death of sundry passengers of the steamboat *Henry Clay*." The bond for these accused was also set at ten thousand dollars.[2]

The owners of the *Henry Clay* arranged for the necessary bonding from several sources for each of the named defendants. J. L. Knapp and Lewis Radford posted bond for the pilot, Edward Hubbard. The steam engine makers, Joseph Belknap and Francis Cunningham posted for the engineer, John Germain. William Radford and Thomas Collyer posted bail for the clerk, James Jessup. Captain Tallman was still sick in bed and his arrest warrant was still outstanding. It was expected that Radford would post the bond for Tallman as he had done for Collyer.[3]

With federal warrants already acted upon, the newspapers were quick to criticize Coroner Lawrence for delaying the issuance of local arrest warrants within

STEAMBOAT HENRY CLAY—ARREST —
Warrants were issued by the U. S. Marshal, on Saturday afternoon, against Thomas Collier, one of the owners of the Henry Clay, and on board of her at the time of the calamity,) Capt. Talman, John Germaine, engineer, James L. Jessup, clerk, and Edward Hubbard, pilot, on a charge of Manslaughter, in causing the death of Stephen Allen. A. J. Downing, Mrs. Maria Bailey, Miss Maria Bailey, Mary Ann Robinson, Elizabeth Hilman, Matilda Wadsworth, J. J. Speed, and many others. The warrants were given to Marshal De Angelis, who yesterday afternoon arrested Mr. Collier, who gave bail in the sum of $10,000, to answer the charge. Mr. Radford, (said to be wealthy,) became his bail. The others have not yet been arrested.

The arrest was made under the act of Congress of July, 1838, which provides that if by the misconduct of the captain, pilot, or other persons employed on board, in their respective duties, the life or lives of any person or persons shall be destroyed, said captain or others shall be deemed guilty of manslaughter, (the trial to be before any Circuit Court of the U. S.,) and punished by imprisonment at hard labor for a period of not more than 10 years.

The arrest of Mr. Collier was based on the idea that being an owner of the vessel, and on board at the time, he came under the denomination of person employed on board. Mr. Radford was also one of the owners, but was not on board at the time. The same amount of bail, we understand, will be required (should they be arrested and give bail,) for the captain and other officers against whom warrants have been issued, as has been required in the case of Mr. Collier.

The proprietors of the steamboat Henry Clay, with her captain, pilot, engineer and clerk, have been arrested by the U. S. Marshal for the Southern District of New York, by authority of warrants issued against them under the law of the United States for securing the safety of passengers in steamboats. The amount of bail for each was fixed at $10,000, which was given. They stand charged with having caused the death of the passengers burned or drowned by the Henry Clay, for which the punishment we believe is imprisonment in the state prison for three, or ten years.

Now let the infamous scoundrels, upon whose guilty heads rests the blood of at least eighty human beings murdered by their recklessness, be followed up and put through to the end, until they are securely incarcerated within the state prison walls and decorated with the appropriate uniform, and for some time following people will travel with safety. To allow them to escape will be simply to practice cruelty to the innocent who will hereafter suffer in consequence, after the manner of the murdered passengers on the Clay. We protest against that mercy to the guilty which experience has shown to be cruelty to the innocent.

Left: *New-York Daily Tribune*, Tuesday, 3 August 1852. Collyer was the first to go before a judge regarding the charge. His bail was ten thousand dollars and was posted quickly.
Right: *The Eagle* (Poughkeepsie), 7 August 1852. As soon as the verdict was decided, arrests were made. There was no sympathy for the accused.

the jurisdiction of Westchester County. The official inquest records had been given to the district attorney of Westchester, Edward Wells, for review, which caused a delay. Coroner Lawrence deferred on issuing county warrants pending a decision by the grand jury. [4]

The issuing of both federal and county warrants created a quandary over jurisdiction in the pending case. United States authorities had made the first arrests. The defendants were held for bail of ten thousand dollars each and charged with manslaughter under the July 1838 Act of Congress (the 1838 Steamboat Act). The defendants were all freed on bond to await trial.[5]

However, the county of Westchester planned to charge the defendants with murder, not manslaughter, under county jurisdiction in accordance with the findings of the Westchester County inquest. Because of this warrant, the *Henry Clay* case became a habeas corpus situation. The defendants were placed in a position

☞ The Coroner's Inquest upon the late criminal destruction of life on the steamer Henry Clay has not yet made its verdict, and we trust will not do so without the most complete investigation of every particular. It is true that the opinion of the public at large is fully made up on the subject, and so, we can hardly doubt, is that of the individual jurors; but propriety manifestly requires a hearing of all the testimony bearing upon the case, before the promulgation of an official judgment. We, therefore, do not agree with those who complain of the slowness of the jury in coming to a decision.

At the same time it seems to us that the magnitude of the case requires from the officers of justice a more active participation in the inquiry before the Coroner than is usually regarded as their duty. If the owners and officers of the Henry Clay had killed a hundred persons in a more common-place manner, the public prosecutor of the County would doubtless have used efforts to have the truth fully brought out on this preliminary investigation, and in the verdict which concludes it. We do not understand that he has yet appeared before the inquest, though we learn that a well-known advocate, rejecting the request of the parties implicated in this awful event to serve them as their counsel, has of his own accord, rendered assistance in clearly eliciting the truth. It is not too late, however, for the proper law officer of the State to act in the matter, and we earnestly invite his attention thereto.

Meanwhile we observe with satisfaction that the United States District Attorney has caused a warrant to be issued for the arrest of the officers, and of one of the owners, who was on board the Clay at the time of the race and conflagration. They are accused of manslaughter, and will, we do not doubt, be brought to trial. This will, we trust, do something to put an end to the suspicion so generally expressed, that when people are massacred in public conveyances, justice cannot be obtained, nor anything done to prevent a recurrence of the catastrophe, especially if there be money on the side of the offenders.

New-York Daily Tribune, Tuesday, 3 August 1852.
An editorial before the inquest jury had made its decision.

to be charged under federal jurisdiction for manslaughter and county jurisdiction for murder. It was an impossible circumstance since state law forbade any person to be tried twice for the same crime.[6]

The defense and prosecution each fought for their position before Judge Edmonds who was assigned to preside over the case. The defending attorneys argued that the United States federal courts should have exclusive jurisdiction over the case. Understandably, that would be in their defendants' favor with the lesser charge of manslaughter and the opportunity for bail. The defense team also argued "the attempt to bring this case within the operation of the second subdivision of the section of Revised Statutes defining murder, is not warranted by law and reason, as no bodily harm was intended." Also for the defendants, if convicted on a manslaughter verdict, the sentence would be less, no more than ten years in prison, compared to harsher sentencing for murder.[7]

On the prosecution side, the district attorney of Westchester County brought up the point that "the conduct of the defendants, though not intended to produce death, was unnecessarily dangerous to the passengers, and evinced a depraved mind regardless of human life." The district attorney for Westchester wanted the stiffer charge of murder, which meant no bond could be posted and the defendants would be required to remain in jail through the trial.[8]

Arguments from both sides continued. After a day of deliberations in court there was no resolution as to which charge, murder or manslaughter, would prevail. Honorable Edmonds ordered the defendants to be placed in the custody of the Westchester County sheriff until the issues at hand could be resolved. A sticky point since bond was already posted for the defendants under the manslaughter charge. The lawyers finally agreed that the accused may leave on parole until the next court appearance while Judge Edmonds spent the following few days pondering his decision.[9]

However, the freedom of the defendants was short-lived. Judge Edmonds barely had time to begin review of the case when he received a petition from the defendants. Although they had been officially and legally freed until the next court date, the Westchester County sheriff had them rounded up and placed under arrest by order of a warrant for murder issued by a Westchester County judge. The charge read: "That they were the officers in charge of the steamboat *Henry Clay*. . . they engaged in a race. . .when it was run ashore. . .one of the passengers was burned to death and fifty-seven of them drowned. . .thereby the defendants had been guilty of murder in having killed those persons without authority of law, by an act imminently dangerous to others, evincing a depraved mind regardless of human life. . . ."[10]

The defendants' attorneys, F. C. Cutting, Dennis McMahon and C. O'Connor scrambled to intervene for the quick release of their clients, stating that the federal authorities had taken over the case. The attorneys argued that their clients should not be tried for murder because "there was no charge of an intention to do bodily harm to any one." They also argued that their clients were not guilty of first degree manslaughter because the accused "were not engaged in the perpetration of any crime or misdemeanor" at the time of the deaths.[11]

The legal arguments resulted in no resolution and the defendants were detained in jail. When Judge Edmond's made his final decision, he first addressed the jurisdiction problem. He stated that the federal courts might possibly have premier jurisdiction in cases of "Admiralty and maritime matters." Because this case was a maritime matter, the federal courts may prevail. However, Edmonds added, "the mere grant of Admiralty and maritime jurisdiction does not exclude State authority." [12]

Thus was the legal caveat. Federal authority may rule supreme, but the judge added that Congress "had not legislated as to the offence when committed within State territory." Whose jurisdiction should handle this case? Since Congress had not excluded state authority in maritime issues, then the state may also have jurisdiction. The burning of the *Henry Clay* and the death of several of its passengers had clearly occurred within the boundaries of the state of New York, although the deaths occurred in the water. The judge stated that he was not entirely clear himself that the United States courts had jurisdiction over New York State in this particular case.[13]

Without resolving the jurisdictional issue, the judge proceeded to address the charge of murder versus the charge of manslaughter. He looked at both sides of the issue, first explaining the federal point of view with, "The proceedings of the United States Courts are under the law of Congress, which enacts that every captain, engineer, pilot, or other person employed on board any steamboat, &c. by whose misconduct, negligence, or inattention to his or their respective duties, the life or lives of any person or persons on board said vessel may be destroyed, shall be deemed guilty of manslaughter." [14]

The judge's explanation leaned heavily toward manslaughter as the appropriate charge, but the judge proceeded to discuss the state's position. "The proceedings of the State Courts are under the State Statute, which enacts that the killing of a human being without the authority of law, when perpetrated by an act imminently dangerous to others, evincing a depraved mind, regardless of human life, although without any premeditated design to effect the death of any particular individual is murder."[15]

The judge further clarified that for a charge of murder, there must be evidence of intent to cause harm. The judge openly admitted, "in my view, that a design to do great bodily harm, or an intention to kill must attend an act imminently dangerous, &c., to make the crime murder. I at one time thought that there could be no conviction for murder under this clause of statute, unless there was an intention to take the life of someone, though it was not necessary to prove an intent to take the life of any particular individual." Edmonds continued, "Now, in this case, there is no allegation of an intention to do bodily harm, but, on the contrary, the facts alleged negative that idea; and thus, as one essential element to constitute the crime of murder is wanting, the prisoners ought not to be held on that charge." [16]

With his ruling, Judge Edmonds threw out the murder charge against the defendants. However, he continued, "They ought not, however, to be fully discharged, but may properly be held for manslaughter, and I am inclined to think, in the first degree." The judge added, "if the person having charge of a steamboat navigating our waters, or the person having charge of the boiler, for the purpose of excelling any other boat in speed, or for the purpose of increasing the speed of such boat, create or allow to be created, an undue or unsafe quantity of steam, they shall be guilty of a misdemeanor. (Laws of 1850, ch. 175,63.) Here it is alleged

Above:
**"The United States vs. Thomas Collyer
and Others"**
The grand jury issued an indictment for
manslaughter on 15 September 1852.

Right:
"The People vs. Thomas Collyer and Others"
The indictment for manslaughter was filed
24 September 1852.

in the warrant, in the very language of the statute, that the killing occurred while the prisoners were engaged in performing those very acts. So that although the warrant calls the offense murder, that which it details is, in fact, not murder, but manslaughter . . . ."[17]

The judge, although not resolving the jurisdictional issue, provided a decision based on the actual language presented in the warrant itself, which defines a manslaughter charge, not a murder charge. If the murder accusation had been upheld, the defendants would have been imprisoned until the trial. Since the judge had decided that a manslaughter charge was the appropriate charge, the defendants were set free on ten thousand dollars bond each. The defendants were allowed to leave the courtroom as free men until a federal trial rendered a final verdict in the case.[18]

The owners and officers of the *Henry Clay* returned home to resume their lives, at least for the present. Edward Hubbard, the accused and maligned pilot, returned to his wife and children. He was free until the trial, but it was not really a freedom upon which to be counted. Each day brought him closer to the date of the trial, when his freedom could be taken away for years. During these precarious days of freedom, he and the other officers also suffered the scourge of public opinion.

A week would pass before the grand jury presented their "true bill for manslaughter." On September 15, the official documents were released, carrying seven counts and naming the accused parties with their positions and duties on the day of the disaster. Thomas Collyer was listed as "part owner and acting for the captain of a certain Steamboat." John F. Tallman was described as "captain of said Steamboat and having charge thereof." James L. Jessup was "the Captain's clerk on board of said steamboat and having charge thereof." John Germain was "Engineer of said Steamboat and having charge of the boilers and other apparatus." Charles Merritt was "Assistant Engineer and also having charge of the boilers and other apparatus." Edward Hubbard was "the Pilot of said Steamboat and having charge thereof." James Elmendorf was the "second pilot of said steamboat and having charge thereof."[19]

The counts charged against the accused were listed in the indictment. The wording defined the actions of the defendants that allegedly caused injury to the passengers of the *Henry Clay*. The defendants were charged with "willfully, feloniously and unlawfully and for the purpose of excelling another boat. . .(called the *Armenia*) in speed and for the purpose of increasing the speed of the said Steamboat called the *Henry Clay*." [20]

The indictment accused Tallman, Jessup, Merritt, Hubbard, and Elmendorf of "aiding, helping, abetting. . .assisting" Thomas Collyer, John Germain, and John F. Tallman "in the felony and manslaughter." The indictment said that by their actions, the officers "did create and allow to be created in the boilers, and other apparatus for the generation of steam of the said Steamboat Henry Clay, an undue and an unsafe quantity of steam and in so doing did create and maintain and cause to be created and maintained within the furnaces of said Steamboat Henry Clay, by means of which unsafe and excessive fires."[21]

The counts accused John Germain and Thomas Collyer of having "made, built and continued such large[ ]and unsafe fires." The indictment further accused the officers of "feloniously and unlawfully, from ignorance and gross neglect. . .and for increasing the speed of the said Steamboat Henry Clay, did create and allow to be created an undue and unsafe quantity of steam. . . ."[22]

The result of those alleged actions by the accused were described as causing injury to passengers on board the vessel. The first victim identified in the indictment, described in graphic detail, was that of the young Simons boy who was "mortally burned, scalded and wounded in and upon, the head, face, neck, breast,

To the District Court of the United States, in and for the Southern District of New York, in the Second Circuit :—

The Grand Jury of the Southern District of New York, attendant upon the September term of the District Court of the United States, in said district, respectfully present—

That they have had under their consideration the cases of the steamboat Henry Clay and the steamboat Reindeer, involving so great a destruction of human life, laid before them by the District Attorney; and having found bills of indictment against such parties as have seemed to the Grand Jury criminally responsible in these cases, under the law of the land, they beg leave to represent certain matters connected with steamboat navigation on the waters of this district, which deserve the serious attention of the community. In the first place, it has been brought to the notice of the Grand Jury—and they accordingly present—that the steamboats navigating the North river are in the constant habit of violating the provisions of the act of Congress, which requires them to blow off steam at the landings or other stoppages of the boat. The injunction of the statute is found in the 7th section of the act entitled "An act to provide for the better security of the lives of passengers on board vessels propelled in the whole, or in part, by steam," approved, July 7, 1838, and is in distinct and imperative terms, as follows :—"And be it further enacted, that whenever the master of any boat or vessel, or the person or persons navigating said boat or vessel, which is propelled in whole, or in part, by steam, shall stop the motion or headway of said boat or vessel, or when the said vessel shall be stopped for the purpose of discharging or taking in cargo, or fuel, or passengers, he or they shall open the safety valve, so as to keep the steam down in said boiler as near as practicable to what it is when the said boat or vessel is under headway, under the penalty of $200 for each and every offence."

The experience of disasters from the neglect of this precaution, which led to this enactment, has been confirmed by the history of steam navigation since its passage, and the deliberate and habitual contempt of this wise and efficient provision of law, "for the better security of the lives of passengers," exhibited by steamboat owners and masters on the North river, calls for the severest reprobation on the part of the community at large, and a vigorous exaction of the statutory penalties by the law officers of the government. The Grand Jury take occasion to request the attention of the District Attorney to the enforcement of the proper pecuniary fines, and to express the opinion that in case of life lost by explosion, after a stoppage of a steamboat, during which this prudential measure has been omitted, the parties responsible will be subject to the legal and moral guilt of manslaughter. In the second place, the Grand Jury present that the steamboats on the North river are very insufficiently provided with any proper equipment, either for the extinguishment of fire or for securing the lives of the passengers in case of disaster to the boat, from this or other causes, which should drive them from it. An ordinary attention to the responsibilities the owners assume, in conveying passengers on vessels propelled by steam, should require from them a full provision of the appliances of fire engines, fire buckets, boats and life preservers, to meet the casualties incident to that mode of navigation ; and whether the origin of fire on board a steamboat be attributable to mere accident or criminal fault, the history of all such occurrences shows that the loss of life on these occasions, would have been greatly reduced by having the means at hand for saving the passengers from drowning. The Grand Jury therefore present to the consideration of the community, the importance of requiring from steamboat owners, in addition to all due precautions against the occurrence of disaster, a sufficient equipment of proper appliances for the preservation of life when the disaster occurs. The investigation of these cases has called the attention of the Grand Jury to another defect in the management of these steamboats, which they present to the attention of the court. They find that there is no command, discipline, or subordination, on board the boats, at all adequate to the emergencies which may at any time arise in the progress of this navigation. The chief officers of the boat are generally unknown to the passengers; they are designated by no badge of authority, and seem seldom to be selected with sufficient reference to those qualities of self-possession, energy and promptitude so essential to control, direct and inspire with confidence the inexperienced crowd, confused and alarmed by the danger, of the nature and extent of which, and of the means of escape from which, they are alike ignorant. The absence of proper command and discipline on board the Henry Clay, after the danger to the boat was known to the officers, and of suitable efforts to acquaint the passengers as to the means of saving themselves, the Grand Jury believe to have been a principal cause of the great destruction of life in the late calamity which befel that boat, and they earnestly suggest to their fellow-citizens that before a return of confidence in the steamboat navigation of the North river, they should be well satisfied that a better system of discipline, to meet emergencies, is established and kept up on board the boats, than has obtained hitherto.

And lastly, the Grand Jury present, that they find too much evidence that the practice of racing—in the various forms of racing against rival boats, racing against the railroad, and racing against time—has been of late very general and constant with many boats on the North river. Besides the immediate and terrible dangers of explosion and fire, to which this reckless and profligate practice directly leads, the Grand Jury consider the great hurry at landings as involving no inconsiderable risk to life and limb, and the abuse and falsehood which this vehement competition gives rise to, as evils of great magnitude. Cases not unfrequently occur of boats passing their regular landings, in spite of the remonstrances of passengers to such destination, in order to assist or secure a victory in the through trip. All these evils—such great disturbances in the safety, regularity, and comfort of steamboat travelling, for which this river was, for many years, so justly celebrated—it is in the power of the travelling community to repress and correct; and the height and extent which they have now reached demand a thorough, decisive, and persevering exercise of public opinion and public action, to restore this favorite mode of travel to the just conditions of prudence and safety, under which alone can it flourish.

The Grand Jury have confined their suggestions to the steamboat navigation of the North river, as the facts on which they are based have come to their knowledge from their investigations into the two cases of destruction of life which have both happened on that river. They desire, however, to call the attention of the law officers of the United States to the steam navigation on other waters of this district, that if any provisions of law be violated therein, they may be properly proceeded with. And all which is respectfully presented.

Luther C. Carter, Foreman.

Jireh Bull,	Peter J. Bogart,
George Webb,	Henry A. Halsey,
Julius Hitchcock,	Ezra Ludlow,
Wm. S. Stilwell,	David Quackenbush,
John J. Jackson,	Wm. K. Strong,
Thos. Thompson,	Thos. E. Smith,
Augustus L. Wood,	Albert W. Goble,
Joseph T. Bell,	E. S. Dewit,
Thos. McNight,	John W. Salter.

"The United States vs. Thomas Collyer and others"
The grand jury included a letter with the indictment regarding racing on the Hudson.

belly, back, sides, arms and legs, of him the said John K. Simons of which said mortal burns, scalds and wounds the said John K. Simons, there and there instantly dies. . . ."[23]

The document listed the names of several of the other victims who perished: "Elizabeth Hillman, Harriet E. Colby, Emilia C. Bancroft, John Hosier, Maria Bailey, Maria W. Bailey, Mary Thompson, William M. Ray, George M. Marcher, Joan B.M. Hanford, Matthew Crannell, Mary Ann Robinson, Margaret Chatillon, Isaac D. Sands, Jennie B. Thompson, Lucy B. McDaniels, Harriet Kinsley, Abraham Crist, Stephen Allen and Andrew Jackson Downing." The indictment stated that the fires forced those victims to jump overboard and be "drowned and suffocated in the waters of said River. . . ."[24]

The indictment ended with the listing once again of the defendants names and ended by stating that the defendants "feloniously and willfully, did kill and slay, against the form of the Statute in such case made and provides, and against the peace of the People of the State of New York, and their dignity." The indictment papers were signed by Edward Wells, District Attorney.[25]

Making a further point, the grand jury attached a statement to the indictment record illustrating the atrocities of riverboat racing on the Hudson River.[26]

Two more weeks passed after the issuing of the indictment, while the attorneys indulged in more legal maneuvering. United States District Attorney J. Prescott Hall, appearing before Judge Betts of the U.S. District Court, asked that the *Henry Clay* indictment be transferred out of the district court to the circuit court. Judge Betts allowed the motion to transfer. Due to a crowded court calendar, Judge Nelson of the circuit court moved the trial to be heard at a later month.[27]

The legal stage was now set. The inquest and grand jury had done their duties. The indictment had been filed while the wheels of justice turned slowly. More than a year would pass after the fateful death passage of the *Henry Clay* on the Hudson River. During that time, Franklin Pierce was elected president of the United States. Epidemics of cholera and yellow fever were documented in the newspapers. Railroad and river disasters and Indian massacres in the West made headlines, while the families of the victims of the *Henry Clay* waited for justice and mourned the loss of their loved ones.

The seasons passed, autumn, winter, spring, summer. As mid-autumn approached once again, the year was too short to ease the grief, relieve the pain, or erase the anger the burning of the *Henry Clay* brought forth. On October 18, 1853, the trial of "The People of the United States against Thomas Collyer, John F. Tallman, John Germain, Edward Hubbard, James L. Jessup, James Elmendorf and Charles Merritt" commenced to once again open the wounds that were yet to be completely healed.[28]

Judge Ingersoll entered into the crowded courtroom. The prosecution and defense teams took their positions. Former United States district attorney J.

Prescott Hall and current assistant district attorney Mr. Dunning were ready to prosecute the case. The defendants were present before the court: Thomas Collyer, John F. Tallman, James L. Jessup, Edward Hubbard, James Elmendorf, and John Germain. One defendant was noticeably absent—Charles Merritt, the assistant engineer, whose attorney, Dennis McMahon explained, would be present on Saturday. The court ordered that Merritt's "recognizances were forfeited."[29]

From the start of the proceedings, there seemed to be no unified front for the officers and owners. One attorney or one defense team did not represent all of the defendants together. There were four attorneys. A. L. Jordan and George F. Betts represented the boat's builder and owner, Thomas Collyer. H. G. Wheaton was counsel for the engineer, John Germain, and Dennis McMahon represented John Tallman, Edward Hubbard, James Jessup, James Elmendorf, and Charles Merritt.[30]

The defense attorneys began their arguments using the term "antagonism" to describe the situation that would arise between the defendants if there was one trial for all the accused together. Their ploy was to win separate trials for each of the defendants. The lawyers argued that the defendants would each be required to testify for the others, which might jeopardize their own defense. Betts and Jordan argued a separate trial for Thomas Collyer, stating that he had not acted as assistant captain since that command would have gone to another of the officers when Tallman fell ill. The lawyers presented the argument that Collyer was the builder of the boat and merely a passenger on the *Henry Clay*. Further, Collyer was not employed on the boat, took no part in its operation and, therefore, was not covered under the statutes. Collyer's attorneys also said that "some of the parties in the case are material witnesses for him, they could not be used as such if included in the same trial."[31]

Attorney H. G. Wheaton pushed for a separate trial for his client, the engineer, John Germain. Dennis McMahon wanted a trial for his five clients separate from Germain and Collyer. McMahon made use of a list of reasons for delaying the trial. He said that Mr. Myers, a witness, was sick, and the ship's barkeeper, Eagan, was out West. McMahon's assistant in the defense team, Mr. Cutting, happened to be in Europe at the time. McMahon tried to excuse himself, saying that he was ill and had a doctor's note.[32]

Prosecutor J. Prescott Hall was not interested in having any separate trials or delays. He argued, "there was no allegation that the disaster was caused by any one man—the theory is that they were conjointly guilty of misconduct and negligence." Hall also pressed upon the court "that the person most responsible was Mr. Collyer. . .If any man should be held for his responsibility on that day, it was the owner of the boat, who was encouraging the others on board; he ought to be tied to the others, and tried with them for the results of the act in which he was a principal actor."[33]

Prosecutor Hall pointed to the wording in the statutes that had been read before: "every captain, engineer, pilot or other person employed on board any steamboat, or vessel propelled in whole or in part by steam, by whose misconduct, negligence or inattention to his or their respective duties the life of any person or persons may be destroyed, shall be deemed guilty of manslaughter."[34]

Although the defendants were fortunate enough to have the indictment for murder thrown out after the official inquest, they were now on trial for manslaughter, and Hall said, "a conviction before any Circuit Court of the United States shall be sentenced to confinement, with hard labor for a period of not more than ten years." The defendants present at court, Collyer, Tallman, Jessup, Germain, Hubbard, Elmendorf, and the absent Merritt had a lot at stake—ten years of their lives in prison.[35]

Prosecutor Hall added that tradition on the North River faulted the engineer for any harm to a passenger. But Judge Betts redefined that regarding the *Reindeer* disaster, which occurred a few weeks after the *Henry Clay* fire and also resulted in several deaths. Betts said responsibility for the proper navigation of the boat was with the "master," but all the employees on a boat, including the engineer, were responsible for safety.[36]

The prosecutor continued to argue that all of the actions of the defendants together, not the actions of each alone, caused the *Henry Clay* disaster. He said Collyer should be tried along with the rest: "Captain Collyer was the moving cause of all these acts, and he ought to come in and take his peril with the rest, for the result of acts in which he was the prime actor. I submit there ought to be no severance but that the parties should all be tried at the same time."[37]

Judge Ingersoll made the final decision. He pointed to all the defendants as responsible parties according to the statutes. He stated that the Supreme Court ruled that the testimony of codefendants in separate trials cannot be admissible, even if state law allows, as "a separation of the trials would not have the effect desired." Ingersoll stated that he did not think the defendants would be tried unfairly if they were tried together. He also pointed out that he had heard that Cutting, who was on Collyer's defense team, was slated to work for the other defendants as well. From the judge's point of view, there was no "antagonism" between the defendants, and he ended with, "The motion for separation must be denied." [38]

The judge's decision ruled the defendants were to be tried together. The crier called the accused persons present in court, and each responded with their names: Thomas Collyer, John F. Tallman, John Germain, Edward Hubbard, James L. Jessup, and James Elmendorf.[39]

Next came the selection of the jury. Several prospective jurors were called and questioned to determine any prejudices they may have regarding the case. Among them was James R. Brewster who said that after reading about the disaster, "he considered their conduct actionable." He then added that at the current time he could be impartial. Prospective juror John Harlow stated that he previously spoke negatively about the case but that he did not think his previous opinion would influence him for the trial. Benjamin Bennett stated he had an opinion and that would "prevent him giving them a fair trial," and John Hostace stated that he had "formed an opinion" from what he had read. All of these men, and several others, were excused from service on the jury.[40]

When John Thomas was called for questioning as a possible juror, defense attorney McMahon "submitted that the defendants were entitled to five peremptory challenges." There was some discussion, and the decision was put on hold regarding Thomas. Later the judge had Thomas recalled for questioning. The judge said, "there is no law for the exercise of peremptory challenges." Thomas was cleared for jury duty.[41]

More potential jury candidates were questioned. William H. Hallock had formed an opinion, but since that time his opinion on the case was "removed." Oliver Hooker had friends who had been on the *Henry Clay* and said that he had spoken with several prospective witnesses. He was asked to "stand aside." Albert Van Winkle was a ship chandler who had provided certain supplies to the steamboat. He was well acquainted with Captain Tallman and knew some of the other defendants. He had heard stories from them about the disaster but believed "he could try the case without bias." These three men were later found to be competent as jurors.[42]

By 4:00 P.M., the twelve-man jury had been selected:

> William H. Baker
> William Gardner
> William H. Hallock
> John Besson
> James Bebee
> Benjamin G. Forbes
> Oliver Hooker
> James Gilmore
> Albert Van Winkle
> John J. Harkness
> Augustus H. C. Marpe
> John Thomas[43]

The first day of the trial ended without any time spent on testimony. The court proceedings established the plan for the trial. There would be one trial for the defendants, with at least three defending attorneys and two district attorneys. The fate of the accused rested in the hands of the jury. The next day commenced the case for the

PROSECUTION.

Chapter 9

The Case for the Prosecution

JUDGE CHARLES A. INGERSOLL presided before the court. Interest had not waned regarding the disaster, and there were more courtroom spectators than the previous day. Present for the trial were the prosecution, the defense team, and the row of defendants minus the still missing Charles Merritt. Assistant District Attorney Dunning opened the case against the accused "If the Court please, gentlemen of the Jury, the defendants are indicted for a crime under the 12th section of an Act of Congress, approved the 7th of July, 1838, entitled 'An Act to provide for the better security of the lives of passengers on board of vessels propelled in one or any part by steam.' "[1]

Dunning proceeded to read additional wording from the statute, wording that had been read several times before, but wording that was all the more critical to the case: "And let it be further enacted that every captain, engineer, pilot, or other person employed on board any steamboat, or vessel propelled in whole or in part by steam, by whose misconduct, negligence or inattention to his or their respective duties, the life of any person or persons may be destroyed, shall be deemed guilty of manslaughter; and on conviction before any Circuit Court of the United States shall be sentenced to confinement, with hard labor, for a period of not more than ten years."[2]

Within the context of the law, Dunning then tied the explanation of the statute to the wording of the indictment. He said the defendants were carrying out their duties. In the capacity of captain was John F. Tallman, the clerk was James L. Jessup, the engineer, John Germain, the first pilot, Edward Hubbard, and second pilot, James Elmendorf. As such "by their misconduct, negligence and inattention the lives of Stephen Allen, A. J. Downing, and various other persons, passengers on board the boat, were destroyed."[3]

The prosecutor summarized the accounts of the last fatal passage of the *Henry Clay* with the approximate four hundred passengers on board. Prosecutor Dunning described the circumstances by which many passengers were trapped on the stern of the burning boat and added that "more than 80 perished, and were thus suddenly with scarce a moment's warning, summoned to eternity." The prosecutor stated, "It is charged, on the part of the prosecution that this fatal calamity—this dreadful sacrifice of human life—was caused by the misconduct, negligence, and inattention of the defendants."[4]

Speaking directly to the jury, Dunning proclaimed, "This gentlemen, is the question upon which you will be called upon to

NEW-YORK CITY.

THE HENRY CLAY CATASTROPHE.

Trial of the Owners and Officers of the Henry Clay.

UNITED STATES CIRCUIT COURT.

Before Hon. Judge Ingersoll.

FIRST DAY.

The People of the United States against *Thomas Collyer, John F. Tallman, John Germain, Edward Hubbard, James L. Jessup, James Elmendorf and Charles Merritt.*

This long pending case has at last come in a palpable shape before the public, and probably in the course of the next fortnight the arguments and evidence will have been concluded, and the verdict rendered by the Jury.

The Court-room yesterday morning was unusually crowded with spectators anxious to witness the proceedings.

Mr. J. Prescott Hall, assisted by Mr. Dunning, appeared for the prosecution.

The defendant, Thomas Collyer, was represented by Messrs. Jordan and Betts : John Germain, by Mr. H. G. Wheaton, and Mr. McMahon acted as counsel for the remaining five defendants.

New-York Daily Times, 19 October 1853.
The trial of the owners and officers of the *Henry Clay* commenced on 18 October 1853.

pass—this the issue that you will be called upon to determine by your verdict—and it will be for you to say, when you shall have heard the evidence introduced before you, whether this charge is well founded." He elaborated that the current law was "sufficiently stringent," and he asked the jury to weigh the evidence and make a decision that would stop further tragic events from occurring on the nation's rivers. He offered, "It may prevent the recurrence of similar calamities; it may teach a lesson—a much needed and important lesson—to those who have the management and control of our steamboats. . . ."[5]

Prosecutor Dunning said that he wanted the witness testimony to speak for itself, and he planned to prove the facts of the case. The prosecutor itemized the facts one by one as he spoke. He told the jury he would prove the *Henry Clay* was "engaged in a trial of speed—a race, a terrible race. . .and that in consequence of that race this calamity happened." Dunning said that he would provide evidence that the race was planned before the boats left Albany. The passengers were worried and brought their concerns to the attention of Thomas Collyer, who had taken charge of the boat in Captain Tallman's absence. Several passengers left the boat, at least twenty at Poughkeepsie, because of the racing. The boat missed several landings. The two vessels continued to run for several miles in close proximity and then collided. After the incident, the *Henry Clay* continued to push hard in excess of the steam allowed, although the *Armenia* was far behind. The safety valves were tied down. The steamboat had a history of fires. Adequate precautions and equipment were not available, such as life preservers, life-boats, or water filled buckets.[6]

Dunning ended his speech before the court stating that the prosecution would present the facts, but the jury would be charged with making a final determination as to the guilt or innocence of the accused. The district attorney pointed out that the prosecution was not trying to convict innocent people, but to present the evidence in a straightforward manner. "We shall strive to state the case fairly between the government and the accused, and having done so we shall have discharged our duty; and it will then be for you, gentlemen, to discharge yours."[7]

The first witness for the prosecution was called. He was John H. Berry, an enrollment and license clerk in the customhouse. The witness affirmed the ownership of the *Henry Clay* in an enrollment document dated June 28, 1851. The document stated Thomas Collyer owned five-eighths, William Radford owned two-eighths, and John F. Tallman owned one-eighth. There were no more recent enrollments since that date.[8]

Next called was Joseph Curtis, an inspector of steamboats. He detailed the *Henry Clay*'s past inspection history and described how he made his inspection of the boiler. Curtis swore before the court that he gave a copy of the certificate for the vessel and another to the owners while also filing one at the customhouse. He testified that the *Henry Clay* was inspected on June 25, 1851, and was authorized to "carry 60 lbs. of steam to the square inch." Exactly one year later, the capacity was cut in half to thirty pounds of steam. Joseph Curtis explained, "I made so large a reduction in the amount of steam in one year was because the boiler had been used excessively, and become weakened more than usual."[9]

The defense countered that the latter certificate was never delivered to the *Henry Clay*. J. Prescott Hall, the district attorney, read from the statute, which stated a certificate must be brought to the ship and another to the customhouse. A. L. Jordan, Thomas Collyer's attorney, objected because the statute was not proof that the *Henry Clay* had, in fact, received one. Judge Ingersoll interjected and ruled that it was the duty of the inspector to deliver one and therefore "the presumption of law is that he did so." A duplicate certificate from the customhouse was presented as evidence.[10]

Lloyd Minturn was called as witness and asked about the crew's "intention" to race. This question brought on a heated discussion between the prosecution and the defense. The defense objected to the prosecution's question because racing was not the issue in this case. The issue before the court was negligence regarding the fires. The prosecution countered "that the *Henry Clay* violated the 7th section of the Law of Congress by not raising their safety valve on approaching a landing." The judge ruled that any racing that resulted in death is punishable by statute and that "it is proper to show any circumstance exhibiting intention, as well as impropriety and negligence, &c."[11]

Following this aside in the questioning, Lloyd Minturn was allowed to proceed. Because he was the first passenger witness to be called to the stand, he was questioned and cross-examined about many details of the *Henry Clay*'s last trip downriver. His testimony filled the remainder of the court day and continued on into the next day. Minturn testified that he initially "observed an unusual degree of excitement at the wharf at Albany." Defense Attorney A. L. Jordan "objected to evidence of any excitement among the 'rabble' at the wharf." Continuing, Minturn confirmed that the *Henry Clay* left Albany about five minutes ahead of the *Armenia*, with the *Armenia* passing the *Henry Clay* at Hudson and proceeding down the west channel.[12]

Speaking about the owner of the steamboat, Minturn said, "I observed throughout what appeared to me a very unusual—(objected);—I observed Mr. Collyer." Minturn testified that Thomas Collyer was "very much excited during what I supposed to be the contest; this excitement consisted in Mr. Collyer's going repeatedly to his friends, Mr. Ridder and Mr. Harris, and making remarks to them, which were heard by myself and others, 'that the *Armenia* could not pass her.'" [13]

Minturn testified that after Catskill Landing, the *Armenia* traveled on the western side of the river, while the *Henry Clay* inched toward her. He observed that the *Armenia* was slightly ahead when the *Henry Clay* collided with her, and the "*Clay* was lifted a little out of the water and the *Armenia* was on her guards." In his testimony, Minturn first indicated that the collision occurred after Kingston, but later, realizing his mistake, corrected his statement saying the collision happened after Bristol. The newspapers were quick to notice the discrepancy in his testimony.[14]

Lloyd Minturn testified that after the collision, he approached Collyer, telling him the "racing is rascally," to which he testified that Collyer replied, "there was no danger." Minturn said that he remained on the forward deck believing "it was the safest, and I thought that it would be the most secure in case of the accident happening, which I apprehended." Defense Attorney Jordan again objected, and the last part of the testimony was struck from the record.[15]

Defense Attorney Wheaton objected to a question about the safety equipment on the boat. He said that the real question was the "criminal charge against the employes [sic] of the boat who had nothing to do with the equipment—only with the navigation." The court ruled against asking a question about life preservers because the law at the time of the accident did not require life preservers on steamboats.[16]

The questioning of Minturn resumed and he testified, "Above Kingston Point, just before the collision, I observed a particularly strong smell of what I now suppose to have been burning wood—it was a resinous smell." He said that he first noticed the burning smell by the bar that was located behind the boiler and, "heard five or six passengers speak of this strong smell." He noticed the same smell again when the fire broke out about three o'clock that afternoon.[17]

Prosecutor Dunning had hoped to question Minturn about the crew drinking at the bar but Judge Ingersoll overruled the line of questioning. The questioning turned to the speed of the boat and Minturn testified, "After the boat left Newburgh until the time of the accident, I observed no difference in the rate of the boat's speed."[18]

Minturn stated that the *Armenia* was less than five miles behind when the fire started on the *Henry Clay*. He saw no officers at the time of the fire but witnessed two firemen with water buckets. Minturn joined in the water brigade to pass the buckets. Minturn testified that he yelled to the steamboat's pilot to turn the boat ashore, but he did not know if the pilot heard him. When the boat was turned to shore Minturn confirmed, "she ran right head on." [19]

The witness had heard Mr. Eagan, the barkeeper, call the order. The witness added, "I did not hear any orders given by the defendants to the passengers to go aft." Interestingly, Eagan was the one who possibly gave the "Go aft" order that the passengers and the press so criticized. However, he was not charged with any wrongdoing and therefore did not stand trial.[20]

Minturn testified about events following the running of the boat on shore. He helped throw the baggage onto the beach, noticing that there was a considerable amount of baggage on the forward deck.

> *Prosecutor Dunning:* Did you see any dead bodies?
> *Minturn:* Oh, yes, a great many.[21]

The defense team opposed any further discussion of the graphic details of the loss of life, believing such testimony would influence the jury. The prosecution turned attention to the subject of boats. Defense counselor Jordan interjected, "Then come to that question at once. Now we shall show bye and bye, that there were two excellent boats on board, but that they could not be got at in consequence of the rushing of the flames. Of course boats came in from the shore and elsewhere, as they naturally would from compassion, but it cannot be taken as showing that there were no boats on board the *Henry Clay*."

> *The court:* Did you see any boats belonging to the *Henry Clay* used for the purpose of saving passengers, in addition to those that came from the shore and from the *Armenia*?
> *Minturn:* I could not have seen them even if they were. (To a juror) It is not my practice when I go on board a steamer to usually look after the safest place.[22]

Minturn underwent additional cross-examination and defended his answers, saying that things had been fresh in his mind when he testified at the inquest the year before. However, with the passage of time and the varying information in the newspaper reports, the facts had become clouded in his memory.[23]

Defense Attorney Wheaton asked Minturn if he noticed a smell from the aft section of the boat even though he was standing at the bow. Dunning, the prosecutor, objected but it was too late. The question opened a nasty round of bantering between the witness and the defense attorney:

> *Defense Attorney Wheaton:* I put the question for the purpose of seeing how hard the witness is prepared to swear, not that I mean to insinuate anything against him.
> *Minturn:* No, Sir; you had best not to.
> *Wheaton:* Why so, pray?
> *Minturn:* I could answer you that out of Court.
> *Wheaton:* What do you mean by that, Sir?
> *Minturn:* I mean to say that I am here as a disinterested witness, and I will have no insinuations made against me; if there are I will throw myself on the protection of the Court here, and with respect to elsewhere—
> *Wheaton:* Oh, don't imagine you are going to intimidate me.
> *Jordan, defense attorney for Collyer:* We would give you just as much of that sort of thing as you would desire.
> *Minturn:* I can tell you that I am able to protect myself.
> As almost to insult Minturn, Wheaton responded, "Oh, yes, you are very brave when there is no danger."[24]

Judge Ingersoll stepped in to put a stop to the altercations between the parties. The cross-examination continued, and Minturn testified that "after I discovered the smoke at Forrest Point, until the boat was turned, was about three minutes, and about three minutes from the time she was turned till she was beached." In one of his final statements, Minturn testified about the speed, "I never saw any alteration in the speed of the *Henry Clay* during the day, until the time when the fire broke out." This was an important piece of testimony for the prosecution who wanted to prove the *Henry Clay* continued at a high rate of speed all the way downriver. After the grueling questioning, Lloyd Minturn was allowed to step down.[25]

Isaac Dayton was the next witness called. He confirmed that the *Henry Clay* "started at what appeared to me a very high rate of speed." He said, after depart-ing Catskill, the steamboat "went down the river at a very high rate of speed—faster, indeed, than I ever had been carried in a steamer before." Dayton noticed the *Armenia* was doing twenty-four revolutions, and he thought the *Henry Clay* was traveling twenty miles per hour or more. He described the horse race like movements of the two boats after Catskill with each running side by side, one inching forward and then the other with just ten feet between them. Dayton described how the *Henry Clay* moved ahead of the *Armenia* by about a third of her length and then cut across her path until the two collided. He said, "the collision was not a violent one," and continued, "we made the landing at Kingston first." He impressed the fact that the *Henry Clay* "kept down the river at, in my judg-ment, a high rate of speed."[26]

When the fire was discovered near Riverdale, Dayton said that he did not know who gave the "Go aft" order, but he ignored the command and "set out to get forward, which I did by getting into a window of the ladies' saloon, thence to the starboard guard and forward." Defense Attorney Wheaton asked him how he escaped. Dayton answered, "I jumped into the water, and after a considerable time I was picked up and taken ashore; I threw over what chairs and boards I could get hold of, and then jumped over."[27]

The next witness called was Isaac McDaniels. He had lost his wife in the dis-aster and had been quite outspoken about the shortcomings of the officers on the boat. McDaniels testified that he spoke with a gentleman on board and "remon-strated against the boat racing and told him I would rather get into New York ten miles astern of the *Armenia* than jeopardize myself and my family." McDaniels said the reply he heard was "there was no danger." The man McDaniels had referred to was not present in the courtroom. During the questioning, a gentle-man entered the courtroom and seated himself. McDaniels recognized him and exclaimed, "That is the man I bought my ticket from." Prosecutor Hall instructed the man to "Stand up." He did so, and McDaniels identified him; it was James Jes-sup, the ship's clerk.[28]

The witness testified that others had also spoken to Jessup about the racing. He then went into the details of his trip, the circumstances of his escape, and his wife's death. He said that he saw Jessup on shore after the *Henry Clay* was grounded and confronted him with the question "Is there any danger now?"[29]

McDaniels ended his testimony speaking to McMahon: "I never saw Mr. Jes-sup before that day, or since, except in this Court, that I am aware of; I think he was then dressed in a white linen coat, but I cannot say whether he had on a hat or a cap; my alarm did not subside while I was on board the boat; I was in alarm the whole way."[30]

During the trial there was a question about who was actually in charge of the *Henry Clay* on the day of the fires. William H. Shelmyre, another passenger, was called next for his testimony, which shed some light on the subject. Shellmyre testified that when he boarded the *Henry Clay* at Albany, someone pointed out Thomas Collyer to him. He conversed with Collyer about his ticket and, "Mr. Collyer remarked to me that he was acting as captain that day; he made the remark to me after we left Albany; I had not known him before; he told me, in answer to some question I put as to the captain, that he was acting as captain, as the captain was sick."[31]

Shelmyre testified that he spoke to Collyer several times during the day. He mentioned to Collyer that "the boats were racing" and asked Collyer to cease the racing for fear of an accident. He testified that Collyer told him that the boats "were not racing" and that "there was no danger." Shelmyre testified that after the collision, he once again approached Collyer and asked him why the *Armenia* had been run down. Collyer replied that "he did not wish to tow her to New York; that she was in their suction."[32]

Next called was John L. Thompson. At the time of the disaster, he had been the district attorney of Lancaster, Pennsylvania, but in the year since the accident had moved to Fairfield, Connecticut. During the testimony, Thompson was "deeply affected" as he spoke. He said that he lost his wife and two children and, in addition, their nurse. Only he and one of his children survived. Thompson was very critical of the officers and took the opportunity to say, "I did not receive any assistance from any officer of the boat. . .I saw none of the officers of the boat after the fire broke out."[33]

Thompson testified, "I have been on board of boats which did not shake, at all when going; I mean the *Francis Skiddy*, which I went up by that morning; it might be that contrast that made me the more notice the shaking of the *Henry Clay*. . . ." Thompson noticed "the planks seemed anxious to move from their places, and they expressed this by a groaning, creaking sound; this was particularly the case near the boiler."[34]

During the final moments of Thompson's testimony, Defense Attorney Wheaton questioned Thompson about whether or not the engineer was "attending to his duty." Thompson responded that the engineer was "regulating the machinery, and as he did so he went, and frequently looked out, back; besides this he appeared much agitated."

> *Wheaton:* Is that an answer to my question?
> *Thompson:* You asked me if he was attending to his duty.
> *Wheaton:* And do you think that a legitimate answer?
> *Thompson:* The Court will decide that. . . .[35]

Phineas P. Wells was called to the stand. He testified about the pieces of hot coals that had landed on the awning and the deck. Wells was asked, "Have you never been on a boat where you have seen cinders blown on the seats?" Wells replied, "Yes, but not such as these. I have noticed the size of cinders that have fallen, but not frequently; I don't know that I have ever seen them so large. . . ."[36]

Wells testified that at the outset of the fire, he "saw smoke coming up in the front of the starboard water wheel house; that increased, and soon I saw flame mixed with it." He looked for life-boats but did not see any on board and watched as the bow of the boat hit shore at a right angle. The boat landed "possibly thirty feet up the sand beach; the water was deep." Wells escaped from the burning boat by going "forward to the starboard end of the boat and got on the main deck, and then jumped off on the beach, having put off the four females."[37]

Wells was asked who sold him his ticket on the steamboat. "I think I should know the person who sold me my ticket, but none of the others." He pointed to a man in the courtroom saying, "That, man." The solemn decorum in the court-room was briefly interrupted by laughter. Wells had pointed to a lawyer named Colby who was not involved with the *Henry Clay* case but merely present at the proceedings. [38]

Next called to testify was James H. Gilson, who stated that "after we left Albany, about ten or twelve miles down the river, my attention was called by a trembling and a jar about the vessel as something uncommon; this was so much so that I kept myself in the bow of the boat." Gilson stated that several people approached Thomas Collyer about the racing. He observed, "I heard remarks made by passengers to Mr. Collyer, who I understood was in command, and who appeared to be so, and to Mr. Jessup." He added, "I heard Mr. Collyer give orders that day; was in different parts of the vessel."[39]

Gilson said that when he paid his fare at Albany there was a crowd of people also buying tickets, so he had time to look at the official steam certificate, which he read to be authorized at thirty or thirty-five pounds. When Gilson went for a shave at the barber-shop, he first looked at the steam gauge in the engine room. Defense Attorney Wheaton asked, "Did you see those figures distinctly?"

> *Gilson:* If I had seen them distinctly, of course I could swear more positively.
> *Wheaton:* What do you mean by evading the question in that way; where did you learn to do so?
> *Gilson:* In New-York court.[40]

Gilson could not swear that the steamboat was carrying forty pounds of steam. Defense Attorney Wheaton then gave the witness a pencil and paper and asked him to draw the numbers the same size as were on the gauge in the engine room. Gilson complied and drew figures "about a quarter of an inch long."[41]

Wheaton asked Gilson to step down from his chair and look at the court clock at about an eighteen-foot and then twelve-foot distance from where he was stand-ing. Gilson said that he could not read the small figures on the clock. Wheaton questioned him on how he could read the steam gauge if he could not read the courtroom clock. Prosecutor Dunning stepped over to scrutinize the clock and said, "There are no figures in the centre of the clock, as attempted to be established by the counsel." Those present in the courtroom burst into laughter.[42]

Gilson had noted Thomas Collyer's level of authority the day of the disaster and testified that he saw Collyer order the fenders thrown over at the time of the collision. He also noted that Collyer told the "ladies not to be frightened." Defense Attorney Jordan took over the questioning and interrogated Gilson to find out if he really knew who Thomas Collyer was.

Jordan: Will you describe his person?
Gilson: I cannot, but I can, I think, describe the dress he wore that day.
Jordan: Did he wear whiskers?
Gilson: I think he did. . .
Jordan: What color were his whiskers?
Gilson: I cannot say positively that he wore whiskers; he had on a light coat and a black hat.
Jordan: Do you never look at men's whiskers?
Gilson: No, Sir; I have no taste for whiskers, (laughter in the courtroom).
Jordan: Did this man whom you took to be Collyer wear whiskers or not?
Gilson: He might have done so; I am not sure.
Jordan: What color were his whiskers?
Gilson: I do not know; they might have been colored, (laughter).
Jordan: Were they white?
Gilson: I cannot say.
Jordan: What do you think?
Gilson: About what, the whiskers? (more laughter).[43]

It was hard to say who was giving whom the difficult time. Gilson testified that he only knew John Tallman and the barkeeper, and that Thomas Collyer was pointed out to him. Collyer, although present in court on the previous days of the trial was not in the courtroom on this day. Defense Attorney Jordan pointed out a gentleman sitting next to him and said, "Is this like the person whom you heard speak these words?"

Gilson: Yes.
Jordan: Then Sir, I have the pleasure of introducing to you, Mr. Ridder, (laughter erupted in the courtroom).[44]

Judge Samuel Nelson, who had presided for the day, adjourned court early. It was Saturday October 25, and the custom was to have shorter court hours on Saturdays. After the jury had heard the first several days of witnesses, the testimony had become very repetitive. Each new witness called imparted much of the same information as those who came before him. However, as a new week of witnesses were called, there was always, with each testimony, some additional information gleaned from the individual witnesses.[45]

John H. Gourlie was called to start the new week. He testified that the *Henry Clay* left Albany one to two minutes before 7:00 A.M. He later added at the cross-examination that, "Albany time is faster than New York time." He testified that he saw Thomas Collyer giving orders, and he "did not notice that the *Clay* blew off any of her steam at the landings." Gourlie testified that after Kingston Landing, "I discovered that stokers or firemen would come up frequently very much exhausted from the heat. . .nobody told me they were stokers, but I judged so from their dress and general appearance—their black faces; it is no doubt hot work shoveling up coal into a furnace on a hot day; it did not strike me as peculiar that they should come on deck; I remember this circumstance particularly from seeing the poor fellows exhausted by the heat." [46]

On cross-examination, Gourlie confirmed that Captain Tallman had been ill that day. He testified that he overheard someone asking Tallman, "How do you do Captain?" with Tallman answering, "that he was very unwell indeed." Gourlie saw Tallman again on the beach after the fire and testified, "he looked ill, and I have no doubt he was very unwell, if I may judge from his appearance."[47]

John Gourlie described his harrowing escape by running forward through the smoke. He made it to the bow of the promenade deck and jumped off to shore after the steamboat had been beached. Responding to a question regarding the officers, he answered, "I saw them give no assistance; I recognized the pilot, the captain, and Mr. Collyer." Of his own efforts, Gourlie said that he did not go into the water but helped on the beach as best he could. "I did what humanity required," he testified. The defense commented to him, "Humanity, I suppose did not require you to wet your feet." [48]

Charles Goodrich was called as a witness and confirmed much of what earlier witnesses had said. Speaking directly to Judge Samuel R. Betts, who presided that day, Goodrich said, "My attention was particularly called to the speed of the boat; I noticed we were going very fast; I also noticed a great trembling and apparent labor or effort on the part of the boat; I also noticed the great heat which has been spoken of in the gangways, and passageways, fore and aft."[49]

Goodrich looked to prosecutor Dunning and said, "I did not observe any slackening of the speed; I think there was none at all after leaving the *Armenia*; the trembling and great heat continued up to the time of the accident; I did not observe the *Clay* to let off steam at any of the landings that she made."[50]

William N. Wilkes, who had been a fireman on the *Henry Clay*, was asked to take the stand. Due to his background with the *Henry Clay*, Wilkes was a potential dream witness for the prosecution. His testimony was filled with just what the prosecution wanted to learn. Wilkes testified that on July 27, the day before the fire, he traveled north on the *Henry Clay* so that he could collect his final pay at

Albany. He had quit his job the day before. Wilkes said that on the trip to Albany, he overheard Captain Tallman tell Thomas Collyer that he planned "to beat the *Armenia* up and down." Defense Attorney Jordan quickly aired his objection: "That occurred on the 27th, the day before the accident, and had reference entirely to a different trip altogether." Judge Ingersoll, who was once again presiding over the trial, allowed the questioning.[51]

Wilkes said that he had quit his job on the *Henry Clay* because he "did not think she was a safe boat." He testified that on the morning of the disaster, he commented to Collyer, "She will not reach New York." Wilkes confirmed the claim of previous testimony by swearing that the engine room certificate stated a steam limit of thirty pounds. [52]

Prosecutor Dunning wished to continue the questioning to prove the *Henry Clay* often carried in excess of the steam allowed on the certificate. However, Judge Ingersoll ruled that the question had no connection to the present case, and he therefore did not allow the line of questioning to continue. Dunning also planned to prove the *Henry Clay* had previously been on fire, but that also was not admitted.[53]

The witness had a speckled working life, taking various jobs over the years, "I have worked on farms—plowing and planting." He had some experience working on other steamboats, including the *Isaac Newton* and joined the crew of the *Henry Clay* in the early part of July 1852 as a fireman.[54]

One pointed question asked whether he left the *Isaac Newton,* or if he was told to leave. There was also question if he left the *Henry Clay* for fear of safety or another reason. One speculation was that someone else was hired to help him do his job. Another speculation was that he drank. McMahon questioned the witness.

> *McMahon:* Do you not drink at all?
> *Wilkes:* I take a glass of liquor once in a while.
> *McMahon:* Are you in the habit of getting drunk?
> *Wilkes:* No, Sir, I am not.[55]

There was great concern regarding the legitimacy of Wilkes' testimony due to the discrepancies between his grand jury testimony and his testimony at the trial. It was determined that the court was legally barred from asking any member of the grand jury about Wilkes because the grand jury oath stated, "all of which you shall keep secret."[56]

Witness James F. DePeyster was called, and Prosecutor Hall asked him to give a narrative of the events of the fatal day. DePeyster testified that he had been reading on the promenade deck when hot cinders began to fall on his book. He was terribly annoyed by them and went below deck to continue reading near the ladies' saloon until the "alarm of fire" was issued.

Hall: Did you see any of the officers assisting the passengers?
DePeyster: Not one, sir; not one; the only officer I saw was the person whose order we obeyed. . . .some of the passengers were desirous of going forward; but they were not allowed to go forward; they were ordered back. . . .[57]

After further testimony he continued, "I mean that it was the duty of an officer to come and tell the passengers to go forward; if that had been done all the passengers could have escaped as I did." He ended his narrative stating that he remained "perfectly calm" until he jumped to the beach and witnessed the scene of the devastation. He remarked, "subsequently I became much disturbed." [58]

Adam Murray of Chicago was the next witness called to testify. He had been on the steamboat the entire trip, having boarded at Albany. Murray was asked about the collision before Kingston Landing, to which he replied, "The Clay went across or in a slanting direction after the other boat, and kept it between her and the shore, and they continued side by side, and considerable excitement existed during the time." Defense Attorney Wheaton protested saying that it was not necessary to prove over and over again the facts about the collision.

Prosecutor Dunning: But suppose that we show it was so general that it must have come to the officers' notice?
Wheaton: But we are not indicted for exciting the ladies, (laughter in the courtroom).[59]

Murray was called upon to relate his words with Jessup, the ship's clerk, regarding the racing. Murray described the confrontation and said that during the argument, Jessup responded that "he wished people would mind their own business." Murray continued his testimony and later indicated that about 2:00 P.M., "I was on the promenade deck during the day, and I observed that the machinery was remarkably hot—throwing out at very great heat." Just before the fire, Murray explained that he had left his wife and child below deck so she could "dress the child." He had gone forward and saw smoke. Turning, he went back to find his wife "by her calling to me." Then came the order to "Go abaft, all passengers."[60]

Prosecutor Dunning continued his examination of the witness.

Dunning: Did you obey this order, and remain abaft?
Murray: Yes, for I expected help.
Dunning: Now, after that, did you hear any other order, or command, or directions given by any other officer of the boat?
Murray: No, sir.
Dunning: Why did you remain in the after part o' the vessel after you were ordered there?
Murray: For the simple reason that the fire was so strong that I could not go forward.

Dunning: At the time the order was given for you to go abaft, were the flames in such a position that the passengers could not go forward?
Murray: No, Sir.
Dunning: Was it in consequence of the order that you remained abaft?
Murray: By all means; I thought that something would be done for us. [61]

Murray uttered the words that easily could have been said by any one of the survivors. His testimony continued on the next morning, and, after much interrogation about the quality of his answers, he remarked that he would try to answer the questions as best he could, "but you may be sure that, from first to last, the matter is very painful to me."[62]

Murray testified that he jumped off the stern holding his son. He explained that, unfortunately, he lost grip of his little boy in the water when he "was seized hold of by the drowning person, and my child was lost from my hold." He explained his wife "was lost on board" and that he had remained on the stern of the boat "in consequence of the order."

Dunning: What was your condition when you got on shore.
Murray: Very forlorn.

Wheaton objected, saying that Murray's response had "no bearing on the case."[63]

The next witness called was Mr. E. Livermore who had been traveling on the *Armenia* on the day of the disaster. Prosecutor Hall planned to ask him questions about why his traveling party left the boat at Kingston Landing. However, this line of questioning leaned toward being the opinion of the witness regarding perceived danger. The court ruled that only facts, not opinions, were admissible as evidence. Prosecutor Dunning then reworded the question, asking "How did you proceed from Catskill to Kingston?"[64]

At once, Defense Attorney A. L. Jordan aired his objection that he "really did not see the necessity of their thirsting as they did for the blood of his client. If that gentleman's ship-yard was to be closed up, and his family desolated, he (the counsel) supposed it was not to be helped; but at least, let him have the protection of the Court while he was being tried."

Prosecutor Hall: I simply propose to ask, did you come down from Kingston in the *Armenia*. . . .I sympathize personally with Mr. Collyer, as much as any man; but if the shipyard is only to be opened to send forth more *Henry Clays*, the longer it is closed the better.
Jordan: Oh, yes; put him in State Prison at once, without further trial.
The Court ruled that the prosecution could ask a question on how the witness arrived at New York.
Dunning: By what means, then, did you get from Kingston to New-York?

Livermore: I crossed the river by the ferry-boat, and after waiting three hours, met the cars going to New-York.[65]

Livermore was questioned about the collision. He testified that he watched the *Henry Clay* and "observed that when the steam would escape from the steam-pipe, she would gain a little upon us." Livermore said, "she struck us just forward of the wheel-house; I could hear crashing of the wood work, and the grating of the two boats together; the boats went along in this position, locked together, five or ten minutes; I then heard the *Armenia* blowing off steam, and I found that her engine had been stopped; the *Clay* then proceeded ahead of us, and went on and made the landing at Kingston first."[66]

The next witness called was a passenger from the *Henry Clay*. He was Henry Hebbard, a silversmith, who had boarded at Catskill with his wife and eight-year-old son. Hebbard owned a steam engine used for "rolling silver." He was asked many questions regarding the operation of a steam engine. Hebbard also testified that while he was on board the *Henry Clay*, walking by the pilothouse he "discovered that a rope about an inch thick was passed over the safety valve lever. . .the valve was weighted, or the weight of the valve was on the extreme end of the lever; it had a weight of some fifteen to twenty pounds." Hebbard stated, "I was fearful, sir, of losing my life, in consequence of an explosion, knowing the safety valve was closed." [67]

Using Hebbard's testimony, prosecutor Dunning wanted to prove that the steam did not release until after the tied down rope was burned. Hebbard continued that "to the best of my judgment the rope was there for the purpose of keeping down the valve; I could see no other reason, there was no other reason."[68]

Henry Hebbard testified that he had been injured after the wreck and had asked to be carried away from the burning boat. He was concerned that the boilers might explode because he did not hear them blow off steam. Hebbard testified that earlier on the trip he believed, "steam was blown off at one point on the west side, the first landing above Newburgh; it was merely a puff, it was not blown off at any other landing."[69]

Regarding owner Thomas Collyer, Hebbard testified that during the trip down, he saw him "actively engaged in giving directions to the man at the wheel; I did not see him doing anything else except being out and in of the wheelhouse; he was speaking to the man at the wheel. . . .I saw Mr. Collyer use a spyglass; he was looking towards the *Armenia*." Contrary to the testimony of Lloyd Minturn, Hebbard thought "Mr. Collyer was the gentleman who told us to go aft after the fire occurred."[70]

The next witness had boarded at Poughkeepsie. He was identified as George Edwards. He testified that prior to the fire, he noticed that on the main deck "the wood work round the entrance to the smoke pipe was very hot, and in some parts charred so much that it was very dark." He said, at the time of the fire, as the boat was near the Forrest House, he smelled smoke "as if painted oil cloth was on fire." He first did not know there was fire but assumed there was because of the smoke.[71]

George Edwards testified that he had gone to the pilothouse to inform the pilot of the fire. He testified that the pilot told him "he knew his own business." Later in the cross-examination, it was pointed out that during the coroner's inquest, Edwards had testified that the pilot said, "he guessed you didn't know anything about it." The discrepancy between the two testimonies brought doubt upon what Edwards' had testified regarding the pilot's words to him.[72]

The questioning continued, and Edwards testified that he started to climb up the ladder again to the pilothouse, but someone ordered him to stop. Edwards gave the man a shove and proceeded up the ladder to the pilothouse. Before Edwards could say anything, he saw another gentleman give the pilot the order to take the steamboat to the shore because the boat was on fire.[73]

On cross-examination, Edwards stated that he was in the habit of counting the revolutions of steamboats ever since he had worked on one ten years before. On his trip on the *Henry Clay*, he had been on the aft promenade deck and "counted every revolution of the wheel." He later explained that the wheel was not visible, but that he "counted the walking beam." After the steamboat left Newburgh, Edwards counted between twenty-one and twenty-two revolutions. He explained that for timing he used the second hand of his watch. Edwards testified that he took a second counting between Stony Point and Haverstraw, clocking twenty-three and a half revolutions in one minute.[74]

George Edwards had seen two small boats, with a capacity of about fifteen people, located on the promenade deck of the *Henry Clay*. After he jumped off the boat to shore, he yelled to the deck hands to throw the small boat out. He did not know if they heard him. At the time, Edwards also noticed some passengers fall from the gangway into shallow water. He testified, "I went and got two of them out, and tended to one of them, a woman, to try to keep her alive; did what I could afterwards in different places to assist."[75]

The next witness, George F. Conner was called. He testified that he could identify Collyer: "I saw him several times in various parts, forward, at the pilot-house and the after part of the deck, I saw him below near the gangway on the main deck; I spoke to him; I cannot tell what it was; it was something in relation to dinner; he was passing backward and forward on board the boat, and acting, as I supposed—(Objected to); I recollect seeing him give one order to one of the hands, the order was to fix the bell-snap aft. . . ." Conner also testified how he saved himself and his wife from the burning boat.[76]

Jordan cross-examined Conner and asked him to "Point out the differences between those two men (Tallman and Collyer)."

Conner: Captain Tallman is rather the best looking man, (laughter); he keeps his whiskers better trimmed.
Jordan: Will you swear it was not Mr. Ridder, for I confess I can scarcely tell the difference between them?
Conner: It was not Mr. Ridder; I know him as well as I do myself.

Conner ended his testimony saying he saw Thomas Collyer "walk back and forward on the deck; I walked back and forward myself, and I don't know that I saw a passenger on board that did not."[77]

Captain Isaac Polhemus, the pilot of the *Armenia* identified himself to the court: "My occupation is following the water—steamboating—in which I have been engaged for forty years; I have been engaged in slooping and steamboating principally upon the North River." Referring to the *Armenia*, he said "I suppose I hail from her as captain. I was on board the *Armenia* on the 28th of July, 1852, the day on which the Clay burned; I was acting then on board of her as pilot."[78]

Captain Pohlhenus told the story of the *Armenia*'s trip that fateful July day. He said the usual captain of the boat, Isaac P. Smith, had gone home before July 27, and that Mr. Bishop was the captain or the master on the twenty-seventh and the twenty-eighth. Polhemus said that on July 28, there were no passengers that wanted to get off at Hudson Landing, and the first stop he needed to make was at Catskill.[79]

The captain testified the *Armenia* "ran a usual course." He described how the *Henry Clay* first followed in the *Armenia*'s path. At Bristol, the *Armenia* made the stop, the *Clay* passed by and traveled to the east of the *Armenia*, moving closer and closer to her until the collision occurred about four miles above Kingston.[80]

Polhemus said he saw two men in the *Henry Clay*'s wheelhouse. He identified one as Hubbard, while the other man may have been Elmendorf. He testified that he directed some words to those in the *Henry Clay* wheelhouse at the time of the collision: "I asked him whether they meant to push me ashore, or whether they meant to run into me, and destroy the lives of passengers and property." The response he heard was, "We'll bother you." At the time, Polhemus noticed Captain Tallman was standing outside the *Henry Clay* wheelhouse.[81]

Polhemus continued, saying that the *Armenia* was backing up when the *Henry Clay* ran into her and broke a piece above the guard. They were "not together more than a minute; we just struck, glanced and went off." The *Armenia* was "so close to the west channel that the boat would not steer." Polhemus stated, "we were going along at a pretty good jog, but not so fast as we have been." He added that "when two boats are close to each other, and going in the same direction, the suction frequently brings them in contact, without any intent upon the part of either; she was a little ahead of us when we struck, because if she had not been she would have knocked our water-wheel to pieces, and that is the reason why I backed as quickly as I could. . . ."

Hall: Was the *Henry Clay* brought into collision with the *Armenia* by the suction that you have spoken of?
Polhemus: I think not.[82]

Polhemus spoke of the officers who were on the *Henry Clay* that day. He stated about the pilot of the *Henry Clay*, "I have known Hubbard for many years, for some portion, I may say the principal part of that time, he has been employed in piloting steamboats; I believe his standing and reputation have been good; he has been considered among the best of the pilots." Then he said of John Tallman and James Elmendorf, "Tallman I have not known as long as I have Hubbard, but probably for four or five years; his standing and reputation on the river is good; I have known Mr. Elmendorf for five or six years and as an assistant pilot his reputation is good."[83]

The witness was questioned about the remarks made from the *Henry Clay*'s pilothouse, to which Polhemus answered, "the words 'We mean to bother you' came from the pilot-house; I am not positive who spoke them, but I think Mr. Hubbard; I heard them distinctly; I did not understand him to say 'we do not mean to bother you;' I think those were not the words, but I may possibly be mistaken; I am not certain."[84]

Polhemus said that from Albany to Kingston the *Armenia* traveled about seventeen miles an hour but that the boat could do about twenty miles an hour without endangering any lives. He explained that "we broke this blower band at Newburgh," which was unrelated to the collision. He said the *Armenia* then traveled at a slower speed at about ten or twelve miles an hour until the blower was repaired. After that, the steam of the *Armenia* returned to its normal twenty-eight to thirty inches.[85]

Polhemus indicated "it was low water when the *Clay* went ashore; from the time we left Albany we had one ebb and part of another, and part of a flood tide; those are very favorable tides; we could not have had more favorable tides on that day." He also said, "there was a strong breeze all the way down through the bay from the Highlands down."[86]

Regarding the small boats, Polhemus said that the safety boats were usually stored on the promenade deck forward of the water wheel. He thought the *Clay* had two boats on board. He mentioned "water-buckets are sometimes kept on the hurricane deck, and sometimes in other places. . . ."[87]

The witness was extensively cross examined by the defense team. Then Polhemus was asked about the method by which the boat was run to shore.

McMahon: From your experience as a pilot, could a vessel under these circumstances be with safety run ashore sideways or diagonally?
Polhemus: No; if I had been placed in the same position as the *Henry Clay* was, I could not have done any better than those on board; she could not have been got

on sideways; she might haul up to the bank sideways but you could not make her stay there; the proper way was to send the head on the bank, for that is the only way you could make her stay there.[88]

The last witness for the prosecution was Captain George F. Barnard who had been a passenger on the *Henry Clay*, boarding at Hudson Landing. He said, "I was bred to the sea." He testified that after Catskill, the *Henry Clay* "was then gaining fast—at a good speed." He spoke of the collision and then of the fire. At first believing it would be extinguished, Barnard said that he yelled to the passengers, "Don't be alarmed." He soon saw the smoke and climbed the ladder to tell the pilot to head toward shore. The pilot responded, "that's what I am doing."[89]

Barnard was asked about the boat running to shore. The captain stated, "The vessel was put on shore as well as she could be—better than I had supposed when I came to examine it; if the shore had been rocky the pilot might have been injured by the beam or the smoke-pipe falling."[90]

At this point, prosecutor Hall stated, "the prosecution would here rest the case," thus, closing the presentation of testimony for the prosecution. Most of the witnesses called for the prosecution shed an unfavorable light on the officers of the *Henry Clay*. There were several points that the prosecution served to prove through the testimony of its witnesses: there was racing, the boat traveled at a high rate of speed, the collision was their fault, the officers did nothing to assist after the fire, and the safety boats were not brought down for rescue.[91]

However, in an unexpected and unplanned turn, the testimony also proved that the actions of one of the officers on board the *Henry Clay*, Edward Hubbard, the pilot, were properly performed. Contrary to the much publicized negative speculation about the running of the burning steamboat bow first onto shore, the testimony proved that this strategy was the safest and only feasible course of action to save the lives of the passengers.

But did the actions of the pilot matter? Edward Hubbard, the pilot, stood, with the other officers and one owner, all accused of manslaughter. The defendants had been on the steamboat together when dozens of people perished. The defendants were indicted and charged together. They were presently on trial together. Their fate remained in the hands of their attorneys, who must now present the case for the

DEFENSE.

Chapter 10

Witness for the Defense

IT was Friday, October 28, 1853, when Defense Attorney McMahon opened the case for the defense. Although McMahon was one of three defense attorneys, he represented five of the defendants as his clients. The three defense attorneys decided that McMahon would speak for all of them to keep things simple. McMahon addressed Judge Ingersoll, first stating several arguments that were based on the 1838 Steamboat Act of Congress.[1]

McMahon quoted the statues of the Steamboat Act, which stated that any deaths related to steamboat accidents must have resulted from "the misconduct, the negligence or inattention" of the officers and anyone employed on the steamboat. His second point noted that "an error in judgment" was not misconduct. McMahon explained that the "Go aft" order given at a time of chaos and the grounding of the steamboat on shore may be seen as errors in judgment but not "misconduct, negligence or inattention." He made his third point saying, for prosecution, the acts may not be simply "omissive" but must be gross or intentional negligence. Lastly, McMahon stated that the prosecution must prove that the acts of each officer or employee in performing their assigned duties in individual acts of misconduct, negligence, or inattention came together to cause injury.[2]

Defense Attorney McMahon indicated that the prosecution stressed the fact that the defendants may be guilty of racing. However, the prosecution failed to prove that the racing caused the fire. If that was the case, then the defendants should be acquitted. McMahon used the case of the steamboat *Reindeer* as an example. The *Reindeer* exploded just a few weeks after the *Henry Clay* burned. In the *Reindeer* trial, it was proven that the boilers exploded because of excessive steam pressure, which was the direct result of the officers not raising the safety valve at each landing. McMahon stated that the prosecution case against the *Henry Clay* defendants failed to prove such facts.[3]

The defense attorney then addressed the jury, stating the defendants were "six men of high character and respectability" and that at the time of the disaster, the newspapers labeled the incident "the Henry Clay murder." McMahon said that after the accident, it would have not been possible to obtain a fair trial, but because fifteen months had passed, there was a chance for a fair trial to restore the reputation of the defendants.[4]

McMahon stated that the prosecution presented no scientific evidence that proved the fire on the boat resulted from a race that was alleged to have taken place eighty-five miles above the scene of the fire near Yonkers. McMahon and the other defense attorneys planned to use experts to prove several important points. They would prove the collision near Kingston was the result of suction; the *Henry Clay* had traveled in the natural channel; she was not traveling at her higher normal speed of twenty-seven or twenty-eight revolutions, twenty-one or twenty-two miles per hour, but traveling actually at less speed; and, "an arrangement had been made by which the boats should not race." He stated that considering the *Henry Clay* traveled "a distance of 135 miles from Albany, she had made but 15 or 16 miles an hour."[5]

The defense also planned to show that the steamboat was well built with a space between the furnace and the woodwork; the boat used less steam on that day; the firemen used the normal amount of coal; and there were precautions against fire with waterbuckets and two small boats on board. The defense also expected to show that the course taken to run the vessel to shore had been appropriate.[6]

McMahon spoke of the pilot: "I say that the pilot instead of being indicted, should have received from these passengers who now malign him a testimonial for his conduct in putting the vessel on shore. That pilot is of the best men of his class in the State of New York. He has a rough exterior, but a kindly heart; although his pilot-house was in flames, and the boat crackling at his feet, and although he ran the risk of being crushed by the steam-pipe and walking beam, like a Roman sentinel, he stood at his post, and did not abandon it." McMahon said to the jury that he would prove the running of the boat bow first was the best way to bring the boat to shore. McMahon emphasized that "Mr. Hubbard, the pilot was in the pilot-house; he did not abandon his position."[7]

The defense attorney continued, "We shall show to you that Mr. Collyer, Mr. Elmendorf, the engineer, and the barman, were engaged in pouring water down the fire-room, in order to check the fire." The defense would prove that owner Thomas Collyer ran to a fence to rip off boards to reach out to victims; the engineer tried to scuttle the vessel in the hopes of putting the fire out; and Captain Tallman, although suffering from "cholera morbus," went into the water himself. "What as to the pilot? He was in the water, and I could relate to you several touching incidents of his acts when his kindly nature was roused." McMahon continued that the ship's clerk, Jessup, was in the water, although he could not swim, and Elmendorf and other officers were also assisting as well as they were able.[8]

McMahon asked why the prosecution witness Lloyd Minturn was not questioned about the officers' efforts to save people. He suggested that George Edwards, another witness for the prosecution, was not truthful in his testimony about charred wood near the chimney because there was no wood near the chimney. The defense would show there were at least twenty-four water buckets on board, two small safety boats, and that the *Henry Clay* was a seaworthy steamboat. They would prove that the captain of the boat, although sick, was "one of the most experienced masters on the river." The defense would also prove that the boat "had one of the best pilots on the river; one also of the best engineers—the man whom Cornelius Vanderbilt would not go to sea without, and one of the most scientific and careful pilots in the craft; that we also had a good second pilot and good clerk."[9]

Defense Attorney McMahon stated that in the past fifteen months, "The matter was spoken of as the steamboat so and so commanded by Captain Tallman, and piloted by Edward Hubbard. During the entire period, they suffered intensely and agonizingly from the attacks upon their character—many of them having wives and children, . . . suffering the most intense anxiety for the result of this prosecution." McMahon ended his opening speech with "When we get through we will scotch the snake; we will put an end to the malignity of the prosecution."[10]

Following McMahon's opening arguments, the defense called its first witness, Joseph Belknap. He testified that his business, Cunningham, Belknap & Co had built the engines and boilers that were installed in the *Henry Clay* in 1851. Originally, the boilers could safely produce seventy-five pounds of steam, but in 1852, the engine was given an overhaul and a new cylinder was installed that "reduces the pressure of steam." With the new cylinder, the steamboat would have the same power using thirty-five pounds of steam instead of the sixty pounds with the old smaller cylinder. Belknap said he believed this was the true reason for the change in the certificate from sixty pounds of steam to thirty-five. Belknap stated, "the boilers in the spring of '52 were perfectly safe with 50 lbs pressure of steam; I do not mean with safety to the other parts of the vessel, but with safety to the boilers."[11]

A drawing of the boilers and a wooden model of the *Henry Clay* were presented to the court. Belknap said the boilers were constructed of the best iron and were safe. Steam and water surrounded the fire within the boiler. The front access doors were closed with a latch. The rear doors, for accessing the spent ashes, were closed with a latch and a wedge. Belknap said this method was the safe and normal way of fastening the doors shut.[12]

Joseph Belknap testified that there was no danger of fire of the woodwork on the boat from the boilers, the fire room, or the steam chimneys. He stated, "the fire room was well constructed with regard to safety from fire; it was better than ordinary; the floor was covered with sheet iron about an eighth of an inch thick; the fires were drawn out upon sheet iron; the top of these boilers was about six inches thick from the deck above. . . ."[13]

Defense Attorney McMahon continued the questioning of the witness.

McMahon: Is there any danger of fire catching from the smoke pipe to the adjoining woodwork?
Belknap: Yes, if the wood work was near enough.
McMahon: How was it on that vessel [*Henry Clay*]?
Belknap: No danger at all. . . .
McMahon: Is there anything uncommon in seeing cinders or small pieces of coal coming out of the chimney?
Belknap: Not at all, especially with small boilers; when the coal is thrown on the fire the draught carries the coal up; the smoke pipe was forty-eight feet long; some of the coal would not be burned when it would fly off.[14]

Belknap explained that the smoke chimneys had enough clearance to be safe: "the hurricane deck was clear around about ten inches." He testified that the weight on the safety valve lever was one hundred pounds and that it "was a proper weight." During Prosecuting Attorney Hall's cross-examination, Belknap testified that if the steam was brought to a higher temperature where all the water would evaporate and produce only gas, then the wood could set fire.[15]

Next called was John B. Weed, a ship joiner who had worked on the actual construction of the steamboat *Henry Clay*. Defense Attorney Mr. Betts asked him about the locations of various gratings on the boat, to which Weed identified them on the model provided. He testified, "the joiner work was as is, usual in that class of vessels. . . ."

Betts: Was the fire room of the *Henry Clay* as well guarded from danger of fire as boats of that class usually are?
Weed: Yes Sir, I think they were; that is in my judgment the woodwork above the main deck was well constructed with regard to fire.[7]

Commenting on the safety of the vessel, Weed told Defense Attorney Betts, "The *Clay* had two boats; they were carried on the promenade deck forward of the wheelhouses. . .that was the usual number of boats for vessels of her class." He stated that, "she had two dozen buckets," and added, "the smoke pipe on the hurricane deck is the most dangerous place in case of fire."[17]

Peter Crary, a steamboat inspector, was called, and questioned by Defense Attorney McMahon. Crary testified that he was the inspector that looked at the *Henry Clay's* boilers on June 25, 1852. He said another inspector, Mr. Curtis, was not present when he and John Germain, the engineer, went to the furnace room. He looked at the boilers and "did not observe any defect in the furnace."[18]

Crary testified that Germain pointed out a defect in the chimney, which was the reason he changed the certificate to thirty-five pounds. He said that he "observed her fire room; it was constructed with regard to safety from fire, about as well as I generally find them." Crary also stated that he agreed with what Joseph Belknap had said and testified, "there being no danger of fire from the radiation from the boilers."[19]

Prosecutor Hall presented Crary with the *Henry Clay* certificate dated June 1852, stating the steam allowed was at thirty pounds. Crary countered that he had given the *Henry Clay* a rating for thirty-five pounds of steam saying, "I considered the *Henry Clay* in all respects properly equipped for running on the North River." The inspector said that he had signed blank certificates and gave them to Curtis, his fellow inspector, to fill out.[20]

Hall pointedly directed his next question to the steamboat inspector.

Hall: Did you put your name to a certificate that was to go forth to the world, without knowing what was to be put in it?
Crary: Mr. Curtis is my associate, and if he put in a different amount to what we agreed upon that's his business. . . .
Crary (to Defense Attorney Jordan): We inspect jointly, and each take a certain class of the certificates jointly signed, and fill them up.[21]

Another witness, Francis Marvin, was called with relatively short testimony. He worked for Thomas Collyer and was the foreman during the building of the *Henry Clay*. He said of the steamboat, "she had the best frame ever built by Mr. Collyer; I can't say that I ever saw one in the city of New York that was her superior."[22]

The defense team had opened their case by calling four expert witnesses. Next, they called a survivor of the disaster, John R. Harris, who was a former employee of the Troy Steamboat Company. He had boarded the *Henry Clay* at Albany, and his version of the day's events differed from the prosecution's side.[23]

Harris testified that he had commented to Collyer near Coxsackie that he "thought the *Henry Clay* was a fast boat." Harris was of the opinion that "neither boat was going fast; the *Armenia* was half a mile behind at the time." He indicated in his testimony that he was disappointed that the *Henry Clay* was not moving very fast. "Both boats ran at a very ordinary rate of speed from Albany to Hudson; when they came into deep water, about Hudson, they increased their speed, but it was at no time very great." Harris also testified, "there was no attempt on the part of the *Armenia* to pass the *Clay*."[24]

Harris stated that the *Henry Clay* traveled steadily during the trip. He estimated the speed at about sixteen miles an hour and noticed that when the boat reached the Highlands, a breeze came up.[25]

Defense Attorney Jordan continued further with a line of questioning regarding the breeze on the day of the fire.

> *Jordan:* Do you know how the tide was running when you met the breeze?
> *Harris:* I do not.
> *Jordan:* Well, Captain, I want to ask you the effect of a stiff breeze against the tide, —say the tide was ebbing, and that there was a stiff breeze from the south?
> *Harris:* Why, the effect would be to make the water rough.
> *Jordan:* Now, Sir, doesn't that necessarily produce a greater agitation and shaking in the vessel than when they are running with the breeze, and when the water is smooth?
> *Harris:* Yes, Sir, always.[26]

Contrary to previous testimony from the prosecution, Harris testified that the steam gauge before Bristol read no more than twenty pounds of steam. He also said that after the *Armenia* left Bristol, she "sheered out from the west shore so as to come up parallel with us." The *Armenia* was only thirty to forty feet away and was caught in the *Henry Clay*'s suction. Harris testified that it appeared the *Henry Clay* was attempting to move away from the *Armenia* by passing a sloop on the east to "break the power of the suction." He stated the *Armenia* again came into the suction, and the two boats collided near Turkey Point, a location about three to five miles above Kingston.[27]

The interrogation of the witness had been taken over by Defense Attorney McMahon.

> *McMahon:* Is it a common thing on the Hudson River for two boats of equal size to run side by side?
> *Harris:* Well, it is a very common thing.[28]

Regarding the heat around the steam chimneys, Harris testified, "I found it to be very hot in the vicinity of the steam machinery and boiler; on the promenade deck, or on the main deck, the heat may be said to have been uncomfortable, from the radiations of heat from the chimney." He explained that the steam chimneys were not covered, causing the increased heat.[29]

Harris informed the court that he was traveling with his brother-in-law, Mr. Williams, on the *Henry Clay*. He had been sitting "on the after deck, in front of the ladies' saloon" with Mr. Ridder and Ridder's daughter. He continued that he did not hear any order to go aft but remained aft anyway because he was afraid there would be an explosion when the boat hit shore. He jumped off and then stayed in

FROM A PASSENGER.

Mr. Editor: A desire was expressed and I think a resolution adopted at the meeting of the passengers saved from the ill-fated steamer Henry Clay, held at the Astor House this morning, that each passenger should write out a statement of what came under his observation during the passage and at the late terrible disaster.

I took passage, together with an invalid friend, on board the Henry Clay on the 28th inst., and soon after stepping on board we started, followed by the Armenia. We proceeded along, very pleasantly, in advance of the A., and landed at Coxsackie. As we neared Hudson I looked astern for the A. and saw her on the other side the river going down the Athens channel—a straighter course, by which she saved a mile in distance, and enabled her to make the landing at Catskill ahead of the Henry Clay.

We waited at the latter place for the A. to make her landing and get out of the way, after which the Clay came along side the dock. After we started, I supposed, from what I had heard of the speed of the Clay, we would overtake the Armenia before reaching Bristol the next landing-place, but so far as I could judge we gained little, if any, on her, and only overtook her as she stooped at Bristol landing. The Clay passed this place without landing.

The Armenia got under way before we came up, and as they saw we were going ahead she was steered directly for the "suction," as it is termed, of the Clay, which she reached. She "hung on" to the suction, and we ran together side by side for some distance, but a small space apart.

At length by a sheer of the Clay, the bow of the Armenia was brought into the action of the "quick water" of the Clay's wheel, which caused the forward guard of the A. to come in contact with the after quarter of the H. Clay. The Armenia then slacked her speed and dropped astern. I am particular in detailing this affair just as I viewed it at the time, for when I went aft from the forward deck, I found much excitement prevailing, and have since heard statements respecting it, which do not agree with my view of the occurrence.

This was the only part of the passage where there appeared anything like racing on the part of the Henry Clay. Two such boats, running side by side, doubtless appeared dangerous and frightful to many passengers, but I must say that, from the very position of the boats, I knew there could be no serious collision, and the only danger I did apprehend was the breaking of the state-houses or paddle-wheels, by the boat having the higher guard riding the guard of the other.

When the Armenia dropped astern, we gained gradually of her the rest of the way. I thought from the appearance of matters that those having charge of the Armenia had given up the contest and were coming at their ordinary speed. The excitement among the passengers on the Clay seemed fast passing away, and matters were going on pleasantly again, without a thought, so far as myself was concerned, about the Armenia.

From all that I saw and heard, I am bound in candor to state my impression, that each boat, from the time we passed Kingston till the time of the disaster—a distance of 80 or 90 miles—was managed without reference to the other. During the passage I had conversation with Mr. Collyer, one of the owners, who was on board. I was not acquainted with any of the officers. Mr. Collyer informed me the Captain, for whom I inquired, was sick in his room. I had noticed the Clerk, assisted by the Barkeeper, had discharged the duties of Captain at the landings.

In speaking with Mr. Collyer about the comparative speed of the different boats on the river, he took occasion to say, there was an agreement between the owners of the Henry Clay and Armenia that they should not race. I told him the Armenia, by taking the other channel, showed a determination to get ahead. He said it was all wrong and a violation of their agreement not to race.

I was sitting on the after deck enjoying a view of the beautiful villages and country seats on the Eastern shore, and having just passed Forrest's country seat I noticed an unusual stir forward and heard the boat was on fire. Mr. Ridder, of New-York, by whom I sat, requested me to sit by his daughter until he could go and see what was the matter. He soon returned and announced that the boat was on fire, and they were heading her for the shore. I then went for my friend who was in the after cabin laying down. I assisted him on deck, but by that time the gangways were so filled with smoke and fire, that our retreat forward was cut off.

The boat soon struck the shore with much force. We being on the after part of the boat, were 150 feet from shore. The flames were rapidly approaching our deck, and the only way of escape was by the water. I hastily seized all the floating articles near, and threw them over to the crowd that were struggling in the water. At length I took the leap, but my sick friend was nearly helpless. I could not prevail on him to jump over with me. He said, to go or stay, would prove equally fatal. Scorched by the flames, he at length got over the rail and dropped into the water.

We succeeded in reaching a brace under the guard, where we were supported for a long time until rescued by a boat. I left the brace after my companion was secured, and swam out from under the guard to see if there was no help approaching.

I saw Mr. Collyer swimming towards us from the shore, shoving boards from the Railroad fence. I swam towards him and aided in scattering the boards around among the passengers, and within reach of those who were sustaining themselves by chairs and settees. Mr. Collyer was enabled to save many lives by the aid of these boards.

I swam with one of these boards to my friend, but his strength was gone, his hold of the brace relaxed, and down he sank in the water. With much difficulty I succeeded in getting his head above water again, and by clinging to the brace with one hand, and aided by a settee near me, I was enabled to keep my hold till we were both rescued by some men in a small boat.

I feel, I trust, suitably thankful to a merciful Providence for my safety. I am overwhelmed with horror, in view of the awful destruction of human life, still I do not feel disposed to join in the indiscriminate censure and condemnation of the officers of the ill-fated boat. So far as they are culpable, let them be held to account, but with more freedom from excitement, let the facts be ascertained before pronouncing judgment.

Dated, New-York, July 29, 1852.

JNO. R. HARRIS, Bellowsfalls, Vt.

New-York Daily Tribune, 31 July 1852. Editorial letter from Jno. R. Harris.

the water to assist his brother-in-law. Harris testified that he witnessed Collyer pushing boards to people, and he "was indebted to him for one of them which I made use of."[30]

The defense questioning turned to the capacity of the forward deck. Harris was asked how many people could fit there. He estimated that there were forty to fifty trunks and some gang-planks, allowing room to accommodate possibly one to two hundred people. He explained that it was customary to store baggage on the deck on day boats for the convenience of loading and unloading.[31]

Defense Attorney McMahon continued the questioning regarding the forward deck.

> *McMahon:* If the smoke-pipe or walking beam had fallen forward what would have been the consequence?
> *Harris:* I think the consequence would have been the death of a great number of persons.[32]

Lastly, Harris was asked if he saw Collyer take an active roll in the operation of the boat. Here again Harris' testimony was contrary to that of the prosecution witnesses. Harris said, "I did not see either that he assumed any command or gave any orders." Entered as evidence was a letter Harris wrote after the accident addressed to the newspapers, where he stated that Mr. Collyer told him there had been an agreement that the two boats would not race.[33]

The second day of defense testimony opened on the morning of Saturday, October 29. David Morris, the pastor of the Baptist church in Cross River, was called to testify. He had boarded the *Henry Clay* for the first time on July 28, 1852, at Poughkeepsie Landing. Morris testified that he saw nothing unusual regarding the landing at Poughkeepsie or on the trip downriver, no creaking, no excessive heat, nothing unusual about the boat's speed. He testified, "all was peaceable."[34]

Pastor Morris stated that he was an owner of a boat, adding, "I have had a great deal of experience in river navigation; I was on the water before the era of steam navigation." He confirmed that a strong southerly breeze and an ebb tide would create rough water. Morris testified at the time of the fire, "I saw smoke issuing from what I thought then was the coalhole; but it was a place over the boiler; I went there with the intention of rendering any assistance I could." He stated that he saw someone get the water for the fire, but he "knew from the smoke no one could breathe more than once, and consequently water was no use." He said that he did not hear any orders given at the time of the fire.[35]

Defense Attorney Jordan took the opportunity to question Morris, a boat owner, about the method the *Henry Clay* was run aground.

> *Jordan:* What would have been the effect in your opinion of running the boat sideways to the shore?
> *Morris:* The effect would, perhaps have emptied us all into the water; if I was pilot and knew the state of her below, I would not have brought her sideways to the shore.[36]

After further questioning, Morris testified that he "looked to the safety-valve to see whether it was free so that we might escape an explosion, and I saw that it was free when we came on shore." A juror asked if it would have been possible to bring the boat to shore in a diagonal fashion, and Morris responded saying that it would have been difficult to find a place without rocks. The witness ended his testimony with a comment to Jordan: "I could not have managed the boat otherwise, nor selected a better place for going ashore if I had an hour to select it."[37]

Next called to the stand was Thomas B. Ridder, who, with his daughter, had survived the *Henry Clay* disaster. Ridder testified that the *Henry Clay* departed Albany "a few minutes before 7 o'clock, according to New-York time; I know that the latter is a little faster than the time at Albany." Ridder was asked about the conversations between Collyer and Harris before the landing at Hudson. Ridder clarified that Collyer had said that the *Henry Clay* was not traveling fast. When Harris remarked that the *Armenia* may pass them, Collyer replied, "She will not; there is an understanding with the owners of the *Armenia* to run behind. . . ."[38]

The questioning of Ridder continued regarding the details of the journey of the *Henry Clay* downriver. Defense Attorney Jordan proceeded with interogatory related to the collision before Kingston.

> *Jordan:* What direction on leaving Bristol did the boats take?
> *Ridder:* The *Clay* bore a little to the eastward, and the *Armenia* with the bow about to the *Clay*'s forward quarter; both boats bore southeasterly towards Tivoli; after leaving there they proceeded on their course both of them, each taking opposite sides of a sloop which they passed, the *Clay* east and the *Armenia* west; their course then was southerly, and both of them bore to the west towards Turkey Point in the Kingston channel; it was about there that the boats came together about opposite the ice-house.[39]

Ridder explained what occurs with suction. The slower boat would hold the faster one back, and the faster one would draw the other toward it due to the suction. He testified that at the time of the collision, he had asked the passengers to move to the larboard side, "that by raising the starboard guard the boats would come together easier than they otherwise would."[40]

Ridder said that he timed the *Henry Clay* from Hudson to Catskill and said the boat was traveling sixteen miles an hour. He said that he "also timed her during the contest from Bristol and her average time then was less than from Hudson to Catskill." He said that after Kingston, the boat traveled at reduced speed. He noticed, "after leaving the Highlands, the wind rose to a stiff breeze, which the forward motion of the boat increased, and the tide was running up; in my experience, such a state of things would make the boat heave more." Ridder continued his testimony, describing the way he brought his daughter and four other passengers to safety during the fire. He said that he saw Collyer passing boards and that the engineer, Germain, tried to scuttle the burning steamship.[41]

There was some questioning about Ridder's statements at the Astor House meeting the day after the disaster. Newspaper reports initially stated that Ridder had blamed the officers for having too much fire in the boat's furnace, for running the boat hard after the passenger complaints about racing, and for the lack of fire buckets. At the trial, Ridder testified that he had been at the meeting to defend the officers, but that the newspapers misinterpreted what he said. He defended himself to a juror saying, "To-morrow I will be 55 years of age; the first steamboat was placed on the river in 1807; I recollect it well, for I was swimming at Albany when it came up; I do not recollect whether it was the *Hudson*, the *Fulton*, or the *Chancellor Livingston*; I was in the war of 1812 and my name stands recorded at Washington."[42]

The brief testimony of Kingston attorney John Van Buren followed. He had been on the *Henry Clay* from Albany to Kingston. Van Buren confirmed that the two steamboats had traveled side by side and that the *Armenia* appeared to have gotten into the *Henry Clay*'s suction near Turkey Point. He confirmed the events of the collision and stated that the *Henry Clay* reached Kingston at about 11:00 A.M., being "a few minutes behind the usual time." Meanwhile, "the *Armenia* then slowed, making a few revolutions backward."[43]

Hewlett Lake, a pilot on another boat the day of the disaster, testified next. He had been about a half mile behind the *Henry Clay* when he first realized she must have been on fire. He testified that he witnessed twenty-five to fifty passengers jump overboard about five hundred feet from shore. He neared the burning boat, and with four of his crew in a small boat, proceeded to assist. Lake said that he saw Collyer in the water pushing boards to passengers. He also saw Elmendorf who was wet.[44]

The defense team afforded itself another opportunity to question an expert witness about the manner in which the steamboat was brought to shore.

> *McMahon:* What is your judgment, as a pilot, of the manner in which the vessel was put on shore?
> *Lake:* I think she could not have been put on shore any different from what she was, to save the lives of passengers on board the steamboat.
> *McMahon:* What danger was incurred by the pilot in running the boat on shore in this manner?
> *Lake:* I would have expected the machinery to have been all thrown back, and that the walking-beam would fall back on the pilot-house, I would also imagine that the vessel would break across. There would be danger of the steam connections breaking, and the steam rushing out on the passengers.[45]

Another pilot, Judson Morey, was examined next. On the day of the *Henry Clay* disaster, he was the pilot on the *Alida* for her run from New York City to Albany. He testified that he passed the *Henry Clay* at Esopus Island, which was eighty-five miles north of New York City. This was the halfway mark on the river for the trip. Morey stated that the *Henry Clay* usually ran between twenty and twenty-three miles per hour and usually arrived in New York City at 3:00 P.M.[46]

Once again, the defense team directed the questioning to the way the *Henry Clay* was run aground. One of Collyer's defense attorneys interrogated the witness.

> *Betts:* What is your judgment as to the manner the *Henry Clay* was put shore?
> *Morey:* It could not be done better.

By this time, during the defense testimony, everyone understood this point of running the vessel to shore. The court responded, "All the nautical witnesses seem to agree in that."[47]

William L. Simmonds was called and testified that he had boarded at Newburgh and had just gone to the third session of the dinner service. He was with Collyer at the time, and there was an unusual level of noise on deck. The two proceeded upstairs and found the boat on fire. Captain Tallman was aroused from his sickbed and immediately came on deck. Simmonds testified that after the boat was brought to shore, Tallman was in a rescue boat "going backward and forward from the shore; he had ladies in the boat; I saw Collyer step along on the side of the boat, and lead some ladies by the hand along the guard, from part of the boat forward to the shore; I saw him do this twice; I saw him in the water."[48]

Earlier, during the prosecution's case, John Cubbage had testified that the bell ringing from the pilothouse signaled for more fire. To contradict that testimony, the defense called Allen Seaman, who had been a steamboat pilot for forty years. Seaman explained the signals of the bells on board. "The pilot communicates with the engineer by a bell; when he wants to slow the vessel he rings one bell; rings the bell again to stop her; rings two to go back." He continued, "The pilot communicates with the deckhands by a bell when he wants a man to trim the deck, or wants one to the wheel." Seaman confirmed that he "never saw a bell on board a boat for the purpose of making hotter fires, or to put on more steam. . . .it is the duty of the engineer to obey the pilot's bells." Seaman confirmed that with twenty-seven turns, the *Henry Clay* would have been traveling at a speed of seventeen to eighteen miles an hour.[49]

Ambrose Bradley testified that he saw a woman in the pilothouse but he did not know if she was Mrs. Elmendorf. Among Bradley's other comments, he said "the afterpart of the pilot house was on fire when the boat got on ashore, and that spread about in the vicinity very rapidly."[50]

The twelfth day of the trial and the last day of witness testimony had arrived. Several more witnesses were called to verify specific bits of information. The first witness called was Philomel H. Smith. On the day of the *Henry Clay* disaster, he had been captain on the steamboat *Mazeppa*. He said that he met up with the *Henry Clay* near Tivoli, Upper Red Hook, and noticed the *Clay* was doing twenty-two revolutions per minute. In the past, Smith had seen the *Henry Clay* do up to twenty-seven turns. He testified that he was behind his schedule, as was the *Henry Clay* on that day. He normally met the *Henry Clay* at Lower Red Hook.[51]

Next, John Squire Jr. of Wm. Radford & Company testified that Radford was the "agent for the Henry Clay." Squire had been called primarily for one reason—to testify regarding the amount of steam the *Henry Clay* was allowed to carry. He said, "I have seen the Inspector's certificate of that vessel, in the month of July '52; it was in a frame in the Captain's office, the ordinary place—on the right hand side fronting the ladies' cabin."

> *McMahon:* Can you state the pounds of steam she was allowed to carry by that certificate?
> *Squire:* Thirty-five.[52]

Witness Addison Brown was a passenger on the Henry Clay on the day of the disaster and had been in the pilothouse several times since Newburgh. He stated that Edward Hubbard, James Elmendorf, the woman in the pilothouse he identified as Mrs. Elmendorf, and Brown were present. Brown testified that he counted the revolutions at "twenty-two or twenty-two and a half, the highest time." Brown was sitting at the window of the pilothouse when someone warned them of a fire on board. Brown testified that he "did not hear the pilot make any such remark to that person as to 'mind his own business.'" He said the pilot, Edward Hubbard, "kept on his course; he told his assistant, Mr. Elmendorf, to go below and see what the matter was."[53]

Brown testified that after the fire started, he remained near the wheelhouse with his wife and daughter. When the boat was grounded on shore, Brown took his family to the main deck and then to safety. Brown also remarked that he "saw Mr. Hubbard, the pilot, afterward, at the water shoving out boards."[54]

Alexander Cunningham testified that he had boarded the *Henry Clay* at Newburgh and walked about the decks of the boat during the trip downriver. In the afternoon, he sat about fifteen feet from the steam chimney where the fire had started. He was there because it was "a pretty hot day" and the location was cooler with "a draft of air and shaded from the sun."[55]

Cunningham explained that during the fire, Tallman attempted to extinguish the flames with buckets of water. After the boat was grounded, Cunningham took a small boat to assist in the rescue, and Tallman accompanied him for the second trip out. To another question, Cunningham added that he heard the steam blow off while he was on the bow of the boat before he jumped off the burning vessel.[56]

Witness Hazzard Moray verified that Captain Tallman had been ill that day. Moray had boarded the *Henry Clay* at Hudson on the day before the disaster, taking her to Albany. Moray testified that he noticed Captain Tallman "in his stateroom, wringing and twisting, he was sick." Turning to a juror the witness stated,

"I do not know who was the commander; the only officer I saw was the bar-tender; he was assisting passengers on deck."[57]

Joseph Prarie, a Canadian Frenchman, was one of four firemen working on the *Henry Clay* on the day of the fires. The others were John J. Brooks, George Brooks, and another named Conklin who worked the same shift. Prarie said his work schedule began at Poughkeepsie, and he worked until the fire broke out. Prarie said that prior to the fire, he had climbed down the ladder to the fire room to replace Conklin, who had gone on deck to cool off. At the time, he saw no fire.[58]

Prarie testified that he had been in the fire room for about fifteen minutes when he started up the ladder to return to the deck. He had reached the second rung of the ladder when he discovered the fire. He testified that the fire originated "on the starboard side of the starboard boiler, about amidship of the boiler; I mean the middle, speaking as the boiler goes lengthwise." He said that he yelled for Engineer Germain to hand him one bucket and then another bucket of water. Collyer arrived at the scene, and then Germain asked Prarie if he had been scalded. Prarie went up to the deck and witnessed "all the rest of the firemen and the deck hands throwing water around the chimney; as soon as the fire was discovered they began to throw water, and continued till the boat reached shore."[59]

Prarie was questioned about the steam gauge. He testified that "there were no figures on the board of the gauge, but marks which the engineer and I understand. A person not acquainted with it could not understand it." He then explained that "on the front of the engine there was a silver plate; there was a patent gauge in front of the engine which I did not understand. . . . Any one who understands reading and writing could tell the number of pounds by the patent gauge." However, he said that a person would have to enter the engine room to view it.[60]

Prarie confirmed several other important facts. He said that there were seventeen pounds of steam at the time of the accident; they only carried the usual amount of Lackawanna coal for the trip, no extra fuel, no extra fire; and the boilers were at least a foot away from the woodwork. He reaffirmed that the engineer came up on deck after the boat hit shore "and struck the ball and let off the steam." There was a rope from the fire room to the safety valve, but that had burned off, so Engineer John Germain hiked himself up through a grate to get to deck and release the safety valve. [61]

The assistant district attorney Dunning questioned the witness about the furnace.

Dunning: What was the condition of the furnace doors of the *Henry Clay*?
Prarie: Very tight; as tight as any I have seen on any vessel.[62]

Judge Ingersoll asked the fireman, "What did you do with the ashes? Did you throw them out? Prarie replied, "No Sir, they remained in the ash pit." Looking to Defense Attorney Jordan, he added, "Mr. Collyer did not give any directions that day about the fire."[63]

Belknap was called again to explain details about the engine. He stated, "the rests on which the boiler stood were of cast iron; there were about eight or ten inches of water under the boilers, for the flue; the iron pieces under the boiler were open-work, so that the air could circulate." He explained the mathematics involved in calculating "the number of pounds of steam to the square inch." Turning to a juror to explain the safety valve mechanism, Belknap said, "this safety valve was raised by a block and fall, made fast on the upper deck with a rope running down to the engine room."[64]

Joseph Prarie was called again and stated, "We blew off steam at Newburg and Cozzens' Dock that day." Belknap said to Mr. Dunning, "The boilers were twenty one feet in length."[65]

With those final words of defense testimony, Defense Attorney Wheaton closed the case for the defense with the statement, "I believe, sir, we rest our case for the defense here."[66]

However, this was not the end of the trial. The prosecution was allowed to question witnesses for a rebuttal and called James W. Simonton, who, in July 1852, was the assistant editor of the *New-York Daily Times*. He had been present at the meeting at the Astor House the day after the *Henry Clay* burned. Simonton testified that he heard Mr. Ridder speak at that meeting and that he aired "his objections to the conduct of the officers on board the boat." In further questioning, Simonton stated that Ridder also said the cause of the fire was due to "making the fire hotter than was necessary. . .that the officers were remonstrated with for racing. . .that there were no fire buckets on board to extinguish the flames."[67]

The next prosecution witness was Augustus Maverick, an assistant editor with the *New-York Daily Times* in July 1852. He had attended and reported about the Astor House meeting for the newspaper. Maverick testified that what he had written was correct. Prosecutor Hall questioned Maverick about the statements Ridder made at the meeting.

Hall: Did Mr. Ridder give any causes of the calamity?
Maverick: Yes, sir, three.
Hall: What are they?
Maverick: First, for firing up to a dangerous extent; second for continuing to run the boat after remonstrances; and, third that there were no fire buckets on board to extinguish the flames.[68]

Jas Cochran, an engineer, was called next for the prosecution. He had been on the wreck of the burned out *Henry Clay* the day after the disaster. He said that Engineer Germain was with him and "the weight was on the lever, but not properly in its place; it was hanging on the nitch; that would prevent its coming to its proper place; it was hanging as if on a nail." John Germain said to Cochran, "I came away that night; it was so the next morning."[69]

Prosecutor Hall said that he wished to call the residents of the neighborhood to prove they helped rescue passengers. Defense Attorney Wheaton said that he would concede to that if it was also agreed that the officers had assisted too. Thus both sides agreed "that everybody helped." Prosecutor Hall stated, "Then I will not call any more witnesses."[70]

The testimony for the prosecution and the defense had come to an end. The next morning brought the closing arguments. Defense Attorney Wheaton began his summations to the court, saying the defendants were all "men of respectability," and that there was no evidence to support the indictment. He referred to the twelfth section of the Act of Congress entitled "An Act to provide for the better security of the lives of passengers on board vessels impelled in whole or in part by steam." He continued that the wording in the act states "And every person employed on such steamboat . . .by whose misconduct, negligence or inattention to his or their respective duties, the life or lives of any person or persons on board may be destroyed, shall be deemed guilty of manslaughter. . . ."[71]

Wheaton instructed the jury that they must determine if the defendants were employed on the boat. If so, what acts did they perform that could be proven as misconduct, negligence, or inattention to their duties. "What has been done which ought not to have been done? What has been omitted which duty imposed upon them to do?"[72]

Wheaton asked for what omission the engineer, the clerk, or the pilot was responsible. He knew that public sentiment cried out for punishment because so many people had perished. Moreover, the public decided that the officers must be punished. However "the law was not vindictive; it punishes not the innocent that life may be protected." He later added, "there was no direct evidence of culpable negligence," on the part of the accused.[73]

Wheaton referred to Ridder's statements at the Astor House and said that he was speaking to a group of excited, emotional people. At the trial, Ridder testified under oath. Wheaton asked the jury, "has there been a culpable omission on the part of either of those defendants?" He asked the jury to look into themselves, and, if they had doubts, they need decide, "In our opinion you are not guilty."[74]

Defense Attorney Jordan followed with statements regarding his client Thomas Collyer. He said that "Mr. Collyer, the only person with whose defense he was particularly charged, is entirely beyond the pale and scope of this indictment, and that to punish him under this act of Congress is out of the question." Jordan was most likely referring to the fact that Collyer was not employed on the boat. The Steamboat Act of 1838 specifically refers to officers and those others employed on the boat as being solely responsible for the safety of the boat. Collyer was the owner, he was not an employee.[75]

Jordan also added that the prosecution witnesses were too excited at the time to objectively see the true facts. "Our courts of justice are for the purpose of arriving at the truth; they were formed for that purpose, and it was a framework which was wisely and justly made." Jordan continued his speech referencing the twelfth section of the Act of Congress and brought attention to the word "employed" in the act. Collyer was not an employee and Jordan brought up the point that, "Mr. Collyer was one of the owners, but the act of Congress has nothing to do with owners of a vessel, and it has purposely omitted them."[76]

Jordan later added that Thomas Collyer "had performed his duty as owner by providing one of the best vessels that was ever built in this port, or that ever ran upon the Hudson River, and so far as he was concerned, together with his co-owners, he provided one of the best set of men who were ever employed upon this river—all young, active, intelligent, vigilant men."[77]

The defense attorney said that the testimony proved the boat had water buckets, safety boats, a good hull, and that the pilot running the boat ashore proved the strength of the structure of the boat. In addition, Jordan reviewed the testimony of several prosecution witnesses, including Conner, Gilson, Gourlie, and Minturn, pointing out contradictions and deficiencies in what they had said. McMahon felt that there was no need to further sum up the defense position since Wheaton and Jordan had argued most respectably.[78]

The prosecution gave the final words to the jury as J. Prescott Hall summed the case for the prosecution. He spent several minutes describing the necessity for the twelfth section of the Act of Congress. Hall expressed his opinion on the case, stating, "I as a man, think that gross misconduct exhibited itself on the part of the officers of the *Henry Clay* on the fatal 28th July 1852." He said that Congress controlled commerce as dictated by the United States Constitution. However, since steam power was not available at the time of the ratification of the Constitution, it became necessary for Congress to pass the Act of 1838.[79]

Hall continued by stating the legislation was "an act to provide for the better security of lives of passengers onboard vessels propelled in whole or in part by steam." He then explained the specifics of the act requiring that steam vessels must be licensed, that hulls must be inspected once a year, and boilers must be inspected every six months. Hall added it was "the duty of officers of vessels to let steam at every landing place, or whenever the headway of the vessel should be stopped. . . ."[80]

The prosecutor refuted the defense's ploy of considering the "respectability" of the defendants. He argued, "What! because they had shut up Mr. Collyer's shipyard is he to be held irresponsible for this act?" Hall also mentioned that the defense attorneys had joked, saying, "there was no racing, but a little maneuvering."[81]

Hall explained the prosecution's theory that "the calamity occurred to this vessel by a series of acts on the part of these defendants committed on the river that day." Later in his closing arguments, Hall identified the opposing defense theory, "that every man brought here as a witness on the part of the government has come with such feelings as indicated a desire of revenge against the officers of that vessel, and that these witnesses, some of them the most respectable citizens of New York, had come on the stand to forswear themselves." The prosecutor continued in his summation for more that two hours, going over the specific details of the case. At the conclusion, several people in the audience applauded.[82]

The prosecution and the defense had completed their summations to the jury. Judge Ingersoll proceeded to direct the jury in their charge. He went over the twelfth section of the Act of Congress:

> That every captain, engineer, pilot, or other person employed on board of any steamboat or vessel propelled in whole or in part by steam, by whose misconduct, negligence or inattention to his or their respective duties, the life or lives of any person or persons on board said vessel may be destroyed, shall be deemed guilty of manslaughter, and upon conviction thereof before any Circuit Court in the Untied States, shall be sentenced to confinement at hard labor for a period of not more that ten years.[83]

Judge Ingersoll further stated, "The indictment which you are to pass upon is founded upon this provision of this act of Congress. It charges that Thomas Collyer, John F. Tallman, John Germain, Edward Hubbard, Jas. L. Jessup and Jas. Elmendorf, the parties now on trial, in July 1852, were employed on the *Henry Clay*. . .the individuals named therein, and against whom the charges are made have severally pleaded that they were not guilty." Ingersoll instructed each member of the jury, "upon your oaths are to determine is, whether they are guilty as charged in the indictment." He told the jury they must decide that if there were deaths, were the deaths the result of the "misconduct, negligence, or inattention of any one?" Also, were those on trial employed on the boat at the time the lives were lost, and were those lives lost due to the "misconduct, negligence or inattention to his or their respective duties?"[84]

The judge also mentioned that the jury needed to consider if the actions of the defendants were misconduct, negligence, inattention, or "an error in judgment," which is not punishable by the law. He instructed the jury on "rules of law," which provided that a defendant "shall be presumed to be innocent until the contrary appears." He continued, "it is the duty of the government to convince the jury, beyond a reasonable doubt, of the guilt of him who may be indicted." He noted that enough time had passed since the disaster to temper emotions, allowing the jury to proceed open-mindedly.[85]

Next, Judge Ingersoll defined the duties of each of the defendants. Tallman was captain and therefore had "the general command of the boat." James L. Jessup, the clerk, sold tickets and acted "as the assistant of the captain." John Germain, the engineer, had duties of "attending to the engine, regulating and directing that, and having control of the firemen." "Edward Hubbard was the pilot of the boat, and his duty was to correct the course of the boat." James Elmendorf, assistant pilot, had duties to "assist the pilot."[86]

The situation with Thomas Collyer was somewhat different. Ingersoll pointed out that Collyer was not an employee on the boat. The jury need ask themselves, "Did he take the place of the regular captain? If he did, he was employed within the meaning of the law, as captain on board the boat." The judge continued to explain that Collyer "must at least assume to exercise the control and authority of the captain." He said that only one witness "testified that Collyer admitted to him that he was captain." Ingersoll instructed the jury that if they believe "Collyer did act as captain, he is responsible under the Act of Congress for any misconduct, negligence or inattention of which he may be found guilty, in the capacity of such office."[87]

The judge also explained that to convict the defendants, "it must be proved that they have done that which they ought not to have done, or done that improperly, or in a negligent manner, which they ought to have done in a proper and careful manner, or neglected to do that which they ought to have done, by which, the disaster occurred and which disaster would not have occurred had it not have been for such misconduct or neglect of duty."[88]

Ingersoll made several additional points and examples to clarify his instructions to the jury. He noted that Joseph Belknap, in his testimony, stated the *Henry Clay* was a well-built and safe boat manned by skilled officers. The judge also said that if one officer's misconduct could be proved then that officer was guilty, but not the rest of the defendants. He also spoke of the government's theory that excessive speed and excessive use of fuel caused the fire. Ingersoll cautioned that "if there was a race six or eight hours before, and if you cannot connect the fire with that race, then you cannot convict the defendants on the grounds of a race."[89]

Ingersoll pointed out that the *Henry Clay*'s normal time of arrival in New York City was 3:00 P.M. On the day of the fire, the steamboat was at Yonkers, fourteen miles north of the city near 3:00 P.M. "This, therefore shows that there was no extraordinary rate of speed, and, if not, where is the evidence of misconduct, negligence, or inattention on the part of the defendants as regards this point?"[90]

The judge stated the testimony showed the pilot brought the steamboat "to shore in the best possible manner." The judge commented the "Go aft" order seemed reasonable to assist the boat in getting up onto the beach. The judge noted the testimony of those who had gone aft and then ran forward to safety. He alluded that those left on the stern may have been overcome with panic. The judge noted the hull and equipment had been inspected.[91]

The judge summarized his comments saying, "If it was but an error in judgment they are not responsible. But if you find they were guilty of willful misconduct, or negligence, or inattention, then they are culpable, and you will render your verdict accordingly. With these remarks you will take the case under your consideration and give it such careful attention and deliberation as it deserves."[92]

Ingersoll concluded his remarks with, "It is admitted, gentlemen, on the part of the prosecution, that the reputation of the defendants is fair—that they are skilful and competent officers, and that their private character is good. This ought to go far, gentlemen—a great way—to turn the balance in favor of the accused."[93]

The jury began their deliberation, but their verdict was decided upon in short order. A half hour after they left the courtroom, the court crier announced that the jury had made their decision. After they returned to their jurors' seats, and the courtroom was called to attention, the clerk addressed the jury. The defendants, Thomas Collyer, John F. Tallman, John Germain, James L. Jessup, Edward Hubbard, James Elmendorf, and the absent Charles Merritt would learn their fate. If innocent, they go free, if guilty, up to ten years of hard labor awaited them.

Clerk: Gentlemen, have you agreed?
Foreman: We have.
Clerk: How do you find?
Foreman:

"NOT GUILTY."[94]

Epilogue

THE LAST ENTRY in the circuit court records stated, "Charge is thereupon given by the Court to the Jury, who retire under charge of Officers duly qualified to attend them and on their return say that they find the defendants not Guilty, and so they say all."[1]

The final chapter of the trial had been written. Had the defendants been villains or victims? There would be no punishment; they were all were tried together and acquitted together. Only the passing of time would determine whether the outcome was a justified and satisfactory one or a travesty of blind justice.

The time did pass, and the families of the more than seventy lost souls of the terrible *Henry Clay* disaster endured months and years of mourning. The tragic event forever changed their lives, and although their lives went on, there was the sadness, the aching, that was buried deep inside, from which they may never be fully released.

Nathaniel Hawthorne completed his biography of Franklin Pierce in August 1852, shortly after the *Henry Clay* disaster. Franklin Pierce won the presidential election in the autumn of that year. In subsequent years, Hawthorne went on to complete other celebrated works. Too few years passed, and so did Nathaniel Hawthorne's life. Twelve short years after his sister Maria's death, Hawthorne entered the same eternity. He died at sixty years of age in 1864.[2]

A. J. Downing did not live to see many of his dreams come to fulfillment. His business partner Calvert Vaux, completed Downing's projects before moving to New York City. In 1857, Vaux became a member of the American Institute of Architects, and the once protégé of the gifted Downing was afforded the opportunity to participate in what had been a desire of his mentor. Vaux collaborated on the design of Central Park in New York City with another of Downing's acquaintances, Frederick Law Olmsted. The collaboration spanned several years.[3]

Ironically, Vaux came to a death by drowning like his former partner A. J.

423

November 3 1853

Wednesday November 2nd 1853.

The Court Meets pursuant to adjournment
and is opened by Proclamation

Present   The Honorable Charles A. Ingersoll
                                    District Judge

The United States
            vs.
Thomas Collyer
John F. Tallman
John Germain
Edward Hubbard
James L. Jessup and
James Elmendorf

                                    This cause being still on Trial
the Jurors are called and severally answer to their names.

Mr Jordan, concludes on part of the defendants
Mr J. Prescott Hall, sums up on the part of the Prosecution

        Charge is thereupon given by the Court to the Jury, who
retire under charge of Officers duly qualified to attend them
and on their return say that they find the defendants not
Guilty, and so they say all.

The Court adjourned until 10 O'clock tomorrow.

The gatehouse at Springside in Poughkeepsie is one of
the few remaining examples of A. J. Downing's work.

Downing. While visiting his son, Vaux drowned in what appeared to be a fatal mishap, falling into the waters of Brooklyn's Gravesend Bay on a foggy day.[4]

A. J. Downing's widow Caroline Downing moved out of the Downing home in Newburgh. She and the executors of her husband's estate sold the property in 1853. Caroline married Judge John Monell of Newburgh, who had been a friend of the family for several years; he was an executor of Downing's estate. Caroline was said to have lived to about ninety years of age.[5]

Times changed and progress served to destroy much of what Downing had produced. His home in Newburgh, Highland Gardens, no longer stands. There are precious few reminders of Downing still in existence, but there is Springside. This gatehouse home in Poughkeepsie, built for Matthew Vassar, exemplifies Downing's philosophy and taste. One could reflect that Downing's presence remains today in the fruit orchards of the Hudson Valley and in the design of Central Park.[6]

Facing page: The Trial Verdict: "The United States vs. Thomas Collyer and Others,"
2 November 1853.

Before the nineteenth century came to a close, Newburgh honored its hometown boy. In 1897, Downing Park was completed. It was a final tribute designed by Downing's business partner Calvert Vaux and his friend Frederick Law Olmstead. A home to him in life, Newburgh is Downing's last resting place. His remains were moved to Cedar Hill Cemetery.[7]

The Kinsley family retained its residence in Highland Falls for some years. Edward V. Kinsley, the sole surviving member of the tragic Z. J. D. Kinsley family, studied law at Yale College. He married but had no children. In April 1888, Edward passed into eternity, dying unexpectedly in his sleep.[8]

Edward Kinsley had, in his lifetime, refused any offer to sell the Kinsley family lands. He had lost his entire family and believed that every time his father had sold land, some tragedy befell the family. The younger Kinsley was determined to keep the family lands intact, thus fueling hope that he could avoid the repetition of such occurrences. Tragedy struck anyway; his plan could not save him from a premature death or save his lands.[9]

After Edward Kinsley's death, the governor of New York State approved "the purchase by the United States of the whole or a part of the lands of the estate of the late E.V. Kinsley lying to the south of and adjoining the Government lands at West Point, New York, in the County of Orange, and now the property of the heirs of said Kinsley." The following year, Elizabeth Hale Kinsley, Edward's widow, signed the papers that turned the land over to the military academy. West Point planned to use the tract for "the erection and maintenance thereon of Forts, Magazines, Arsenals, Dock Yards, Military Academy, Hospitals and other needful buildings. . . ."[10]

Several of the gravesites of Kinsley family members, including Z. J. D., his wife Eliza, and their children Annie, Mary, Julia, Joseph, Harriet, and Eliza were moved from the family burial ground in Highland Falls, New York, to the West Point Cemetery. There appeared in the *News of the Highlands* the following notice: "A monument is to be erected at West Point to the memory of the Kinsley family, some of whom died years ago. Two of them perished when the steamer *Henry Clay* was burned. It is lettered on all sides, a copper inscription plate on one side containing these words: 'On the incorporation of the Kinsley estate into the domain of the US Military Academy these remains, were removed from the family burial ground and re-interred beneath this monument.'" For eternity, the members of this family so beset by tragedy rest together including Eliza and Harriett Kinsley, who lost their lives on the *Henry Clay*.[11]

The residents of the military academy at West Point were dealt another blow with the death of Maria Slaughter Bailey and her daughter Maria. They left behind a grieving family of men, who, for the remainder of their lives, would carry the burden of their tragic loss. Maria's husband, Jacob Whitman Bailey, continued to teach, research, and write at West Point Military Academy. Their two oldest sons, Samuel and Loring, were sent to boarding school to receive a good education. The youngest son, and also a survivor of the disaster, William Whitman Bailey, remained home with his father.[12]

Five years later, in 1857, Jacob Bailey was named the president of the American Association for the Advancement of Science. It was a position that he would never fill. Bailey was unable to adjust after his wife and daughter drowned, and this contributed to his increasingly failing health. The "honest and reserved" Jacob W. Bailey died in 1857 at forty-six years of age. Three years later, his son Samuel died.[13]

Bailey's two remaining sons lived professionally illustrious lives, following in their father's footsteps, in the field of academics. Loring Woart Bailey studied at Harvard and then moved to the University of New Brunswick in Canada to become a professor of chemistry and natural science.[14]

Young William Whitman "Whitty" Bailey, like his father, never fully recovered from the effects of the *Henry Clay* disaster and experienced lapses of poor health throughout his life. He persevered, nonetheless, and studied at Brown University until 1864. He procured several teaching and research jobs, and in 1867 participated in the 40th parallel geological survey expedition. However, his poor health forced him to leave the expedition the following year, but he returned to Brown University to teach the first botany class offered at the institution. In 1881, he became a professor of botany at the university and continued in his work there until his retirement in 1906.[15]

As he neared retirement, William Bailey paused to write a letter to *The Rocks*, a publication in Highland Falls, New York. His purpose was to clarify the details of the *Henry Clay* disaster that were printed in an anniversary article in the July 27, 1905, issue. He began his letter: "Dear Sir:. . .as one of the probably very few survivors of that dreadful event, I can add some details to your narrative. . . ." So the letter progressed, describing the events that changed his life and that of his family. More than fifty years had passed, but the details remained fresh in his mind.[16]

In those fifty years, much had changed on the Hudson River. The steamboats continued to run, but it was a different business. Congress passed the Steamboat Act of 1852, which outlawed river racing. The act included stronger provisions for the inspection of steamboats and the safety of passengers. It provided for the licensing of pilots and engineers by the Steamboat Inspection Service.[17]

The expansion of train travel through the Hudson Valley also served to change the pace of steamboat travel on the river. If a traveler wanted speed, the train was available. Otherwise the steamboats offered a slower alternative. The new steamboat passenger was one where time didn't seem to matter as much. Taking a steamboat cruise on the river held a romance of its own, and the precious moments of the experience were far more important than a fast pace. Day boats like the famous *Mary Powell*, the "Queen of the Hudson," graced the waters of the old river, not to race, but to casually cruise up or down its waters slow enough for its passengers to enjoy the sunshine, the fresh air, and the beautiful riverside scenery.[18]

The *Henry Clay*, being virtually destroyed by the fire, no longer graced the waters of the Hudson River. The derrick, E. K. Collins, the same derrick used in the recovery operations, towed the remaining charred remnants to New York City. The engine of the *Henry Clay* was refurbished and used in the steamboat *Glen Cove*.[19]

The true cause of the fire on the *Henry Clay* would remain a mystery. One of the defense witnesses, Joseph Prarie, testified during the trial that the ashes had not been cleaned out of the ash pit for the entire trip downriver. Could this have contributed to the fire? There was witness testimony that the latches on the furnace doors were fastened tight. But, it was conjectured "that the furnace doors of the Clay had not been fastened securely by the firemen, when replenishing the fuel. . . ." This theory appears to be the accepted explanation for the cause of the *Henry Clay* fire, as it is stated in Morrison's *History of American Steam Navigation*:

> It is supposed that just previous to the fire, the blower having been put in operation for increasing the draft of the furnaces, and that the furnace doors not being securely fastened, the strong blast from the blower had forced open the furnace doors and drove the flames from the furnaces against the wood-work in the vicinity of the boiler, that was in the hold of the vessel, which took fire immediately and burned with alarming rapidity.[20]

The owners of the *Henry Clay* lost more than two hundred thousand dollars as a result of the fire. The *Henry Clay* had been built at a cost of about forty to fifty thousand dollars, but the owners carried insurance of just twenty-five thousand dollars. However, the loss of the *Henry Clay* did not destroy Thomas Collyer's business, and he continued to build more boats. He named the last boat he built, before his death in 1863, the *Thomas Collyer*, after himself.[21]

Captain Isaac Smith retained ownership of the *Armenia* until 1863 when he sold her to Commodore Van Santvoord and John Davidson. She was kept on the Hudson River day line route for several years and even had employment as a milk boat and also served as a spare boat. In 1883, the *Armenia* was sold to the Baltimore based Henry Brothers & Co. who moved her to service on the Potomac River. Ironically, life for the famed steamboat ended somewhat in the same fashion as the *Henry Clay*. She burned on January 5, 1885, at Alexandria, Virginia.[22]

Captain Tallman left the steamboats in disgrace after the trial. He managed Cozzens' Hotel for a couple of years until things settled down. However, by 1855, he was back on the Hudson River, a captain once again. He died fifteen years later at the age of fifty-four.[23]

There was a record of a James L. Jessup who had lived in Newburgh. This Jessup died at age thirty-eight in 1863. The age gives a clue that perhaps this may be the same James L. Jessup of the *Henry Clay* who was described as a young man at that time. Jessup's obituary stated he had worked for many years as a ticket agent for the Erie Railway Company. One could speculate that he perhaps left the steamboat business for a safer, quieter job on land. He was described in the obituary "a modest, retiring, and highly respected citizen."[24]

If this person was indeed the James L. Jessup of the *Henry Clay*, he was the son-in-law of Thornton M. Niven. Niven had owned a house on Montgomery Street in Newburgh, which land records show was sold to John Peter DeWint. How ironic if his daughter, Caroline Downing, may have walked the same hallways as did Jessup, the man accused as a responsible party in her first husband's death.[25]

Finally, what of the pilot, Edward Hubbard, who was credited with bringing the *Henry Clay* to shore? The testimony at the trial proved that he was correct to run the burning steamboat bow first to shore. After the trial, he returned home, an exonerated man, to continue his work on the river, on steamboats like the *L. Boardman* and the famous *Thomas Powell*. Time passed, and during those years he earned the honored title of "Captain."[26]

He eventually left the steamboat lines to work on the *Storm King Ferry*. This job kept him close to his family and his home on Hudson Street in Cornwall in the Hudson Highlands. He was close enough to be home for his supper after a day's work, a small yet welcome privilege after spending his life on the river.[27]

He was a respected member of his community, as were his children and grandchildren, some of whom stayed on to live in the town that was his home for over forty years. His life was peppered with joys and sadness, from the birth of his several children, he would be a father to more than a dozen in all, to the death of his second wife, Laneretta, who had shared the tragedy of the *Henry Clay* with him. In the end, his third wife, Sarah Jane, and several of his children were left to mourn him. He rests eternally in Old Town Cemetery in the heart of Newburgh.[28]

Edward Hubbard lived to an old age, and through those years his precious gold watch was a treasured gift. Perhaps time and truth brought the final judgment regarding this one member of the crew of the steamboat, *Henry Clay*. He had been honored with this gold watch, a testament to his bravery so many years before. In fitting tribute, the inscription tells it all. He was:

"THE PILOT WHO SO NOBLY STOOD TO HIS POST
IN THE HOUR OF DANGER."[29]

Appendix 1: Names of the Saved

NAMES OF THE SAVED.

Jacob B. Jewett and lady, of Poughkeepsie.
Prof. Bailey and son, of West Point.
Mr. and Mrs. Johnson, of Norwalk, Ct.
T. B. Ridder and daughter, of 198 Prince st.
Mrs. D. Tilton, of New York.
Louis Myres, of Fishkill.
Mary Derwint, of Fishkill.
Mrs. A. J. Downing, of Newburgh.
Mr. and Mrs. Van Dyck, Philadelphia.
Mr. and Mrs. Merrill,   do.
Mrs. Woodward,   do.
John C. Carpenter,   do.
James Craig, W. H. Shelmire, G. M. Grier.
Mrs. Romaine, and two children, Brooklyn.
Miss Austin, Brooklyn.
James Brewster and two daughters.
Anna M. Wilson, Norfolk, Va.
Miss M. Wilson,   do.
A. Foreman,   do.
N. Foreman,   do.
J. G. Martin,   do.
Miss M. Wilson, (slightly injured.)
J. R. Harris, Bellows Falls.
W. R. Williams,   do.
Captain S. Dean, lady and daughter, Pittsburg, Pa.
Capt. C. W. Batchelor, lady and servt., Pittsburg, Pa.
G. W. Manning, Pittsburg, Pa.
P. A. Spring, Cincinnati, Ohio.
R. Cooper, Memphis, Tenn.
Joseph Pierce, Cambridge, Mass.
Wm. A. Irvin, Pittsburg, Pa.
S. Farrow, Montreal, Canada.
James Henry, Baltimore, Md.
John W. Whiting and lady, New Orleans.
John Steele, Albany.
[Mr. Steele is an aged man, and came within an ace of losing his life. He was in the water nearly half an hour, and when rescued was nearly exhausted.]
J. L. Thompson, child and servant, Lancaster, Pa.

T. Y. Mills, Columbus, Ohio.
Master Ray, of Cincinnatti, Ohio—his father, mother and sister were drowned.
S. W. D. Cook, of Cincinnati, Ohio.
Mr. and Mrs. Way, of Mellville, Ohio.
Dr. P. P. Wells, of Brooklyn.
J. H. Gourlie, 1 Hanover-street.
J. Isaac Dayton, 319 West 24th street.
Mrs. T. Romeyn and daughter, New York.
Miss Doty, Rochester.
J. W. Ostrander, 356 West 18th-street.
Pierson A. Spinning, Cincinnati, Ohio.
N. F. Ott, Monson.
S. H. Shelnuyer, Philadelphia.
Henry Lawrence, 718 Broadway.
J. H. Longbottam, 93 John street, N. Y.
J. W. Mullen and lady, Pittsburgh.
James H. Kelly, 125 Navy street, Brooklyn.
J. G. Corley, 54 Wall street.
A. Shepherd, Melville, Ohio.
Thomas H. Phelps, Scipioville,
Thomas A. Phelps,   do.
Miss Phelps,   do.
Edward Cooper, Memphis, Tenn.
Geo. F. Connor, 65 Pearl st., Albany.
Wm. R. Irvin, Pittsburgh.
Joseph Locket, Brooklyn.
Francis Carpenter, Webster, Mass.
Samuel M. Beck, New York.
W. B. Prescott and lady, Holmesville, La.
J. W. Prescott, Alexandria, La.
Miss M. M. Tucker, Milledgeville, Ga.
Mrs. H. Livingston, Brooklyn,
Miss M. Livingston   do.
J. Randolph, 1bberville, La.
Marcus Bosbom, Rock Island, Ill.
James M. McGregor, 179 Forsyth st., N. Y
L. Mintum, New York.
G. W. Greer, Philadelphia.
E. R. Cubbage,   do.
Isaac Dayton, New York.
Capt. George F. Barnard, 370 Broadway.

The Eagle (Poughkeepsie), Saturday, 31 July 1852.
The names of the saved per the newspaper's tally.

Appendix 2: List of Passengers Missing

List of Passengers Missing.

1. Wm. B. Tuman, aged 15, No. 96 Mott-street.

2. Helena Chatillon, aged 14 months, daughter of John Chatillon, of Perry.

3 Bessie Williams, an aged colored woman, of Pough-keepsie.

4. Catharine Whitmore, No. 184 Cherry-street. New-York.

5. Mrs. Ostrander, New-York.

6. Isaac Sherman, New-York.

7. Miss Eliza Smith, Philadelphia.

8. Mrs. Geo. Bell, Alexandria. Va.

9. Mrs. Crrwford, Ypsilanti, Mich., aged 57.

10. RANSOM BOTTOMS, a young man, aged 22, from Noton Corner, near Albany, has light hair, wore a white beaver hat, black coat, vest and pants, white linen over-coat, white shirt, name marked on the collar; a gold watch, with name inside; had a set of false teeth in his pocket.

11. THOMAS LEMON, Albany, aged 35; dark complex-ion, with black curly hair; black cloth coat and vest, blue pants, Canton flannel inside shirt; his name thought to be in his pocket-book, he was on his way to Dover, Jersey, in search of work as harness-maker; and left his wife and two children in Albany.

New-York Daily Times, Wednesday, 4 August 1852.
List of Passengers Missing. The *New-York Daily Tribune* noted on 6 August 1852 that Mrs. Bell was not on the *Henry Clay* when it burned and Thomas Lemon had taken the *Armenia*.

Appendix 3: Number of Lost

The number lost proves to be a trifle less than it was reported last week, a few of the missing having been found.   The total of the deaths sums up as follows:

Bodies recognized by name at Yonkers	51
Unrecognized bodies at Yonkers	7
The bodies found in the waters of New York	3
The bodies found on the Jersey shore	9
Dead bodies recognized	70
Missing	11
Total	81

The Eagle (Poughkeepsie), 7 August 1852.
This tally has seventy bodies recognized and
eleven missing as of 7 August 1852.

Appendix 4: Additional Inquest Testimony

Mary Cooper: Identified by William G. Cummings of West Farms who testified that she was burned and drowned. (*New-York Daily Times*, 30 July 1852.)

Sarah Dennison: Also identified by William G. Cummings of West Farms. (*New-York Daily Times*, 30 July 1852.)

Christopher Hill: Identified by his mother, Maria Hill. He was fifteen years old and was employed as a server on the *Henry Clay*. (*New-York Daily Times*, 30 July 1852.)

Adeline M. Holmes: Identified by Theophilus Holmes. (*New-York Daily Times*, 30 July 1852.)

John Hoosier: Identified by Norman Colkins. Hoosier was eighteen years old and had been on the *Henry Clay* with a Miss Vervaland. She jumped to shore from the forward deck to save herself. (*New-York Daily Times*, 30 July 1852.)

Julia Hoy: Identified by Michael Kavanagh. (*New-York Daily Times*, 30 July 1852.)

Charlotte Johnson: Identified by Garrett Hepp, her brother-in-law. (*New-York Daily Times*, 30 July 1852.)

Elizabeth Ledyard: Identified by her brother, William Ledyard who said that his other sister, Fanny, had also been on the boat and had suffered serious burns. (*The New York Herald*, 2 August 1852.)

Anna B. Marcher: Identified by George Holberton who said that she drowned. (*New-York Daily Tribune*, 2 August 1852.)

George Marcher: Identified by his father-in-law, Samuel E. Lent. (*New-York Daily Times*, 30 July 1852.)

Elizabeth McAnally: Identified by her sister Ann, who explained that she could not afford to bury her sister. Wm. W. Scrugham and James R. Whiting offered a five-dollar sum to help with the burial costs. (*New-York Daily Times*, 31 July 1852.)

Henrietta Moore: Identified by Samuel Osgood. She was a schoolteacher traveling with Edward Cooper. Cooper tried to coax her to jump overboard, but she was too frightened. She disappeared from sight as the smoke and flames surrounded her while she stood on deck. (*The Eagle*, Poughkeepsie, 31 July 1852, *New-York Daily Tribune*, 2 August 1852.)

Elizabeth Pearsall: Identified by her stepfather, David Tilton of East Brooklyn. Her mother survived the disaster. (*New-York Daily Times*, 30 July 1852.)

Elizabeth Shanckey: Identified by Francis McCabe who confirmed her employment with John Simons. (*New-York Daily Times*, 31 July 1852.)

John Stevens: An assistant cook on the *Henry Clay*. His body was found near Manhattanville. (*New-York Daily Times*, 5 August 1852.)

Teresa Thielman: Her body was found at Gregory's Dock near Bull's Ferry and was originally thought to be unrelated to the disaster. Justice Browning determined by the condition of the body that it was too decomposed to be related to the *Henry Clay* disaster. He ordered the remains to be buried. Contents of her purse and her rings confirmed her identity. Her father had her body disinterred and then reburied in New York City. (*New-York Daily Times*, 2 August 1852.)

Elizabeth Williams: Identified by her son, Henry Williams. She was the mother of Charlotte Johnson, who also perished. (*New-York Daily Times*, 4 August 1852.)

Caroline Whitlock: Identified by Theophilus Holmes. (*New-York Daily Times*, 30 July 1852.)

George F. Whitlock: Identified by Theophilus Holmes. (*New-York Daily Times*, 30 July 1852.)

Appendix 5: Inquest Identifications

28 July 1852
Jacob Hillman (Elizabeth Hillman)
Stoddard Colby (Harriet E. Colby)
Stacy Bancroft (Amelia C. Bancroft)

29 July 1852
Norman A. Colkins (John Hoosier)
Jacob W. Bailey (Maria and Maria W. Bailey)
John L. Thompson (Mary Thompson, Eugene)
Samuel Cook (Mr. and Mrs. William Ray and daughter)
David Tilton (Elizabeth Pearsall)
Michael Kavanagh (Julia Hoy)
Calvert Vaux (Andrew Jackson Downing)
Theophilus Holmes (George, Caroline Whitlock, Adeline Holmes)
William G. Cummings (Mary Cooper, Sarah Dennison)
John W. Simons (John H. Simons, Howard Simons)
Samuel E. Lent (George K. Marcher)
Susan Marsden (Johanna Hanford)
Anthony Robinson (Mary Ann Robinson, Isabella)
Matthew Crannell (Matthew Crannell)
John Chatillion (George Thielmann, Mrs. Chatillion)
Theodore Wing (son of Isaac Sands)
Garrett Hepp (Charlotte Johnson)
Adam Murray (Jane Murray, John Murray)
Maria Hill (Christopher Hill)

30 July 1852
Selah J. Jordan (Phoebe Ann Jordan, Jacob Schoonmaker)
David Crist, George Weller (Abraham Crist)
John Chatillion (Katrina Chatillion)
Walter Harding, Daniel Darcy, William J. Ackerman (J. J. Speed)
Ann McAnally (Elizabeth McAnally)
Francis McCabe (Elizabeth Shanckey)
Aubar Reade (Stephen Allen)

31 July 1852
Susan Marsden (Joan Hanford)
Daniel Sands (Isaac D. Sands)
Elmore Thompson (Jennie B. Thompson)
Isaac McDaniels (Lucy McDaniels)
George Holberton (Anna B. Marcher)
Samuel Osgood, William Ackerman (Henrietta Moore)
Edward LeFort, Robert Manning (Maria Hawthorne)
William Ackerman (unrecognized bodies # 1, 2, 3, 4, 5)
Charles Boughter, Franklin Reigert (Elizabeth C. Thompson)
John Allen Smith, James Mackin (Caroline DeWint)
William Rowley (Eliza Kinsley)
Peter Traux, John Watson (Henrietta Traux, Mary Traux)

1 August 1852
William D. Ledyard (Elizabeth Ledyard)
Reverend Abijah Green (Harriet Kinsley)
John Archer (unrecognized #6)
William Ackerman (Bridgit Broderick, unrecognized # 7)
Lewis Costigan (unrecognized # 8)
Anne Marie Thompson (Catherine Schoonmaker)
[] Thielman (Teresa Thielman)
[] (Matilda Fennell)

2 August 1852
William Fling (Ann Hill, Eliza Smith)

3 August 1852
John Milligan (Emeline Milligan)
Theophilus Holmes (Adeline Holmes)
Henry Williams (Elizabeth Williams)
Note: There were no inquest records published for either Matilda Wadsworth or Emily Bartlett. Mrs. Bartlett was on the list of the dead but was not listed in the newspaper report for the verdict of inquest in *The Eagle* (Poughkeepsie) on 7 August 1852 nor in *The New York Herald* of 4 August 1852.

Appendix 6: Trial Witnesses

"The United States vs. Thomas Collyer and Others."
Circuit court minutes 18 October –2 November 1853.

18 October 1853
Charles A. Ingersoll–District Judge
Jurors called and sworn
19 October 1853: Prosecution (Ingersoll)
John H. Berry
Joseph Curtis
Lloyd Minturn
20 October 1853 (Ingersoll)
Lloyd Minturn
Isaac Dayton
21 October 1853 (Ingersoll)
Isaac Dayton
Isaac McDaniels
William Shellmeyer (Shellmyre)
John L. Thompson
22 October 1853 (Hon. Samuel Nelson,
Assistant Justice of the Supreme Court of the
United States)
Phineas P. Wells
James H. Gilson
24 October 1853 (Hon. Samuel R. Betts, District Judge)
John Gourlie
Charles Goodrich
25 October 1853 (Ingersoll)
William N. Wilkes
James F. DePeyster
Adam Murray
26 October 1853 (Ingersoll)
Adam Murray
Edward M. Livermore
Henry Hibbard
G. P. Edwards

27 October 1853 (Ingersoll)
G. P. Edwards
George F. Conner (Connor)
Isaac Polhemus
George F. Barnard
28 October 1853: Defense (Ingersoll)
Joseph Belknap
John N. Weed
Peter Crary (Craig)
Francis Marvin
John R. Harris
29 October 1853 (Ingersoll)
David Morris
Thomas B. Ridder (Riddle)
John Van Buren
Hewlett Lake
Judson Morey
William L. Simmons (Simmonds)
Allen Seaman (Seymour)
Ambrose Bradley
31 October 1853 (Ingersoll)
Philomon Smith
John Squire
Addison W. Brown
Alexander Cunningham
Hazard Morey
Joseph Prairie (Praise)

Additional Prosecution Witnesses Called:
James W. Simonton
Augustus Maverick

Jas. Cochran

Notes

Book 1: Tragedy

Prologue

1. Robert H. Boyle, *The Hudson River: A Natural and Unnatural History* (New York: W.W. Norton & Company, Inc., 1969), 248.
2. U.S. Federal Census for Cornwall, Orange County New York, 1850–1880, Orange County Genealogical Society.
3. Newspaper article, The *Cornwall Times*, 17 September 1881.

Chapter 1: Strife!

1. Oliver A. Rink, *Holland on the Hudson: An Economic and Social History of Dutch New York* (Ithaca and London: Cornell University Press and Cooperstown, New York: New York State Historical Society, 1986), 24; John H. Morrison, *History of American Steam Navigation* (New York: Stephen Daye Press, 1958), 19, 24; Clare Brandt, *An American Aristocracy: the Livingstons* (Garden City, New York: Doubleday & Company, Inc., 1986), 160.
2. Fred Erving Dayton, *Steamboat Days* (New York: Frederick A. Stokes Company, 1925),13; Clare Brandt, *An American Aristocracy: the Livingstons* (Garden City, New York: Doubleday & Company, Inc., 1986),161; John H. Morrison, *History of American Steam Navigation* (New York: Stephen Daye Press, 1958), 26.
3. John H. Morrison, *History of American Steam Navigation* (New York: Stephen Daye Press, 1958), 39; Donald C. Ringwald, *Hudson River Day Line: The Story of a Great American Steamboat Company* (Berkeley, California: Howell-North Books, 1965), 1; Clare Brandt, *An American Aristocracy: the Livingstons* (Garden City, New York: Doubleday & Company, Inc., 1986), 161; U.S. Census records for Cornwall, New York, 1880.
4. Edwin G. Burrows and Mike Wallace, *Gotham: A History of New York City to 1898* (New York and Oxford: Oxford University Press, 1999), 432.
5. Ralph Nading Hill, *Sidewheeler Saga: a Chronicle of Steamboating* (New York and Toronto: Rinehart & Company Inc, 1953), 75; John H. Morrison, *History of American Steam Navigation* (New York: Stephen Daye Press, 1958), 39–41.
6. John H. Morrison, *History of American Steam Navigation* (New York: Stephen Daye Press, 1958), 40–41; Ralph Nading Hill, *Sidewheeler Saga: a Chronicle of Steamboating* (New York and Toronto: Rinehart & Company Inc, 1953), 75, 78; Raymond J. O'Brien, *American Sublime: Landscape and Scenery of the Lower Hudson Valley* (New York: Columbia University Press, 1981), 134; Edwin G. Burrows and Mike Wallace, *Gotham: A History of New York City to 1898* (New York and Oxford: Oxford University Press, 1999), 433; Fred Erving Dayton, *Steamboat Days* (New York: Frederick A. Stokes Company, 1925), 28; Carl Carmer, *The Hudson* (New York and Toronto: J.J. Little and Ives Company, 1939), 197–202.
7. John H. Morrison, *History of American Steam Navigation* (New York: Stephen Daye Press, 1958), 46–51; Fred Erving Dayton, *Steamboat Days* (New York: Frederick A. Stokes Company, 1925), 14, 15, 40, 47.

8. Robert H. Boyle, *The Hudson River: A Natural and Unnatural History* (New York: W.W. Norton & Company, Inc., 1969), 58; Roy Rozenzweig and Elizabeth Blackmar, *The Park and Its People: A History of Central Park* (Ithaca and London: Cornell University Press, 1992), 22; Allan Keller, *Life Along the Hudson* (Tarrytown, New York: Sleepy Hollow Restorations, Inc. 1976), 136.

9. Robert H. Boyle, *The Hudson River: A Natural and Unnatural History* (New York: W.W. Norton & Company, Inc., 1969), 62, 63; Allan Keller, *Life Along the Hudson* (Tarrytown, New York: Sleepy Hollow Restorations, Inc. 1976), 136.

10. Robert H. Boyle, *The Hudson River: A Natural and Unnatural History* (New York: W.W. Norton & Company, Inc. 1969), 60.

11. Allan Keller, *Life Along the Hudson* (Tarrytown, New York: Sleepy Hollow Restorations, Inc. 1976), 173; Stephen P. Stanne, Roger G. Panetta and Brian E. Forist, *The Hudson* (New Brunswick, New Jersey: Rutgers University Press, 1996), 115; Raymond J. O'Brien, *American Sublime: Landscape and Scenery of the Lower Hudson Valley* (New York: Columbia University Press, 1981), 140.

12. Fred Erving Dayton, *Steamboat Days* (New York: Frederick A. Stokes Company, 1925), 40; Carl Carmer, *The Hudson* (New York and Toronto: J.J. Little and Ives Company, 1939), 252–254.

13. Robert H. Boyle, *The Hudson River: A Natural and Unnatural History* (New York: W.W. Norton & Company, Inc. 1969), 20, 21, 28; Arthur G. Adams, *The Hudson: A Guidebook to the River* (Albany, New York: State University of New York Press, 1981), 14.

14. Robert H. Boyle, *The Hudson River: A Natural and Unnatural History* (New York: W.W. Norton & Company, Inc., 1969), 41, 42.

15. Ibid., 34, 43.

16. Clare Brandt, *An American Aristocracy: the Livingstons* (Garden City, New York: Doubleday & Company, Inc., 1986), 161.

17. Stephen P. Stanne, Roger G. Panetta, and Brian E. Forist, *The Hudson* (New Brunswick, New Jersey: Rutgers University Press, 1996), 101; Robert H. Boyle, *The Hudson River: A Natural and Unnatural History* (New York: W.W. Norton & Company, Inc. 1969), 52.

18. Arthur G. Adams, *The Hudson: A Guidebook to the River* (Albany, New York: State University of New York Press, 1981), 14; Robert H. Boyle, *The Hudson River: A Natural and Unnatural History* (New York: W.W. Norton & Company, Inc. 1969), 37, 249.

19. Allan Keller, *Life Along the Hudson* (Tarrytown, New York: Sleepy Hollow Restorations, Inc. 1976), 95; Stephen P. Stanne, Roger G. Panetta, and Brian E. Forist, *The Hudson* (New Brunswick, New Jersey: Rutgers University Press, 1996), 97.

20. Ibid., 97; Carl Carmer, *The Hudson* (New York and Toronto: J.J. Little and Ives Company, 1939), 142–144.

21. Robert H. Boyle, *The Hudson River: A Natural and Unnatural History* (New York: W.W. Norton & Company, Inc., 1969), 51; Arthur G. Adams, *The Hudson: A Guidebook to the River* (Albany, New York: State University of New York Press, 1981), 13–14.

22. Allan Keller, *Life Along the Hudson* (Tarrytown, New York: Sleepy Hollow Restorations, Inc. 1976), 28; Robert H. Boyle, *The Hudson River: A Natural and Unnatural History* (New York: W.W. Norton & Company, Inc. 1969), 48–49; Stephen P. Stanne, Roger G. Panetta, and Brian E. Forist, *The Hudson* (New Brunswick, New Jersey:

Rutgers University Press, 1996), 101, Joanne Michaels and Mary-Margaret Barile *The Best of The Hudson Valley & Catskill Mountains: An Explorer's Guide*, fourth edition (Woodstock, Vermont: The Countryman Press, 2001), 259, 261.

23. Ibid.; Stephen P. Stanne, Roger G. Panetta, and Brian E. Forist, *The Hudson* (New Brunswick, New Jersey: Rutgers University Press, 1996), 105.

24. Eric Homberger, *The Historical Atlas of New York City: A Visual Celebration of Nearly 400 Years of New York City's History* (New York: Henry Holt and Company, 1994), 60; Allan Keller, *Life Along the Hudson* (Tarrytown, New York: Sleepy Hollow Restorations, Inc. 1976), 95.

25. Robert H. Boyle, *The Hudson River: A Natural and Unnatural History* (New York: W.W. Norton & Company, Inc., 1969), 48, 83; Eric Homberger, *The Historical Atlas of New York City: A Visual Celebration of Nearly 400 Years of New York City's History* (New York: Henry Holt and Company, 1994), 60; Allan Keller, *Life Along the Hudson* (Tarrytown, New York: Sleepy Hollow Restorations, Inc. 1976), 28.

26. Robert H. Boyle, *The Hudson River: A Natural and Unnatural History* (New York: W.W. Norton & Company, Inc., 1969), 56; Allan Keller, *Life Along the Hudson* (Tarrytown, New York: Sleepy Hollow Restorations, Inc. 1976), 102, 136.

27. Ralph Nading Hill, *Sidewheeler Suga: a Chronicle of Steamboating* (New York and Toronto: Rinehart & Company Inc, 1953), 80; Edwin G. Burrows and Mike Wallace, *Gotham: A History of New York City to 1898* (New York and Oxford: Oxford University Press, 1999), 432; Raymond J. O'Brien, *American Sublime: Landscape and Scenery of the Lower Hudson Valley* (New York: Columbia University Press, 1981), 134; Fred Erving Dayton, *Steamboat Days* (New York: Frederick A. Stokes Company, 1925), 63; John Mylod, *Biography of a River: The People & Legends of the Hudson Valley* (New York: Hawthorne Books, Inc. Publishers, 1958), 63; John H. Morrison, *History of American Steam Navigation* (New York: Stephen Daye Press, 1958), 97.

28. Robert H. Boyle, *The Hudson River: A Natural and Unnatural History* (New York: W.W. Norton & Company, Inc., 1969), 56; Fred Erving Dayton, *Steamboat Days* (New York: Frederick A. Stokes Company, 1925), 53.

29. John H. Morrison, *History of American Steam Navigation* (New York: Stephen Daye Press, 1958), 46, 54.

30. "Thirteenth Day," closing comments by Hall, *The New York Herald*, 3 November 1853; John Mylod, *Biography of a River: The People & Legends of the Hudson Valley* (New York: Hawthorne Books, Inc. Publishers, 1958), 63; Robert H. Boyle, *The Hudson River: A Natural and Unnatural History* (New York: W.W. Norton & Company, Inc., 1969), 57.

31. John H. Morrison, *History of American Steam Navigation* (New York: Stephen Daye Press, 1958), 68, 119; Donald C. Ringwald, *Hudson River Day Line: The Story of a Great American Steamboat Company* (Berkeley, California: Howell-North Books, 1965), 5, 7.

32. John H. Morrison, *History of American Steam Navigation* (New York: Stephen Daye Press, 1958), 144, 567.

33. Donald C. Ringwald, *Hudson River Day Line: The Story of a Great American Steamboat Company* (Berkeley, California: Howell-North Books, 1965), 8; Allan Keller, *Life Along the Hudson* (Tarrytown, New York: Sleepy Hollow Restorations, Inc. 1976), 112, 157.

34. Fred Erving Dayton, *Steamboat Days* (New York: Frederick A. Stokes Company,

1925), 56, 60; Robert H. Boyle, *The Hudson River: A Natural and Unnatural History* (New York: W.W. Norton & Company, Inc., 1969), 57; Ralph Nading Hill, *Sidewheeler Saga: A Chronicle of Steamboating* (New York and Toronto: Rinehart & Company Inc, 1953), 84–85; Arthur G. Adams, *The Hudson: A Guidebook to the River* (Albany, New York: State University of New York Press, 1981), 266.

35. John H. Morrison, *History of American Steam Navigation* (New York: Stephen Daye Press, 1958), 106–111.

36. "Steamboat Accidents in the United States in 1852," *The Eagle* (Poughkeepsie), 14 August 1852.

Chapter 2: Wednesday, July 28, 1852—An Ordinary Day

1. Fred Erving Dayton, *Steamboat Days* (New York: Frederick A. Stokes Company, 1925), 394–395.

2. Ibid., 60; John H. Morrison, *History of American Steam Navigation* (New York: Stephen Daye Press, 1958), 144.

3. Fred Erving Dayton, *Steamboat Days* (New York: Frederick A. Stokes Company, 1925), 60.

4. Ibid., 60.

5. Donald C. Ringwald, *Hudson River Day Line: The Story of a Great American Steamboat Company* (Berkeley, California: Howell-North Books, 1965), 15; "Terrible Steamboat Calamity," *Daily Albany Argus*, 30 July 1852; John H. Morrison, *History of American Steam Navigation* (New York: Stephen Daye Press, 1958), 107, 144, 145; "Coroner's Inquest at Yonkers—Sixth Day," testimony of Phineas Wells, *New-York Daily Times*, 3 August 1852; "Incidents," *New-York Daily Times*, 30 July 1852.

6. "Traveling—Change of Hour," *The Eagle* (Poughkeepsie), 24 July 1852; "Letter from Mr. Livermore," *New-York Daily Times*, 2 August 1852.

7. The Mariners' Museum in collaboration with Anthony J. Peluso Jr., *The Bard Brothers: Painting America Under Steam and Sail* (Harry N. Abrams, Inc., Publishers with The Mariners' Museum, 1997), 68; John H. Morrison, *History of American Steam Navigation* (New York: Stephen Daye Press, 1958), 144.

8. "Terrible Catastrophe!," initial coverage of the Henry Clay disaster, *New-York Daily Tribune*, 29 July 1852; "The Coroner's Inquest at Yonkers—Seventh Day," testimony of William Radford, *New-York Daily Times*, 4 August 1852.

9. "The Coroner's Inquest at Yonkers—Seventh Day," testimony of William Radford, *New-York Daily Times*, 4 August 1852.

10. Ibid.

11. Ibid.

12. Ibid.

13. "The Henry Clay Calamity," Radford testimony, *The New York Herald*, 4 August 1852.

14. "The Coroner's Inquest at Yonkers—Seventh Day," testimony of William Radford, *New-York Daily Times*, 4 August 1852.

15. "Meteorological Observations," for Albany, *The New York Herald*, morning edition, 29 July 1852; "The Coroner's Inquest at Yonkers—Seventh Day," testimony of William Radford, *New-York Daily Times*, 4 August 1852.

16. Ibid.

17. "Ninth Day," Polhemus testimony, *New-York Daily Times*, 28 October 1853; The Mariners' Museum in collaboration with Anthony J. Peluso Jr., *The Bard Brothers: Painting America Under Steam and Sail* (Harry N. Abrams, Inc., publishers with The Mariners', Museum, 1997), 55, 58.

18. "The Coroner's Inquest," Adam Murray testimony, *New-York Daily Tribune*, 30 July 1852; "Coroner's Inquest at Yonkers," Murray testimony, *New-York Daily Times*, 30 July 1852.

19. "Coroner's Inquest at Manhattanville," Peter Traux testimony, *New-York Daily Times*, 2 August 1852; "Incidents—Further Particulars," *New-York Daily Times*, 2 August 1852; "Second Day of the Inquest," John Simons testimony, *New-York Daily Times*, 30 July 1852.

20. James R. Mellow, *Nathaniel Hawthorne in His Times* (Boston: Houghton Mifflin Company, 1980), 411; "Rumors and Incidents," *New-York Daily Times*, 30 July 1852.

21. "Mr. Dunning's Opening Speech and Testimony," testimony of Lloyd Minturn, *New-York Daily Times*, 20 October 1853.

22. Ibid.; "The Henry Clay Steamboat Calamity," testimony of Lloyd Minturn, *The New York Herald*, 20 October 1853; "Third Day," testimony of Lloyd Minturn, *New-York Daily Times*, 21 October 1853; "The Late Disaster Burning of the Henry Clay," *The Eagle* (Poughkeepsie), 7 August 1852.

23. "Case for the Prosecution," Minturn testimony, *The New York Herald*, 20 October 1853; "The Coroner's Inquest at Yonkers—Seventh Day," testimony of John E. Cubbage, *New-York Daily Times*, 4 August 1852.

24. Ibid.

25. "Seventh Day," Radford testimony, *New-York Daily Times*, 4 August 1852; "Dreadful Calamity," *New-York Daily Times*, 29 July 1852.

26. "Fifth Day," testimony of James H. Gilson, *The New York Herald*, 23 October 1853; "Third Day," testimony of Lloyd Minturn, The *New York Herald*, 21 October 1853; "Meeting of Survivors at the Astor-House," comment made by Mr. Way, *New-York Daily Times*, 30 July 1852.

27. "Meteorological Observations," *The New York Herald*, 29 July 1852; Robert H. Boyle, *The Hudson River: A Natural and Unnatural History* (New York: W.W. Norton & Company, Inc., 1969), 105, 108.

28. "Tenth Day—Opening of the Case for the Defense," testimony of John R. Harris, *The New York Herald*, 29 October 1853; "Tenth Day," testimony of John R. Harris, *New-York Daily Times*, 29 October 1853.

29. Letter to the editor from John. R. Harris, *New-York Daily Tribune*, 31 July 1852; "Tenth Day—Opening of the Case for the Defense," testimony of John R. Harris, *The New York Herald*, 29 October 1853; "Eleventh Day," testimony of Thomas B. Ridder, *New-York Daily Times*, 31 October 1853; "Second Day," testimony of Lloyd Minturn, *New-York Daily Times*, 20 October 1853; "Third Day," testimony of Isaac Dayton, *New-York Daily Times*, 21 October 1853.

30. "Sixth Day," testimony of John H. Gourlie and Charles Goodrich, *The New York Herald*, 25 October 1853; "Statement of a Passenger," from John Gourlie, *New-York Daily Times*, 2 August 1852; "Fourth Day," testimony of Isaac Dayton, *New-York Daily Times*, 22 October 1853.

31. "Sixth Day," testimony of Charles Goodrich, *The New York Herald*, 25 October 1853; "Third Day," testimony of Isaac Dayton, *New-York Daily Times*, 21 October 1853; Robert H. Boyle, *The Hudson River: A Natural and Unnatural History* (New York: W.W. Norton & Company, Inc., 1969), 106.

32. William Wade, *Panorama of the Hudson River*, 1848, *http://www.hhr.highlands.com/wade-text.html*.

33. Ibid.; Allan Keller, *Life Along the Hudson* (Tarrytown, New York: Sleepy Hollow Restorations, Inc. 1976), 173.

34. Ibid.; "Letter from Mr. Livermore," *New-York Daily Times*, 2 August 1852.

35. "Second Day of the Inquest," testimony of Samuel W. D. Cook, *New-York Daily Times*, 30 July 1852.

36. "The Inquest-Third Day," Harding testimony, *New-York Daily Times*, 31 July 1852; "The Body of Mrs. Hill Recognized," *New-York Daily Times*, 3 August 1852.

37. "Particulars and Incidents," *New-York Daily Times*, 4 August 1852.

38. "Third Day," testimony of Isaac Dayton, *New-York Daily Times*, 21 October 1853; "Statement of a Passenger," from John Gourlie, *New-York Daily Times*, 2 August 1852.

39. John H. Morrison, *History of American Steam Navigation* (New York: Stephen Daye Press, 1958), 145; "Twelfth Day," testimony of Joseph Prairie *New-York Daily Times*, 1 November 1853.

40. "The Coroner's Inquest at Yonkers—Seventh Day," testimony of William Radford, *New-York Daily Times*, 4 August 1852.

41. "The Coroner's Inquest at Yonkers—Seventh Day," John E. Cubbage testimony, *New-York Daily Times*, 4 August 1852; "Sixth Day," James F. DePeyster testimony, *New-York Daily Times*, 3 August 1852.

42. Joanne Michaels and Mary-Margaret Barile, *The Best of the Hudson Valley & Catskill Mountains: An Explorer's Guide*, Fourth Edition (Woodstock, Vermont: The Countryman Press, 2001), 195–196; Arthur G. Adams, *The Hudson: A Guidebook to the River* (Albany, New York: State University of New York Press, 1981), 255; Clare Brandt, *An American Aristocracy: The Livingstons* (Garden City, New York: Doubleday & Company, Inc., 1986), 185–187.

43. "Third Day," Lloyd Minturn testimony, *New-York Daily Times*, 21 October 1853; "The Late Disaster Burning of the Henry Clay," *The Eagle* (Poughkeepsie), 7 August 1852.

44. Ibid.

45. "Eleventh Day," testimony of John Van Buren, *New-York Daily Times*, 31 October 1853; Third Day," testimony of Isaac Dayton, *New-York Daily Times*, 21 October 1853; "Second Day–Case for the Prosecution," testimony of Lloyd Minturn, *The New York Herald*, 20 October 1853.

46. "Eighth Day," testimony of Henry Hebbard, *The New York Herald*, 27 October, 1853; "Fifth Day," testimony of James H. Gilson, *The New York Herald*, 23 October 1853; "Sixth Day," testimony of John Gourlie, *New-York Daily Times*, 25 October 1853; "Coroner's Inquest at Yonkers," testimony of Samuel W. D. Cook, *New-York Daily Times*, 30 July 1852.

47. "The Inquest," testimony of Stoddard B. Colby, *New-York Daily Tribune*, 29 July 1852; "Coroner's Inquest at Yonkers—Sixth Day," testimony of John H. Gourlie, *New-York Daily Times*, 3 August 1852.

48. "The Henry Clay Steamboat Calamity," testimony of Adam Murray, *The New York Herald*, 26 October 1853.
49. "The Coroner's Inquest—Fourth Day," testimony of Isaac McDaniels, *New-York Daily Times*, 2 August 1852.
50. "The Late Disaster Burning of the Henry Clay," *The Eagle* (Poughkeepsie), 7 August 1852.
51. Ibid.
52. "The Coroner's Inquest at Yonkers," testimony of John Gourlie, *New-York Daily Times*, 3 August 1852; "Sixth Day,' testimony of John Gourlie, *New-York Daily Times*, 25 October 1853; "Fourth Day," McDaniels' testimony, *New-York Daily Times*, 2 August 1852.
53. "Coroner's Inquest at Yonkers," testimony of Jacob Hillman and Samuel Cook, *New-York Daily Times*, 30 July 1852; "Ninth Day," testimony of Isaac Polhemus, *New-York Daily Times*, 28 October 1853.
54. "Sixth Day," testimony of John Gourlie, *New-York Daily Times*, 25 October 1853; "Eleventh Day," testimony of John Van Buren, *New-York Daily Times*, 31 October 1853; Donald C. Ringwald, *Hudson River Day Line: The Story of a Great American Steamboat Company* (Berkeley, California: Howell-North Books, 1965), 38–39; Bob Steuding, *Rondout—A Hudson River Port* (Fleischmanns, New York: Purple Mountain Press, 1995), 164; "Coroner's Inquest at Yonkers," testimony of Anthony Robinson, *New-York Daily Times*, 30 July 1852.
55. "Letter from Mr Livermore," *New-York Daily Times*, 2 August 1852; "Meeting of Survivors," *New-York Daily Times*, 30 July 1852.
56. "Opening Case for the Prosecution," testimony of John R. Harris, *The New York Herald*, 29 October 1853.
57. Arthur G. Adams, *The Hudson: A Guidebook to the River* (Albany, New York: State University of New York Press, 1981), 222; " Twelfth Day," Joseph Prairie testimony, *New-York Daily Times*, 1 November 1853; "The Coroner's Inquest—Fourth Day," testimony of Daniel Sands, *New-York Daily Times*, 2 August 1852; "The Inquest–Third Day," testimony of Selah J. Jordan, *New-York Daily Times*, 31 July 1852; "Second Day of the Inquest," testimony of John W. Simons, *New-York Daily Times*, 30 July 1852.
58. William Wade, *Panorama of the Hudson River*, 1848, *http://www.hhr.highlands.com/wadetext.html*.; "Coroner's Inquest at Yonkers," George P. Edwards testimony, *New-York Daily Times*, 30 July 1852.
59. Arthur G. Adams, *The Hudson: A Guidebook to the River* (Albany, New York: State University of New York Press, 1981), 208; William Wade, *Panorama of the Hudson River*, 1848, *http://www.hhr.highlands.com/wadetext.html*.
60. "Coroner's Inquest at Yonkers," testimony of John L. Thompson, *New-York Daily Times*, 30 July 1852; Clement Eaton, *Henry Clay and the Art of American Politics*, edited by Oscar Handlin, eighth printing (Boston and Toronto: Little, Brown and Company, 1957), 194, 198.
61. "Eleventh Day," testimony of William L. Simmonds refers to his boarding between 12:30 and 1:00 at Newburgh, *New-York Daily Times*, 31 October 1853; John A. Garraty and Mark C. Carnes, eds., *American National Biography*, published under the auspices of the American Counsel of Learned Societies, vol. 6 (New York: Oxford Uni-

versity Press, 1999), 843, 844; "List of the Dead," and "Second Day of the Inquest," *New-York Daily Times*, 30 July 1852; "Names of the Dead" and "The Rescued," *Newburgh Telegraph*, 5 August 1852; William H. Ewen, "The Hudson's Blackest Day," *Yonkers Historical Bulletin*, July 1965, 13; *William Alex, Calvert Vaux: Architect and Planner (New* York: Ink, Inc. 1994), 57; The DeWint name also was spelled DeWindt.

62. "Andrew J. Downing," *Newburgh Telegraph*, 12 August 1852, vol. 3, no. 15; "Downing and His Wife," *Newburgh Telegram,* 22 August 1914, 4.

63. "Coroner's Inquest at Yonkers," John L. Thompson testimony, *New-York Daily Times*, 30 July 1852; "The Inquest—Third Day," testimony of David Crist and George Weller, *New-York Daily Times*, 31 July 1852; "Fourth Day," testimony of Elmore Thomspson, *New-York Daily Times*, 2 August 1852; "The Henry Clay Steamboat Calamity," James F. DePeyster testimony, *The New York Herald*, 26 October 1853.

64. "Second Day of the Inquest," George P. Edwards testimony, *New-York Daily Times*, 30 July 1852; "The Coroner's Inquest at Yonkers," testimony of James F. DePeyster, *New-York Daily Times*, 3 August 1852; "Coroner's Inquest at Yonkers," John L. Thompson testimony, *New-York Daily Times*, 30 July 1852.

65. A newspaper report in the *New-York Daily Tribune* of 30 July 1852 initially referred to Mrs. Elmendorf as the wife of the "principal pilot." It was later learned that she was the wife of James Elmendorf who was the second pilot. U.S. Circuit Court, *New-York Daily Times*, 1 November 1853; John Mylod, *Biography of a River* (New York: Hawthorne Books, Inc. 1969), 54; Benson J. Lossing, *The Hudson From Wilderness to the Sea* (Somersworth: New Hampshire Publishing Company, 1972), 251; U.S. Federal Census for Cornwall, Orange County New York, 1850, Orange County Genealogical Society.

66. Raymond J. O'Brien, *American Sublime: Landscape and Scenery of the Lower Hudson Valley* (New York: Columbia University Press), 48; Robert H. Boyle, *The Hudson River: A Natural and Unnatural History* (New York: W.W. Norton & Company, Inc., 1969), 124.

67. "Tenth Day," testimony of John R. Harris, *New-York Daily Times*, 29 October 1853.

68. Stephen P. Stanne, Roger G. Panetta, and Brian E. Forist, *The Hudson* (New Brunswick, New Jersey: Rutgers University Press, 1996), 115, William Whitman Bailey, "A Survivor Tells the Story and Makes Corrections," *Newburgh Sunday Telegram*, 12 August 1905, first appeared in *The Rocks*, 8 August 1905; George W. Cullum, BVT, MAJ.GEN, *Biographical Register of the Officers and Graduates of the U.S. Military Academy of West Point From Its Establishment in 1802–1890*, vol. 1, nos.1–1000 (Boston and New York: Houghton Mifflin and Company, Cambridge: The Riverside Press, 1891), 211, 501, 504; "Second Day of the Inquest," Jacob Bailey testimony, *New-York Daily Times*, 30 July 1852; Jacob Whitman Bailey letter to Mrs. Cole dated 4 August 1852, Selected Letters of Jacob Whitman Bailey, compiled by Alfred G. Bailey, Dean of Arts in the University of New Brunswick, 1962; Prof. W. Whitman Bailey, "Recollections of West Point—Part I of the Henry Clay Disaster," *News of the Highlands*, May 5, 1900; "Fifth Day," Phineas P. Wells testimony, *The New York Herald*, 23 October 1853.

69. "Fifth Day," Phineas P. Wells, *New-York Daily Times*, 24 October 1853, "Fifth Day," Phineas P. Wells testimony, *The New York Herald*, 23 October 1853; "Coroner's Inquest," *New-York Daily Times*, 30 July 1852.

70. "Second Day of the Inquest," Adam Murray testimony, *New-York Daily Times*, 30 July

1852; "The Inquest," testimony of Stacy B. Bancroft, *New-York Daily Tribune*, 29 July 1852; "Seventh Day," William Radford testimony, *New-York Daily Times*, 4 August 1852.

71. John H. Morrison, *History of American Steam Navigation* (New York: Stephen Daye Press, 1958), 144; Donald C. Ringwald, *Hudson River Day Line: the Story of a Great American Steamboat Company* (Berkeley, California: Howell-North Books, 1965), 15.

72. "Meteorological Table," *The Eagle* (Poughkeepsie), 31 July 1852; "Third Day," Lloyd Minturn testimony, *The New York Herald*, 21 October 1853.

73. "Fourth Day," testimony of John L. Thompson, *The New York Herald*, 22 October 1853, "Coroner's Inquest at Yonkers," John L. Thompson testimony, *New-York Daily Times*, 30 July 1852.

74. Robert H. Boyle, *The Hudson River: A Natural and Unnatural History* (New York: W.W. Norton & Company, Inc., 1969), 182, 206; Joanne Michaels and Mary-Margaret Barile, *The Best of the Hudson Valley & Catskill Mountains: An Explorer's Guide*, Fourth Edition (Woodstock, Vermont: The Countryman Press, 2001), 259.

75. Robert H. Boyle, *The Hudson River: A Natural and Unnatural History* (New York: W.W. Norton & Company, Inc., 1969), 241; William Wade, *Panorama of the Hudson River*, 1848, *http://www.hhr.highlands.com/wadetext.html*.

76. Robert H. Boyle, *The Hudson River: A Natural and Unnatural History* (New York: W.W. Norton & Company, Inc., 1969), 231.

77. "Rumors and Incidents," information about Stephen Allen, *New-York Daily Times*, 30 July 1852; "Statements of Eye Witnesses," statement of John Dike, *New-York Daily Times*, 30 July 1852; James R. Mellow, *Nathaniel Hawthorne in His Times* (Boston: Houghton Mifflin Company, 1980), 411; "Fourth Day," Isaac McDaniel testimony, *New-York Daily Times*, 22 October 1853; "Law Intelligence," testimony of Isaac Dayton, *New-York Daily Tribune*, 21 October 1853; Wade, *Panorama of the Hudson River*, 1848, *http://www.hhr.highlands.com/wadetext.html*.

78. "Twelfth Day," testimony of Joseph Prairie, (his name was spelled, Prairie, in newspapers but Praise in circuit court trial records filed at NARA in New York City) *The New York Herald*, 1 November 1853; "The Passage from Albany," *Newburgh Telegraph*, 5 August 1852.

79. William Wade, Master Engraver, 1846, "Virtual Trip Up the Hudson," *http://hhrhighlands.com/virtual.htm*; "Sixth Day," testimony of John Gourlie, *The New York Herald*, 25 October 1853; Raymond J. O'Brien, *American Sublime: Landscape and Scenery of the Lower Hudson Valley*, (New York: Columbia University Press, 1981), 141; Arthur G. Adams, *The Hudson: A Guidebook to the River* (Albany, New York: State University of New York Press, 1981), 105; Harmon H. Goldstone and Martha Dalrymple, *History Preserved: A Guide to New York City Landmarks and Historic Districts* (New York: Simon and Schuster, 1974), 350.

80. "The Inquest," Stacy Bancroft testimony, *New-York Daily Tribune*, 29 July 1852.

Chapter 3: Fire at Riverdale

1. "Second Day of the Inquest," testimony of John Thompson, *New-York Daily Times*, 30 July 1852.

2. Ibid.; "Seventh Day," Cubbage testimony, *New-York Daily Times*, 4 August 1852; "Second Day of the Inquest," testimony of John Thompson, *New-York Daily Times*, 30 July

1852; "The Burning of the Henry Clay," *Newburgh Telegraph*, 5 August 1852; "Fourth Day," Thompson testimony, *New-York Daily Times*, 22 October 1853.

3. "Twelfth Day," Alexander Cunningham testimony, *New-York Daily Times*, 1 November 1853; "The Late Disaster, Burning of the Henry Clay," *The Eagle* (Poughkeepsie), vol. 9, 7 August 1852.

4. "Ninth Day," George Conner testimony, *The New York Herald*, 28 October 1853; newspapers reported his name as "Connor," his name noted in trial records as "Conner;" Circuit court records for the trial of the officers of the Henry Clay, "The United States vs. Thomas Collyer and others, National Archives and Records Administration, Northeast Region, New York, 418.

5. Comments of John Dike, *New-York Daily Times*, 30 July 1852, "Eleventh Day," David Morris testimony, *New-York Daily Times*, 31 October 1853.

6. "The Burning of the Henry Clay," *Newburgh Telegraph*, 5 August 1852; "Incidents of Escape," *New-York Daily Tribune*, 29 July 1852; "Statement from a Passenger," John Gourlie, *New-York Daily Times*, 2 August 1852.

7. "The Finale of a Race," *New-York Daily Times*, 29 July 1852; "Ninth Day," Polhemus testimony, *The New York Herald*, 28 October 1853.

8. William Whitman Bailey, "A Survivor Tells the Story and Makes Corrections," *Newburgh Sunday Telegram*, 12 August 1905, first appeared in *The Rocks*, 8 August 1905; Professor William Bailey, "Recollections of West Point," *News of the Highlands*, 5 May 1900; Jacob Whitman Bailey letter to Mrs. Cole dated 4 August 1852, Selected Letters of Jacob Whitman Bailey arranged by Professor Loring Woart Bailey of the University of New Brunswick, and letters and papers relating to the Bailey family of West Point, compiled by Alfred G. Bailey, 1962.

9. Ibid.; Prof. W. Bailey, "Recollections of West Point," *News of the Highlands*, 5 May 1900; William Whitman Bailey, "A Survivor Tells the Story and Makes Corrections," *Newburgh Sunday Telegram*, 12 August 1905, first appeared in *The Rocks*, 8 August 1905.

10. "Third Day," Isaac Dayton testimony, *The New York Herald*, 21 October 1853; "Eleventh Day," Hewlett Lake testimony, *New-York Daily Times*, 31 October 1853; "Tenth Day," Harris testimony, *The New York Herald*, 29 October 1853.

11. "Twelfth Day," Addison Brown testimony, *New-York Daily Times*, 1 November 1853; "Tenth Day,"McMahon arguments, *New-York Daily Times*, 29 October 1853; "Annotations," and grave numbers 164 and 166, Old Town Burying Ground, archives of Orange County Genealogical Society; U.S. Census for Cornwall, New York, 1850.

12. "Third Day," Lloyd Minturn testimony, *New-York Daily Times*, 21 October 1853; "Fifth Day," Wells testimony, *The New York Herald*, 23 October 1853;"Incidents of Escape," *New-York Daily Tribune*, 29 July 1852.

13. "Eleventh Day," Ridder testimony, *New-York Daily Times*, 31 October 1853; "Ninth Day," Edwards testimony, *The New York Herald*, 28 October 1853; "Facts and Rumors," *New-York Daily Tribune*, 30 July 1852; "Sixth Day," Gourlie testimony, *New-York Daily Times*, 3 August, 1853.

14 "Seventh Day," Cubbage testimony, *New-York Daily Times*, 4 August 1852.

15. "Second Day of the Inquest," John Thompson testimony, *New-York Daily Times*, 30 July 1852.

16. "The Henry Clay Calamity," *The New York Herald*, 5 August, 1852; "Eleventh Day,"

Hewlett Lake testimony, *New-York Daily Times*, 31 October 1853; "Incidents of Escape," *New-York Daily Tribune*, 29 July 1852.

17. "Second Day of the Inquest," John Thompson testimony, *New-York Daily Times*, 30 July 1852.

18. Ibid.

19. Ibid.

20. "Ninth Day," George Conner testimony, *The New York Herald*, 28 October 1853.

21. William Whitman Bailey, "A Survivor Tells the Story and Makes Corrections," *Newburgh Sunday Telegram*, 12 August 1905; Jacob Whitman Bailey letter to Mrs. Cole dated 4 August 1852, Selected Letters of Jacob Whitman Bailey arranged by Professor Loring Woart Bailey of the University of New Brunswick and letters and papers, relating to the Bailey family of West Point compiled by Alfred G. Bailey, 1962.

22. Ibid.; "Second Day of the Inquest," Jacob Bailey testimony, *New-York Daily Times*, 30 July 1852.

23. Ibid.; Jacob Whitman Bailey letter to Mrs. Cole dated 4 August 1852, Selected Letters of Jacob Whitman Bailey arranged by Professor Loring Woart Bailey of the University of New Brunswick, and letters and papers relating to the Bailey family of West Point, compiled by Alfred G. Bailey, 1962.

24. Ibid.; "Second Day of the Inquest," Jacob Bailey testimony, *New-York Daily Times*, 30 July 1852; "Incidents," *New-York Daily Times*, 3 August 1852.

25. Prof. William W. Bailey, "Recollections of West Point," *The News of the Highlands*, 5 May 1900.

26. Ibid.

27. "Fourth Day," Elmore Thompson testimony, *New-York Daily Times*, 2 August 1852.

28. Ibid.

29. "Additional Particulars—Incidents, Etc." report on Mrs. Sands, *New-York Daily Times*, 31 July 1852.

30. Ibid.

31. "The Injured and the Dead," *New-York Daily Times*, 29 July 1852.

32. Jacob Whitman Bailey letter to Mrs. Cole dated 4 August 1852, Selected Letters of Jacob Whitman Bailey arranged by Professor Loring Woart Bailey of the University of New Brunswick, and letters and papers relating to the Bailey family of West Point, compiled by Alfred G. Bailey, 1962.

33. "Seventh Day," DePeyster testimony, *The New York Herald*, 26 October 1853; "Incidents of Escape," *New-York Daily Tribune*, 29 July 1852.

34. "Seventh Day," DePeyster testimony, *The New York Herald*, 26 October 1853; "Sixth Day," Gourlie testimony, *New-York Daily Times*, 3 August 1852.

35. "Fifth Day," Wells testimony, *The New York Herald*, 23 October 1853.

36. "Account of a Passenger," written by Isaac Dayton, *New-York Daily Tribune*, 30 July 1852.

37. "The Inquest," Jacob Hillman testimony, *New-York Daily Tribune*, 29 July 1852.

38. "Coroner's Inquest at Yonkers," Stacy Bancroft testimony, *New-York Daily Times*, 30 July 1852.

39. "Fourth Day," Isaac McDaniels testimony, *New-York Daily Times*, 22 October 1853.

40. Ibid.

41. "Seventh Day," DePeyster testimony, *New-York Daily Times*, 26 October 1853; "Heart

Rending Scenes," *New-York Daily Times*, 29 July 1852; "Sixth Day," Gourlie testimony, *New-York Daily Times*, 25 October 1853.

42. "The Burning of the Henry Clay," *Newburgh Telegraph*, 5 August 1852; "Twelfth Day," Alexander Cunningham testimony, *New-York Daily Times*, 1 November 1853.

43. "Seventh Day," Lloyd Minturn testimony, *New-York Daily Times*, 4 August 1852.

44. "Rumors and Incidents," *New-York Daily Times*, 30 July 1852; Several other men were listed as rescuers including Edward Cooper of Memphis (*New-York Daily Times*, 29 July 1852), T. B. Ridder (*New-York Daily Times*, 31 October 1853), Peter Hand, and Charles Woodruff (*New-York Daily Times*, 3 August 1852), Morgan O'Brien (*Newburgh Telegram* 29 July 1905), TY Mills of Columbus, Ohio (*New-York Daily Times*, 29 July 1852). Also in a letter to the editor it was noted that J. H. Longbottom of New York saved "Mrs. W.J. Pease, Mrs. Rev. J. C. Baughman and the baby of Mrs. B. C. Webb," (*New-York Daily Tribune*, 31 July 1852). In another letter, Samuel M. Beck wrote of his rescue of a young women. (*New-York Daily Tribune*, 31 July 1852.)

45. "Tenth Day," Harris testimony, *New-York Daily Times*, 29 October 1853; "Rumors and Incidents," *New-York Daily Times*, 30 July 1852; "Eleventh Day," Ridder testimony, *New-York Daily Times*, 31 October 1853; "The Injured and Dead," *New-York Daily Times*, 29 July 1852.

46. "Additional Particulars," *New-York Daily Times*, 31 July 1852; "Seventh Day," Minturn and Wells testimony, *New-York Daily Times* 4 August 1852; "Twelfth Day," Addison Brown and Joseph Prarie testimony, *New-York Daily Times*, 1 November 1853; "Tenth Day," McMahon, *New-York Daily Times*, 29 October 1853; "Eleventh Day," Ridder testimony, *New-York Daily Times*, 31 October 1853; "Testimony," Edwards, *New-York Daily Tribune*, 30 July 1852.

47. "Statement of Mr. Polhemus," *The New York Herald*, 29 July 1852; "Incidents," *New-York Daily Times*, 3 August 1852; "Eleventh Day," Hewlett Lake testimony, *The New York Herald*, 30 October 1853; "Letter from Captain Verrel," dated 31 July 1852, to the editors of the *New-York Daily Tribune*, 3 August 1852.

48. "Statement of Mr. Polhemus," *The New York Herald*, 29 July 1852.

49. Ibid., "Statement of Captain Tallman," *The New York Herald*, 29 July 1852; "The Finale of a Race," *New-York Daily Times*, 30 July 1852; "Sixth Day," Gourlie testimony, *New-York Daily Times*, 25 October 1853; "Terrible Disaster," *Daily Albany Argus*, 29 July 1852.

50. "Incidents," *New-York Daily Tribune*, 29 July 1852.

51. "Terrible Disaster," *The Eagle* (Poughkeepsie), 31 July 1852; "Letter from Mr. Livermore," *New-York Daily Times*, 2 August 1852.

52. Ibid.

53. Ibid.

54. "Incidents," *New-York Daily Times*, 29 and 30 July 1852.

55. "The Henry Clay Calamity," *The New York Herald*, 4 August 1852; "Incidents of Escape, &c.," *New-York Daily Tribune* 29 July 1852.

56. "Rumors and Incidents," *New-York Daily Times*, 30 July 1852; "Scenes and Incidents," *The New York Herald*, 31 July 1852; "Incidents," *New-York Daily Times* 3 August 1852.

57. Ibid.; Jacob Whitman Bailey letter to Mrs. Cole dated 4 August 1852, Selected Letters of Jacob Whitman Bailey arranged by Professor Loring Woart Bailey of the Universi-

ty of New Brunswick, and letters and papers relating to the Bailey family of West Point compiled by Alfred G. Bailey, 1962.

58. "From the Wreck of the Henry Clay," *Daily Albany Argus*, 2 August 1852.

59. "The Burning of the Henry Clay," *Newburgh Telegraph*, 5 August 1852; "Incidents of Escape," *New-York Daily Tribune*, 29 July 1852; "Scenes and Incidents," *The New York Herald*, 31 July 1852.

60. "Coroner's Inquest at Yonkers," *New-York Daily Times*, 30 July 1852.

61. "The Finale of a Race," *New-York Daily Times*, 29 July 1852; "Hotel List," *New-York Daily Times*, 29 July 1852.

62. Ibid.; The Old Trinity Church remained the tallest building in New York City until 1892. Eric Homberger, *The Historical Atlas of New York City: A Visual Celebration of Nearly 400 Years of New York City's History* (New York: Henry Holt and Company, 1994), 104.

Chapter 4: Meeting at the Astor

1. Headline to news story printed in *New-York Daily Tribune*, 29 July 1852; headline to news story printed in *New-York Daily Times*, 29 July 1852; front page headline to news story printed in *The New York Herald*, 29 July 1852.

2. "Terrible Steamboat Calamity," *The New York Herald*, 29 July 1852.

3. "Coroner's Inquest at Yonkers," "Second Day of the Inquest" and "Passengers Missing," *New-York Daily Times*, 30 July 1852.

4. "Meeting of the Passengers," front page notice, *The New York Herald*, 29 July 1852.

5. "Meeting of Survivors at the Astor-House," *New-York Daily Times*, 30 July 1852; "Meeting of Passengers," *New-York Daily Tribune*, 30 July 1852.

6. "Meeting of Passengers," *New-York Daily Tribune*, 30 July 1852.

7. "Meeting of Survivors at the Astor-House," *New-York Daily Times*, 30 July 1852; "Meeting of Passengers," *New-York Daily Tribune*, 30 July 1852; "Indignation Meeting of the Passengers at the Astor House," *The New York Herald*, morning edition, 30 July 1852.

8. "Meeting of Survivors at the Astor-House," *New-York Daily Times*, 30 July 1852.

9. Ibid.

10. "Meeting of Passengers," *New-York Daily Tribune*, 30 July 1852.

11. Ibid.

12. "Meeting of Survivors at the Astor-House," *New-York Daily Times*, 30 July 1852.

13. Ibid.

14. Ibid.

15. "Indignation Meeting of the Passengers at the Astor House," *The New York Herald*, morning edition, 30 July 1852; "Meeting of Passengers," *New-York Daily Tribune*, 30 July 1852.

16. Ibid.; "Meeting of Survivors at the Astor-House," *New-York Daily Times*, 30 July 1852; "Indignation Meeting of the Passengers at the Astor House," *The New York Herald*, morning edition, 30 July 1852.

17. Ibid.; "Meeting of Survivors at the Astor-House," *New-York Daily Times*, 30 July 1852; "Indignation Meeting of the Passengers at the Astor House," *The New York Herald*, morning edition, 30 July 1852.

18. "Meeting of Passengers," *New-York Daily Tribune*, 30 July 1852; "Meeting of Survivors at the Astor-House," *New-York Daily Times*, 30 July 1852.

19. "Indignation Meeting of the Passengers at the Astor-House, " *The New York Herald*, morning edition, 30 July 1852.

20. "Meeting of the Survivors," *New-York Daily Times*, 30 July 1852.

21. "To the Survivors of the Henry Clay," written by Isaac McDaniels, *New-York Daily Times*, 30 July 1852.

22. "Resolutions," *New-York Daily Times*, 30 July 1852.

23. "Meeting of Survivors at the Astor-House," *New-York Daily Times*, 30 July 1852.

24. Ibid.

25. "Incidents," *New-York Daily Tribune*, 29 July 1852.

26. "Incidents" *New-York Daily Times*, 30 July 1852.

27. "Editorial: The Henry Clay Calamity," *The New York Herald*, 4 August 1852.

Chapter 5: The Living and the Dead

1. "Incidents," *New-York Daily Times*, 30 July 1852.

 2. "Incidents of Escape &c.," *New-York Daily Tribune*; 29 July 1852.

 3. Ibid.

 4. "Recovery of Bodies—Interesting Items," *New-York Daily Tribune*, 3 August 1852; "The Inquest," testimony of Jacob Hillman, *New-York Daily Tribune,* 29 July 1852.

 5. "The Inquest," testimony of Stoddard Colby, *New-York Daily Tribune,* 29 July 1852; Colby death notice, *New-York Daily Tribune*, 29 July 1852; Proctor Cemetery, *http://freepages.genealogy.rootsweb.com/~colby/colby*family / d391.html.

 6. "Coroner's Inquest at Yonkers," testimony of Stacy Bancroft, *New-York Daily Times*, 30 July 1852.

 7. "Statement of a Passenger," *New-York Daily Times*, 30 July 1852. The Presidential election campaign drew much coverage in the newspapers.

 8. "Statement of Captain Tallman of the Henry Clay," *New-York Daily Times*, 30 July 1852.

 9. "To the Public," a card from the owners of the Henry Clay, *New-York Daily Times*, 31 July 1852.

10. "Incidents," *New-York Daily Times*, 30 July 1852; "Interesting Particulars," *New-York Daily Times*, 31 July 1852; "More Accounts by Passengers," *New-York Daily Tribune*, 31 July 1852; "Fourth Day," *New-York Daily Times*, 2 August 1852.

11. "Incidents," *New-York Daily Times*, 30 July 1852; "Sixth Day," *New-York Daily Times*, 3 August 1852.

12. "Incidents," *New-York Daily Times*, 30 July 1852.

13. Ibid.

14. "Second Day of the Inquest," Bailey testimony, *New-York Daily Times*, 30 July 1852; "William Whitman Bailey, "A Survivor Tells the Story and Makes Corrections," *Newburgh Sunday Telegram*, 12 August 1905.

15. "Second Day of the Inquest," Cook testimony, *New-York Daily Times*, 30 July 1852.

16. "Inquest at Yonkers," McDaniels testimony, *New-York Daily Tribune*, 2 August 1852; "Fourth Day," McDaniels testimony, *New-York Daily Times*, 2 August 1852.

17. "Second Day of the Inquest," Murray testimony, *New-York Daily Times*, 30 July 1852.

18. "Second Day of the Inquest," Chatillion testimony, *New-York Daily Times*, 30 July 1852; "The Inquest," *New-York Daily Times*, 31 July 1852; "List of Passengers Missing," *New-York Daily Times*, 4 August 1852.
19. "Second Day," Simons testimony, *New-York Daily Times*, 30 July 1852; "Additional Particulars," *New-York Daily Times*, 31 July 1852.
20. "Second Day," Marsden testimony, *New-York Daily Times*, 30 July 1852.
21. "Fourth Day," Marsden testimony, *New-York Daily Times*, 2 August 1852; "Coroner's Investigation," *New-York Daily Tribune*, 2 August 1852; "Fourth Day," *The New York Herald*, 1 August 1852.
22. "Coroner's Investigation," *New-York Daily Tribune*, 2 August 1852. The newspapers differed on spelling of Handford/Hanford.
23. "Terrible Disaster," *Daily Albany Argus*, 29 July 1852; "Second Day of the Inquest," Crannell testimony, *New-York Daily Times*, 30 July 1852.
24. "Second Day of the Inquest," Wing testimony, *New-York Daily Times*, 30 July 1852; "Interesting Particulars," *New-York Daily Times*, 31 July 1852.
25. "Fourth Day," Elmore Thompson testimony, *The New York Herald*, 1 August 1852.
26. "Second Day of the Inquest," John Thompson testimony, *New-York Daily Times*, 30 July 1852.
27. "Third Day," Selah Jordan testimony, *New-York Daily Times*, 31 July 1852.
28. Ibid.; "List of Dead," *New-York Daily Times*, 30 July 1852.
29. From a private letter to a friend of the Editors of *The Express*," dated 1 August 1852, *New-York Daily Tribune*, 4 August 1852.
30. "Second Day," Vaux testimony, *New-York Daily Times*, 30 July 1852.
31. "Statements of Eye Witnesses," comments by John Dike, *New-York Daily Times*, 30 July 1852; "Fourth Day," testimony of Edward Lefort. *New-York Daily Times*, 2 August 1852.
32. "Fourth Day," testimony of Robert Manning, and "Incidents and Further Particulars," *New-York Daily Times*, 2 August 1852; "Owners and Officers of the Vessel &c." *The New York Herald*, 4 August 1852.
33. "Second Day," Robinson testimony, *New-York Daily Times*, 30 July 1852.
34. "Additional Particulars," *New-York Daily Times*, 31 July 1852.
35. "Third Day," David Crist and George Weller testimonies, *New-York Daily Times*, 31 July 1852.
36. "Particulars and Incidents," *New-York Daily Times*, 4 August 1852; "Finding the Body of Hon. Stephen Allen," *The New York Herald*, 31 July 1852.
37. "More Accounts by Passengers, &c.," *New-York Daily Tribune*, 31 July 1852; "Interesting Particulars," *New-York Daily Times*, 31 July 1852.
38. "Third Day," Reade testimony, *New-York Daily Times*, 31 July 1852.
39. "Third Day," Harding, Darcy, and Ackerman testimony and "The Death of J. J. Speed," *New-York Daily Times*, 31 July 1852.
40. "Interesting Particulars," *New-York Daily Times*, 31 July 1852.
41. Ibid.; "Further and Later Particulars," The *New York Herald*, 1 August 1852.
42. "Interesting Particulars," *New-York Daily Times*, 31 July 1852.
43. "William G. Ackerman," *New-York Daily Times*, 3 August 1852.
44. "Incidents," *New-York Daily Times*, 2 August 1852; "Raising the Wreck," *The New York*

Herald, 1 August 1852.

45. "Inquest at Yonkers," Daniel Sands testimony, *New-York Daily Tribune*, 2 August 1852; "Friends Burial Grounds," *http://www.usgennet.org/usa/ny/county/dutchess/data/cems/hicksite2.htm*.
46. "Fifth day," Green testimony, *The New York Herald*, 2 August 1852.
47. "Coroner's Inquest at Manhattanville," *New-York Daily Times*, 2 August 1852.
48. Ibid.
49. Ibid.
50. Ibid.; Phyllis Lee Levin, *Abigail Adams: A Biography* (New York: Thomas Dunne Books, St. Martin's Griffin, 2001), 464, 465.
51. "Coroner's Inquest at Manhattanville," *New-York Daily Times*, 2 August 1852.
52. "Particulars and Incidents," *New-York Daily Times*, 4 August 1852.
53. "Three Bodies," *New-York Daily Times*, 2 August 1852.
54. Ibid.
55. "Coroner's Inquest at Manhattanville," *New-York Daily Times*, 2 August 1852; "More Bodies Found," *The New York Herald*, 2 August 1852.
56. "Interesting Particulars," *New-York Daily Times*, 31 July 1852.
57. "Fourth Day," *New-York Daily Times*, 2 August 1852.
58. "Interesting Particulars," and "Funeral of the Unrecognized," *New-York Daily Times*, 31 July 1852; "Scene at the Grave," *New-York Daily Tribune*, 3 August 1852.
59. "Interesting Particulars," "Notice of Funeral," *New-York Daily Times*, 31 July 1852; "Notice of Funeral," *New-York Daily Times*, 2 August 1852.
60. "Funeral of the Unrecognized," *New-York Daily Times*, 31 July 1852 and 2 August 1852; "Scene at the Grave," *New-York Daily Tribune*, 3 August 1852.
61. Ibid.

Chapter 6: Remembrance

1. James R. Mellow, *Nathaniel Hawthorne in His Times* (Boston: Houghton Mifflin Company, 1980), 392; Edwin Haviland Miller, *Salem Is My Dwelling Place: A Life of Nathaniel Hawthorne* (Iowa City: University of Iowa Press, 1991), 378–379.
2. Julian Hawthorne, *Nathaniel Hawthorne and His Wife: A Biography*, vol. 1 (Boston and New York: Houghton Mifflin and Company; Cambridge: The Riverside Press, 1884), 452, 453; James R. Mellow, *Nathaniel Hawthorne in His Times* (Boston: Houghton Mifflin Company, 1980), 410.
3. Julian Hawthorne, *Nathaniel Hawthorne and His Wife: A Biography*, vol. 1 (Boston and New York: Houghton Mifflin and Company; Cambridge: The Riverside Press, 1884), 455.
4. Ibid., 457; Arlin Turner, *Nathaniel Hawthorne: A Biography* (New York and Oxford: Oxford University Press, 1980), 243; James R. Mellow, *Nathaniel Hawthorne in His Times* (Boston: Houghton Mifflin Company, 1980), 411.
5. Arlin Turner, *Nathaniel Hawthorne: A Biography* (New York and Oxford: Oxford University Press, 1980), 244; "The Henry Clay Calamity," *The New York Herald*, 4 August 1852.
6. Julian Hawthorne, *Nathaniel Hawthorne and His Wife: A Biography*, vol. 1 (Boston and New York: Houghton Mifflin and Company; Cambridge: The Riverside Press, 1884),

453; Arlin Turner, *Nathaniel Hawthorne: A Biography* (New York and Oxford: Oxford University Press, 1980), 244; James R. Mellow, *Nathaniel Hawthorne in His Times* (Boston: Houghton Mifflin Company, 1980), 412.

7. Ibid., 412.

8. Ibid., 412; Julian Hawthorne, *Nathaniel Hawthorne and His Wife: A Biography*, vol. 1 (Boston and New York: Houghton Mifflin and Company; Cambridge: The Riverside Press, 1884), 457.

9. "New York City," *New-York Daily Times*, 4 August 1852.

10. "The Man," Smithsonian Institution, Horticulture Services Division, http:*www.si.edu/horticultute/gardens/Haupt/Downing*/down.html; "Downing and His Wife," *Newburgh Telegraph*, 22 August 1914, 4; Phyllis Lee Levin, *Abigail Adams: A Biography* (New York: Thomas Dunne Books, St. Martin's Griffin, 2001), genealogy chart of "The John Adams Family;" "Resurrecting A. J. Downing," Newburgh/Revealed, http;//newburghrevealed.org/photojournalajdowning.htm.

11. William Alex, *Calvert Vaux: Architect and Planner* (New York: Ink, Inc., 1994), 2; "Downing and His Wife," *Newburgh Telegram*, 22 August 1914, 4; "Springside Walking Tour—A National Historic Landmark," leaflet provided at the Matthew Vassar Estate in Poughkeepsie, Springside Landscape Restoration, Poughkeepsie, New York.

12. Notice of A. J. Downing from the *Washington Republic*, printed front page in the *New-York Daily Times*, 4 August 1852.

13. William Alex, *Calvert Vaux: Architect and Planner* (New York: Ink, Inc., 1994), 3; "Downing & Vaux, Architects," *Newburgh Telegraph*, 5 August 1852.

14. Roy Rosenzweig and Elizabeth Blackmar, *The Park and Its People: A History of Central Park* (Ithaca and London: Cornell University Press, 1992), 30, 124; "The Inscriptions," Smithsonian Institution, Horticulture Services Division, http:*www.si.edu/horticulture/gardens/Haupt/Downing/down.html*.

15. "Downing and His Wife," *Newburgh Telegraph*, 22 August 1914, 4; Internments in the St. Luke's Churchyard, Matteawan, from "Old Gravestones of Dutchess County, New York," by J. W. Poucher, 1924, items # 62, 63, 92, 458, 459, 460. *http://www.rootsweb.co/~nydutche/cems//stluke.htm*.

16. "The Death of A. J. Downing," *The New York Herald*," 2 August 1852; Notice of death of Mrs. Wadsworth, *Newburgh Telegraph*, 5 August 1852.

17. Internments in the St. Luke's Churchyard, Matteawan, from "Old Gravestones of Dutchess County, New York," by J. W. Poucher, 1924, items # 62, 63, 92, 458, 459, 460. *http://www.rootsweb.co/~nydutche/cems//stluke.htm*.

18. "From a private letter to a friend of the Editors of *The Express*," *New-York Daily Tribune*, 4 August 1852.

19. "Incidents," *New-York Daily Times*, 2 August 1852.

20. Phyllis Lee Levin, *Abigail Adams: A Biography* (New York: Thomas Dunne Books, St. Martin's Griffin, 2001), 458, 464, 465, genealogy chart of "The John Adams Family."

21. Obituary notice from *Fishkill Standard* printed in *New-York Daily Times*, 4 August 1852.

22. "Death of Abraham Crist," *New-York Daily Times*, 3 August 1852.

23. "Abraham Crist," *Newburgh Telegraph*, 12 August 1852.

24. "Abraham Crist," *Newburgh Telegraph*, 5 August 1852; *New-York Daily Tribune*, 2 August 1852.
25. "Stephen Allen," *Newburgh Telegraph*, 5 August 1852; "Allen, Stephen," *Encyclopedia of New York City* (New Haven: Yale University Press, 1995), 4, 14; "More Accounts by Passengers, &c.," *New-York Daily Tribune*, 31 July 1852; "Interesting Particulars," *New-York Daily Times*, 31 July 1852.
26. "Allen, Stephen," *The National Cyclopedia of American Biography* (New York: James T. White & Company, 1895), 256; "Allen, Stephen," *Encyclopedia of New York City* (New Haven: Yale University Press, 1995), 4.
27. "Stephen Allen," *Newburgh Telegraph*, 5 August 1852.
28. "Death of Stephen Allen," from the *Journal of Commerce*, printed in *New-York Daily Times*, 30 July 1852.
29. "Funeral of Stephen Allen," *New-York Daily Times*, 2 August 1852.
30. Ibid.
31. "Funeral of Stephen Allen," *New-York Daily Tribune*, 2 August 1852; "Funeral of Stephen Allen," *New-York Daily Times*, 2 August 1852.
32. Ibid.; "Hon. Stephen Allen," *Evening Post*, printed in *New-York Daily Tribune*, 30 July 1852.
33. "The Inquest—Third Day," testimony of Daniel Darcy and William Ackerman, *New-York Daily Times*, 31 July 1852.
34. "Latest Intelligence," *New-York Daily Times*, 31 July 1852; "Death of J.J. Speed," *New-York Daily Tribune*, 31 July 1852; "J.J. Speed, Esq.", *New-York Daily Tribune*, 2 August 1852.
35. "Incidents," *New-York Daily Times*, 3 August 1852.
36. "Mr. and Mrs. Schoonmaker of Jordanville," *Newburgh Telegraph*, 5 August 1852.
37. "Schoonmaker Family Ground," Town of Ulster County, New York, cemeteries, copied 15 August 1924 by Dr. J. Wilson Poucher and Byron J. Terwilliger, items # 10, 11, 28, 29, http://www.hopefarm.com/gardicem.htm.
38. "Miss Phoebe Ann Jordan," *Newburgh Telegraph*, 5 August 1852.
39. "Schoonmaker Family Ground," Town of Ulster County, New York, cemeteries, copied 15 August 1924 by Dr. J. Wilson Poucher and Byron J. Terwilliger, items # 10, 11, 28, 29, http://www.hopefarm.com/gardicem.htm.
40. "An Afflicted Family," *Newburgh Telegraph*, August 5, 1852; note on Kinsley property in the *History of Orange County New York*, compiled by E. M. Ruttenber and L. H. Clark (Philadelphia: Evert & Peck, 1881), 819, 820; "The West Point Lands," a map drawn by Capt. H. M. Reeve, General U.S. Army, U.S.M.A., 1892; *The Centennial of the United States Military Academy at West Point*, 1802–1902, vol.1, Addresses and Histories (New York: Greenwood Press, Publishers, 1969).
41. *History of Orange County New York*, compiled by E. M. Ruttenber and L. H. Clark (Philadelphia: Evert & Peck, 1881), 819; George W. Cullum, *Biographical Register of the Officers and Graduates of the U.S. Military Academy at West Point*, third edition, vol. 1 (Boston and New York: Houghton, Mifflin and Company, 1891), 211.
42. Ibid.; "An Afflicted Family," *Newburgh Telegraph*, August 5, 1852.
43. "E. V. Kinsley Found Dead," *Newburgh Daily News*, 2 April 1888.
44. "Later from the Wreck of the Henry Clay," *Cincinnati Inquirer*, 31, July 1852.

45. "The Terrible Catastrophe—Burning of the Henry Clay," *Cincinnati Enquirer*, 1 August 1852.

46. Ray family burial information, St. Paul's Lutheran Church Cemetery, Town of Durham in the Village of Oak Hill, *http://rootsweb.com/~nygreen2/st_paulschurch_cemetery.htm*.

47. "Awful Steamboat Calamity," *The Saturday Express*, Lancaster, 31 July 1852.

48. "City and County Items," *Examiner and Herald*, Lancaster, 4 August 1852.

49. Thompson family burial information, The Princeton Cemetery, *http://princetonol.com/groups/cemetery/mon.html*; "Fourth Day," Thompson testimony, *New-York Daily Times*, 22 October 1853.

50. Selected Letters of Jacob Whitman Bailey, West Point Military Academy Special Collections and Archives Division, with commentaries by Loring Woart Bailey and compiled by Alfred G. Bailey.

51. "Scene at the Grave," *New-York Daily Tribune*, 3 August 1852; "Funeral of the Unrecognized," *New-York Daily Times*, 31 July 1852.

52. *New-York Daily Times*, 5 August 1852.

53. Updates on the missing, *New-York Daily Times*, 5 August 1852; Obituary of Ann Hill and Eliza Smith, *Philadelphia Public Ledger*, 2 August 1852.

54. William H. Ewen, "The Hudson's Blackest Day," *Yonkers Historical Bulletin*, July 1965.

Book 2: Retribution

Chapter 7: Truth Under Oath

1. "Washington," *New-York Daily Times*, 4 August 1852.

2. "List of the Dead," *New-York Daily Times*, 2 August 1852; "Fourth Day," Elmore Thompson testimony, *New-York Daily Times*, 2 August 1852; "Sixth Day," Gourlie testimony, *New-York Daily Times*, 3 August 1852; "Second Day of the Inquest," John Thompson and George Edwards testimony, *New York Daily Times*, 30 July 1852.

3. "Facts and Rumors," *New-York Daily Tribune*, 30 July 1852; "Fourth Day," McDaniels testimony, *New-York Daily Tribune*, 2 August 1852; The "Hudson Canyon" is five miles wide and drops into the Atlantic Ocean to nine thousand foot depth. Robert H. Boyle, *The Hudson River: A Natural and Unnatural History* (New York: W.W. Norton & Company, Inc., 1969), 257–262.

4. "The Catastrophe," *New-York Daily Times*, 2 August 1852.

5. Ibid.; "Letter from Mr. Romeyn," *New-York Daily Times*, 2 August 1852. Newspaper reports spelled the name, Romaine.

6. "The Steamboat Massacre," *The New York Herald*, 31 July 1852.

7. "To the Coroner and Jury," *New-York Daily Tribune*, 3 August 1852.

8. "The Coroner's Inquest at Yonkers," "Sixth and Seventh Days," *New-York Daily Times*, 3, 4 August 1852.

9. "Seventh Day," testimony of William Radford, *New-York Daily Times*, 4 August 1852.

10. Ibid.

11. Ibid.

12. "The Henry Clay Calamity," Radford testimony, *The New York Herald*, 4 August 1852.

13. "Seventh Day," testimony of William Radford, *New-York Daily Times*, 4 August 1852.
14. Ibid.
15. Ibid.; "Incidents," It was noted "that the Henry Clay was insured for $13,000 among the three owners," *New-York Daily Times*, 2 August 1852.
16. "Second Day of the Inquest," Murray testimony, *New-York Daily Times*, 30 July 1852; "Fourth Day," Elmore Thompson testimony, *New-York Daily Times*, 2 August 1852.
17. "Seventh Day," Minturn testimony, *New-York Daily Times*, 4 August 1852.
18. Ibid., Cubbage testimony.
19. "Second Day of the Inquest," John Thompson testimony, *New-York Daily Times*, 30 July 1852.
20. "The Coroner's Inquest," Crannell testimony, *New-York Daily Tribune*, 30 July 1852; "Seventh Day," Cubbage testimony, *New-York Daily Times*, 4 August 1852.
21. "Second Day of the Inquest," Cook testimony, *New-York Daily Times*, 30 July 1852; "Fourth Day," McDaniels testimony, *New-York Daily Times*, 2 August 1852.
22. "Seventh Day," Minturn and Cubbage testimonies, *New-York Daily Times*, 4 August 1852; "Sixth Day," Gourlie testimony, *New-York Daily Times*, 3 August 1852.
23. "The Coroner's Inquest," Bailey testimony, *New-York Daily Tribune*, 30 July 1852; "Second Day of the Inquest," John Thompson testimony, *New-York Daily Times*, 30 July 1852.
24. "Sixth Day," Gourlie testimony, *New-York Daily Times*, 3 August 1852; "Second Day of the Inquest," Colby and Cook testimonies, *New-York Daily Times*, 30 July 1852; "Testimony," Murray testimony, *New-York Daily Tribune*, 30 July 1852.
25. "The Inquest," Bancroft testimony, *New-York Daily Tribune*, 29 July 1852; "The Coroner's Inquest," *New-York Daily Tribune*, 30 July 1852; "Second Day of the Inquest," Cook, *New-York Daily Times*, 30 July 1852.
26. "Sixth Day," Wells testimony, *New-York Daily Times*, 3 August 1852; "Second Day of the Inquest," Edwards, Murray, and Cook testimonies, *New-York Daily Times*, 30 July 1852.
27. "Seventh Day," Minturn and Cubbage testimonies, *New-York Daily Times*, 4 August 1852.
28. "Sixth Day," *New-York Daily Times*, 3 August 1852; "The Coroner's Inquest," Crannel testimony, *New-York Daily Tribune*, 30 July 1852; "Seventh Day," Cubbage testimony, *New-York Daily Times*, 4 August 1852.
29. "Sixth Day," DePeyster testimony, *New-York Daily Times*, 3 August 1852; "Second Day of the Inquest," John Thompson and Cook testimonies, *New-York Daily Times*, 30 July 1852; "Seventh Day," Minturn testimony, *New-York Daily Times*, 4 August 1852.
30. "Second Day of the Inquest," Edwards testimony, *New-York Daily Times*, 30 July 1852; "Seventh Day," Minturn testimony, *New-York Daily Times*, 4 August 1852; "The Coroner's Inquest," Bailey testimony, *New-York Daily Tribune*, 30 July 1852; "Sixth Day," Wells testimony, *New-York Daily Times*, 3 August 1852.
31. "Seventh Day," Minturn testimony, *New-York Daily Times*, 4 August 1852; "The Coroner's Inquest," Edwards testimony, *New-York Daily Tribune*, 30 July 1852.
32. "Second Day of the Inquest," Murray testimony, *New-York Daily Times*, 30 July 1852; "Incidents of Escape," *New-York Daily Tribune*, 29 July 1852; Letter to the editor, "Management of the Henry Clay," *New-York Daily Times*, 30 July 1852.

33. "Seventh Day," Cubbage and Minturn testimonies, *New-York Daily Times*, 4 August 1852.
34. "Sixth Day," Gourlie and DePeyster testimonies, *New-York Daily Times*, 3 August 1852.
35. Seventh Day," Minturn testimony, *New-York Daily Times*, 4 August 1852.
36. "Letter to Editor," *New-York Daily Times*, 2 August 1852; "Letter from Mr. Livermore," *New-York Daily Times*, 2 August 1852; "Letter from Dr. Wells," *New-York Daily Times*, 30 July 1852.
37. "Seventh Day," Minturn testimony, *New-York Daily Times*, 4 August 1852.
38. Ibid.
39. Ibid.
40. "Verdict," *New-York Daily Times*, 5 August 1852; There was no James Hubbard as listed on the indictment. The name should have been listed as James Elmendorf, who was the second pilot.

Chapter 8: Indictment

1. Correction to previous report, *New-York Daily Times*, 4 August 1852; "Henry Clay-More Arrests," *New-York Daily Times*, 5 August 1852.
2. Ibid.
3. "United States District Court," *The New York Herald*, 5 August 1852. There was no report of the bond posted for Elmendorf.
4. "Verdict—Subsequent Proceedings," *New-York Daily Times*, 5 August 1852.
5. "The Henry Clay Habeas Corpus Case," *New-York Daily Times*, 2 September 1852.
6. Ibid.
7. Ibid.
8. Ibid.
9. Ibid.
10. "The Henry Clay Disaster," *New-York Daily Times*, 7 September 1852.
11. Ibid.
12. Ibid.
13. Ibid.
14. Ibid.
15. Ibid.
16. Ibid.
17. Ibid.
18. Ibid.
19. "U.S. District Court—Wednesday—The Henry Clay Catastrophe," *New-York Daily Times*, 16 September 1852; "The People vs. Thomas Collyer and Others," and "Copy Indictment for the Manslaughter 1st Degree," E. Wells, District Attorney, state of New York, Westchester County, dated 15 September 1852 and filed 24 September 1852, National Archives and Records Administration, Northeast Region, New York, New York, district court minutes, first count.
20. Ibid.
21. Ibid., second, third and fourth count.
22. Ibid., fifth and sixth count.

23. Ibid., first count.
24. Ibid., third and seventh count.
25. Ibid.
26. "Grand Jury Letter dated 2 October 1852," Indictment record for "The People vs. Thomas Collyer and Others," National Archives and Records Administration, Northeast Region, New York, New York.
27. "U.S. District Court," *New-York Daily Times*, 1 October 1852.
28. "Trial of the Owners and Officers of the Henry Clay," *New-York Daily Times*, 19 October 1853.
29. "Law Intelligence," *New-York Daily Tribune*, 19 October 1853; "United States Circuit Court," *The New York Herald*, 19 October 1853.
30. "Law Intelligence," *New-York Daily Tribune*, 19 October 1853; "United States Circuit Court," *The New York Herald*, 19 October 1853.
31. Ibid.
32. "Trial of the Owners and Officers of the Henry Clay," *New-York Daily Times*, 19 October 1853; "Law Intelligence," *New-York Daily Tribune*, 19 October 1853.
33. "United States Circuit Court," *The New York Herald*, 19 October 1853.
34. "Trial of the Owners and Officers of the Henry Clay," *New-York Daily Times*, 19 October 1853.
35. Ibid.
36. Ibid. A few weeks after the *Henry Clay* burned, the *Reindeer* exploded at Bristol, resulting in several deaths. Manslaughter charges were pressed against Captain Farnharm and John Howlett. *New-York Daily Times,* 6 September 1852 and 5 October 152.
37. Ibid.
38. "Raw Intelligence," *New-York Daily Tribune*, 19 October 1853.
39. "Trial of the Owners and Officers of the Henry Clay," *New-York Daily Times*, 19 October 1853.
40. "United States Circuit Court," *The New York Herald*, 19 October 1853.
41. Ibid.
42. Ibid., "Law Intelligence," *New-York Daily Tribune*, 19 October 1853.
43. "Minute entries for the United States vs. Thomas Collyer et. al." Circuit court records, dated 18 October 1853, National Archives and Records Administration, Northeast Region, New York, New York, p. 406.

Chapter 9: The Prosecution

1. Circuit court records for the "United States vs. Thomas Collyer and Others," National Archives and Records Administration, Northeast Region, New York, New York, p. 407; "U.S. Circuit Court," *New-York Daily Times*, 20 October 1853.
2. Ibid.
3. Ibid.
4. Ibid.
5. Ibid.
6. Ibid.
7. "U.S. Circuit Court," *The New York Herald*, 20 October 1853.

8. "U.S. Circuit Court," *New-York Daily Times*, 20 October 1853; "U.S. Circuit Court," *The New York Herald*, 20 October 1853.
9. "U.S. Circuit Court," *New-York Daily Times*, 20 October 1853.
10. Ibid.
11. "U.S. Circuit Court," *New-York Daily Tribune*, 20 October 1853.
12. "U.S. Circuit Court," *The New York Herald*, 20 October 1853.
13. Ibid.
14. Ibid.
15. "U.S. Circuit Court," *New-York Daily Times*, 20, 21 October 1853; "U.S. Circuit Court," *The New York Herald*, 20, 21 October 1853.
16. "U.S. Circuit Court," *New-York Daily Times*, 21 October 1853.
17. Ibid.
18. Ibid.
19. Ibid.
20. "U.S. Circuit Court," *The New York Herald*, 21 October 1853.
21. "U.S. Circuit Court," *New-York Daily Times*, 21 October 1853.
22. Ibid.
23. Ibid.
24. Ibid.
25. Ibid.
26. Ibid.; "U.S. Circuit Court," *The New York Herald*, 21 October 1853.
27. "U.S. Circuit Court," *New-York Daily Tribune*, 21 October 1853; "U.S. Circuit Court," *The New York Herald*, 21 October 1853.
28. "U.S. Circuit Court," *The New York Herald*, 22 October 1853; "U.S. Circuit Court," *New-York Daily Times*, 22 October 1853.
29. "U.S. Circuit Court," *New-York Daily Times*, 22 October 1853.
30. Ibid.
31. "U.S. Circuit Court," *The New York Herald*, 22 October 1853; The name Shelmyre and Shelmire that appeared in newspapers was spelled "Shellmeyer" in the court documents for the trial, "The United States vs. Thomas Collyer etc." dated 21 October 1853, p. 410, National Archives and Records Administration, Northeast Region, New York, New York.
32. Ibid.
33. "U.S. Circuit Court," *New-York Daily Times*, 22 October 1853; "U.S. Circuit Court," *The New York Herald*, 22 October 1853.
34. "U.S. Circuit Court," *New-York Daily Times*, 22 October 1853.
35. Ibid.; "U.S. Circuit," *The New York Herald*, 22 October 1853.
36. "U.S. Circuit Court," *The New York Herald*, 23 October 1853.
37. Ibid.; "U.S. Circuit Court," *New-York Daily Times*, 24 October 1853.
38. "U.S. Circuit Court," *New-York Daily Times*, 24 October 1853.
39. "U.S. Circuit Court," *The New York Herald*, 23 October 1853; "U.S. Circuit Court," *New-York Daily Tribune*, 24 October 1853.
40. "U.S. Circuit Court," *The New York Herald*, 23 October 1853; "U.S. Circuit Court," *New-York Daily Times*, 24 October 1853.
41. Ibid.

42. Ibid.

43. Ibid.

44. "U.S. Circuit Court," *New-York Daily Tribune*, 24 October 1853; "U.S. Circuit Court," *New-York Daily Times*, 24 October 1853.

45. Ibid.; "U.S. Circuit Court," *The New York Herald*, 23 October 1853.

46. "U.S. Circuit Court," *The New York Herald*," 25 October 1853; "U.S. Circuit Court," *New-York Daily Times*, 25 October 1853.

47. Ibid.

48. Ibid.

49. "U.S. Circuit Court," *The New York Herald*, 25 October 1853.

50. Ibid.

51. "U.S. Circuit Court," *The New York Herald*, 26 October 1853; "U.S. Circuit Court," *New-York Daily Times*, 26 October 1853.

52. Ibid.

53. "U.S. Circuit Court," *The New York Herald*, 26 October 1853; "U.S. Circuit Court," *New-York Daily Times*, 26 October 1853.

54. "U.S. Circuit Court," *New-York Daily Times*, 26 October 1853; "U.S. Circuit Court," *The New York Herald*, 26 October 1853.

55. "U.S. Circuit Court," *New-York Daily Times*, 26 October 1853.

56. "U.S. Circuit Court," *The New York Herald*, 26 October 1853; "U.S. Circuit Court," *New-York Daily Times*, 26 October 1853.

57. "U.S. Circuit Court," *The New York Herald*, 26 October 1853.

58. Ibid.

59. "U.S. Circuit Court," *New-York Daily Times*, 26 October 1853.

60. Ibid.

61. Ibid.

62. Ibid.; "U.S. Circuit Court," *New-York Daily Times*, 27 October 1853.

63. Ibid.

64. Ibid.

65. Ibid.; "U.S. Circuit Court," *The New York Herald*, 27 October 1853. *New-York Daily Times* reported a three-hour wait; *The New York Herald* reported a two-hour wait.

66. "U.S. Circuit Court," *New-York Daily Times*, 27 October 1853.

67. "U.S. Circuit Court," *The New York Herald*, 27 October 1853.

68. Ibid.; "U.S. Circuit Court," *New-York Daily Times*, 27 October 1853.

69. "U.S. Circuit Court," *The New York Herald*, 27 October 1853.

70. "U.S. Circuit Court," *The New York Herald*, 27 October 1853; "U.S. Circuit Court," *New-York Daily Times*, 27 October 1853.

71. "U.S. Circuit Court," *New-York Daily Times*, 27, 28 October 1853.

72. "U.S. Circuit Court," *New-York Daily Times*, 28 October 1853; "U.S. Circuit Court," *The New York Herald*, 28 October 1853.

73. "U.S. Circuit Court," *New-York Daily Times*, 28 October 1853.

74. Ibid.

75. "U.S. Circuit Court," *New-York Daily Tribune*, 28 October 1853.

76. "U.S. Circuit Court," *The New York Herald*, 28 October 1853.

77. Ibid.

78. "U.S. Circuit Court," *New-York Daily Times*, 28 October 1853.
79. Ibid.
80. Ibid.
81. Ibid.
82. Ibid.
83. Ibid.
84. Ibid.
85. Ibid.
86. Ibid.
87. Ibid.
88. Ibid.
89. "U.S. Circuit Court," *New-York Daily Tribune*, 28 October 1853; "U.S. Circuit Court," *New-York Daily Times*, 28 October 1853; "U.S. Circuit Court," *The New York Herald*, 28 October 1853.
90. "U.S. Circuit Court," *New-York Daily Times*, 28 October 1853.
91. "Hall," "U.S. Circuit Court," *New-York Daily Tribune*, 28 October 1853.

Chapter 10: Witness for the Defense
1. "U.S. Circuit Court," *New-York Daily Times*, 29 October 1853.
2. Ibid.
3. Ibid.
4. "U.S. Circuit Court," *The New York Herald*, 29 October 1853; "U.S. Circuit Court," *New-York Daily Times*, 29 October 1853. Charles Merritt was charged and on trial but he was not present for the trial. No reason for his absence was reported.
5. Ibid.; "Law Intelligence," *New-York Daily Tribune*, 29 October 1853.
6. Ibid.
7. "U.S. Circuit Court," *New-York Daily Times*, 29 October 1853.
8. Ibid.
9. Ibid.
10. Ibid.
11. Ibid.; "U.S. Circuit Court," *The New York Herald*, 29 October 1853.
12. Ibid.
13. Ibid.
14. Ibid.
15. Ibid.
16. Ibid.
17. "U.S. Circuit Court," *The New York Herald*, 29 October 1853.
18. Ibid.; In the newspapers, the witness named was spelled "Crary," in the court records the spelling was "Craig," "Circuit Court Records: U.S. vs. T. Collyer and others," National Archives and Records Administration, Northeast Region, New York, New York, 419.
19. "U.S. Circuit Court," *The New York Herald*, 29 October 1853.
20. Ibid.
21. Ibid.
22. Ibid.

23. "U.S. Circuit Court," *New-York Daily Times*, 29 October 1853.

24. Ibid.; "U.S. Circuit Court," *The New York Herald*, 29 October 1853.

25. "U.S. Circuit Court," *New-York Daily Times*, 29 October 1853.

26. Ibid.

27. "U.S. Circuit Court," *The New York Herald*, 29 October 1853; "U.S. Circuit Court," *New-York Daily Times*, 29 October 1853.

28. Ibid.

29. Ibid.

30. Ibid., "U.S. Circuit Court," *The New York Herald*, 29 October 1853; "Law Intelligence," *New-York Daily Tribune*, 29 October 1853.

31. "U.S. Circuit Court," *The New York Herald*, 29 October 1853; "U.S. Circuit Court," *New-York Daily Times*, 29 October 1853.

32. Ibid.

33. Ibid.; "From A Passenger—Jno. Harris," *New-York Daily Tribune*, 31 July 1852.

34. "U.S. Circuit Court," *The New York Herald*, 30 October 1853.

35. Ibid.

36. Ibid.

37. Ibid.; "U.S. Circuit Court," *New-York Daily Times*, 31 October 1853.

38. Ibid.

39. Ibid.

40. Ibid.

41. Ibid.

42. Ibid.

43. "U.S. Circuit Court," *The New York Herald*, 30 October 1853; "U.S. Circuit Court," *New-York Daily Times*, 31 October 1853.

44. Ibid.

45. Ibid.

46. Ibid.; "U.S. Circuit Court," *The New York Herald*, 30 October 1853.

47. "U.S. Circuit Court," *New-York Daily Times*, 31 October 1853.

48. The name was spelled "Simmonds" in the newspapers but spelled "Simmons" in "Court Records for the trial of the officers of the Henry Clay," National Archives, Northeast Region, New York, New York, 420; "U.S. Circuit Court," *New-York Daily Times*, 31 October 1853.

49. The name was spelled "Seymour" in the newspapers but spelled "Seaman" in "Court Records for the trial of the officers of the Henry Clay," National Archives, Northeast Region, New York, New York, 420; "U.S. Circuit Court," *The New York Herald*, 30 October 1853; U.S. Circuit Court," *New-York Daily Times*, 31 October 1853.

50. "U.S. Circuit Court," *The New York Herald*, 30 October 1853.

51. "U.S. Circuit Court," *The New York Herald*, 1 November 1853.

52. Ibid.

53. "U.S. Circuit Court," *New-York Daily Times*, 1 November 1853; "Law Intelligence," *New-York Daily Tribune*, 1 November 1853.

54. Ibid.

55. "U.S. Circuit Court," *New-York Daily Times*, 1 November 1853.

56. Ibid.

57. "U.S. Circuit Court," *The New York Herald*, 1 November 1853.
58. Witness name was spelled "Prarie" in newspapers but "Praise" in "Court Records for the trial of the officers of the Henry Clay," National Archives, Northeast Region, New York, New York, 421; "U.S. Circuit Court," *The New York Herald*, 1 November 1853.
59. Ibid.
60. Ibid.
61. Ibid.
62. Ibid.
63. Ibid.
64. "U.S. Circuit Court," *New-York Daily Times*, 1 November 1853; "U.S. Circuit Court," *The New York Herald*, 1 November 1853.
65. Ibid.
66. Ibid.
67. Ibid.
68. Ibid.
69. Ibid.
70. "U.S. Circuit Court," *New-York Daily Times*, 1 November 1853.
71. "U.S. Circuit Court," *The New York Herald*, 2 November 1853; "U.S. Circuit Court," *New-York Daily Times*, 2 November 1853.
72. Ibid.; "U.S. Circuit Court," The New York Herald, 2 November 1853.
73. Ibid.
74. Ibid.
75. Ibid.
76. Ibid.; "U.S. Circuit Court," *New-York Daily Times*, 2 November 1853.
77. Ibid.
78. Ibid.
79. "U.S. Circuit Court," *The New York Herald*, 3 November 1853.
80. Ibid.
81. Ibid.
82. Ibid.
83. Ibid.
84. Ibid.
85. Ibid.
86. Ibid.
87. Ibid.
88. Ibid.
89. Ibid.
90. Ibid.
91. Ibid.
92. Ibid.
93. Ibid.
94. Ibid.

Epilogue

1. "Court Records for the trial of the officers of the Henry Clay," National Archives, Northeast Region, New York, New York, 423.

2. Baym, Nina, Ronald Gottesman, Laurence B. Holland, David Kalstone, Francis Murphy, Hershel Parker, William H. Pritchard, Patricia B. Wallace, *Norton Anthology of American Literature*, third edition, vol. 1 (New York and London: W. W. Norton & Company, 1989), 1085.

3. William Alex, *Calvert Vaux: Architect and Planner* (New York: Ink, Inc., 1994), 3, 9, 10, 11.

4. Ibid., 28–29.

5. Land Records for Orange County (New York), 1703–1869: Grantor Index C–D, Liber 133, p. 139–142 (Downing), 1854; "Downing and His Wife," *Newburgh Telegraph*, 22 August 1914.

6. "Springside Walking Tour—A National Historic Landmark," Springside Landscape Restoration, leaflet, Matthew Vassar Estate, Poughkeepsie, New York; Roy Rosenzweig and Elizabeth Blackmar, *The Park and Its People: A History of Central Park* (Ithaca and London: Cornell University Press, 1992), 124; William Alex, *Calvert Vaux: Architect and Planner* (New York: Ink, Inc., 1994), 11; Robert H. Boyle, *The Hudson River: A Natural and Unnatural History* (New York: W.W. Norton & Co., Inc., 1969), 63.

7. William Alex, *Calvert Vaux: Architect and Planner* (New York: Ink, Inc., 1994), 24; Downing Park website, *http://www.newburgh-ny.com/downing_park.htm*; "Downing and His Wife," *Newburgh Telegraph*, 22 August 1914.

8. "E. V. Kinsley Found Dead," *Newburgh Daily News*, 2 April 1888.

9. Ibid.

10. *Information Relating to the Lands Comprising the Military Reservation at West Point N.Y. 1723–1889* (U.S.M.A. Press and Bindery, 1891), 153, 160.

11. Ibid., 158;"A Walking Tour of West Point Cemetery," Section XXX, Row L; Notice of Kinsley monument, *News of the Highlands*, 6 August 1891.

12. Charles Coulston Gillespie, ed. *Dictionary of Scientific Biography*, vol. 1 (New York: Charles Scribner's Sons, 1970), 397; George W. Cullum, BVT, MAJ.-GEN, *Biographical Register of the Officers and Graduates of the U.S. Military Academy of West Point From Its Establishment in 1802 to 1890*, vol. 1 (Boston and New York: Houghton Mifflin and Company, Cambridge: The Riverside Press, 1891), 505; "Introduction," Bailey Family Collection at the University of New Brunswick, Canada, Archives and Special Collections, Harriet Irving Library, 1995, *http://www.lib.unb.ca/archives/Bailey/family.html*.

13. George W. Cullum, BVT, MAJ.-GEN, *Biographical Register of the Officers and Graduates of the U.S. Military Academy of West Point From Its Establishment in 1802 to 1890*, vol. 1 (Boston and New York: Houghton Mifflin and Company, Cambridge: The Riverside Press, 1891), 505; Allen Johnson, ed., *Dictionary of American Biography*, The United States Military Academy Archives (New York: Charles Scribner's Sons), 498.

14. Charles Coulston Gillespie, ed. *Dictionary of Scientific Biography*, vol. 1 (New York: Charles Scribner's Sons, 1970), 397.

15. "Personal Papers–The William Whitman Bailey Papers (1867–1904)," The New York Botanical Garden Archives and Manuscript Collections, The LuEsther T. Mertz

Library, *http://nybg.org/bsci/libr/Bailey1.htm*; William Whitman Bailey Papers, 1843-1914, Harvard University Library of the Gray Herbarium Archives, http://huh.harvard.edu/libraries/archives/BAILEYWW.html.

16. William Whitman Bailey, "A Survivor Tells the Story and Makes Corrections," *Newburgh Sunday Telegram*, 12 August 1905, first appeared in *The Rocks*, 8 August 1905.

17. John H. Morrison, *History of American Steam Navigation* (New York: Stephen Daye Press, 1958), 592–593.

18. Ibid., 118, 120, 155.

19. William H. Ewen, "The Hudson's Blackest Day," Yonkers Historical Bulletin, July 1965.

20. "What Caused the Fire," *The Eagle* (Poughkeepsie), 21 August 1852; John H. Morrison, *History of American Steam Navigation* (New York: Stephen Daye Press, 1958), 110.

21. "Law Intelligence," *New-York Daily Tribune*, 29 October 1863; Fred Erving Dayton, *Steamboat Days* (New York: Frederick A. Stokes Company, 1925), 395; The Mariners' Museum with Anthony J. Peluso, *The Bard Brothers: Painting America Under Steam and Sail* (The Mariners' Museum with Harry N. Abrams, Inc. Publishers, 1997), 40.

22. Donald C, Ringwald, *Hudson River Day Line: The Story of a Great American Steamboat Company* (Berkeley, California: Howell-North Books, 1965), 22, 60.

23. The Mariners' Museum with Anthony J. Peluso, *The Bard Brothers: Painting America Under Steam and Sail* (The Mariners' Museum with Harry N. Abrams, Inc. Publishers, 1997), 55, 58.

24. "Died," *Whig Press* (Middletown, New York), 11 February 1863.

25. Ibid.; Land Records for Orange County (New York), 1703 1869: Grantee Index D–H, Liber 120, p. 165–168 (DeWint), 1853.

26. "Annotations" for Old Town Burying Ground, *Records from Newburgh, New Windsor and Other Nearby Towns*," vol. 2 arranged and indexed for the Orange County Genealogical Society by Marilyn Terry, Dan Burrows, and Helen Benjamin; Orange County Directory 1878–1879, Town of Cornwall, *http://www.usgennet.org/usa/ny/county/orange/cornwall/id4.htm.*; "Death, the Grim Reaper," *Cornwall Local*, 8 June 1893.

27. Newspaper article on E. Hubbard, *The Cornwall Times*, 17 September 1881; Land Records for Orange County (New York), 1703—1869: Grantee Index D—H, Liber 198, p. 368-369 (Hubbard), 1867.

28. Federal census records 1850, 1860, 1870 and 1910 for Cornwall New York; "Annotations" for Old Town Burying Ground, *Records from Newburgh, New Windsor and other Nearby Towns*," vol. 2 arranged and indexed for the Orange County Genealogical Society by Marilyn Terry, Dan Burrows, and Helen Benjamin; Orange County Directory 1878–1879, Town of Cornwall, *http://www.usgennet.org/usa/ny/county/orange/cornwall/id4.htm*.

29. Newspaper article on Edward Hubbard, *The Cornwall Times*, 17 September 1881.

Bibliography

Adams, Arthur G. *The Hudson: A Guidebook to the River.* Albany, New York: State University of New York Press, 1981.

Alex, William. *Calvert Vaux: Architect and Planner.* Introduction by George B. Tatum. New York: Ink, Inc. 1994.

"Annotations," and other burial records for Old Town Cemetery in Newburgh. Orange County Genealogical Society.

"A Walking Tour of the West Point Cemetery." Section XXX Row L. West Point Military Academy. West Point, New York.

Bailey Family Collection at the University of New Brunswick, Canada. Archives and Special Collections. Harriet Irving Library. 1995. *http://www.lib.unb.ca/archives/Bailey/ family.html.*

Bailey, William W., Prof. "Recollections of West Point," *News of the Highlands,* 5 May 1900.

Bailey, Wm. Whitman. "A Survivor Tells the Story and Makes Corrections," *Newburgh Sunday Telegram,* 12 August 1905. First appeared in *The Rocks.* 8 August 1905.

Baym, Nina, Ronald Gottesman, Laurence B. Holland, David Kalstone, Francis Murphy, Hershel Parker, William H. Pritchard, Patricia B. Wallace. *The Norton Anthology of American Literature,* Third edition, Vol. 1. New York and London: W.W. Norton & Company, 1989.

Boyle, Robert H. *The Hudson River: A Natural and Unnatural History.* New York: W.W. Norton & Company, Inc., 1969.

Brandt, Clare. *An American Aristocracy: The Livingstons.* Garden City, New York: Doubleday & Company, Inc., 1986.

Burrows, Edwin G. and Mike Wallace. *Gotham: A History of New York City to 1898.* New York and Oxford: Oxford University Press, 1999.

Carmer, Carl. *The Hudson.* The Rivers of America Series, Illustrated by Stow Wengenroth. New York and Toronto: Farrar & Rinehart by New York: J.J. Little and Ives company, 1939.

Centennial of the United States Military Academy at West Point, New York 1802–1902. Vol. I. Addresses and History. Maps of West Point Lands drawn by Capt. H. M. Reeve, General Staff, U.S. Army, U.S.M.A., 1892. The West Point Military Library. New York: Greenwood Press, Publishers, 1969.

Cincinnati Enquirer, 31 July—1 August 1852.

Cornwall Local, 8 June 1893.

Cornwall Times, The, 17 September 1881.

Cullum, George W. BVT, MAJ.-GEN. *Biographical Register of the Officers and Graduates of the U. S. Military Academy of West Point From Its Establishment in 1802, to 1890.* Third Edition. Vol. 1, nos. 1–1000. Boston and New York: Houghton Mifflin and Company, Cambridge: The Riverside Press, 1891.

Daily Albany Argus, 29 July–7 August 1852.

Dayton, Fred Erving. *Steamboat Days.* Illustrated by John Wolcott Adams. New York: Frederick A. Stokes Company, 1925.

"Died," *Whig Press* (Middletown, New York), 11 February 1863.

Downing Park website. Included description and short history. *www.newburgh-ny.com/downing_park.htm*.

Eager, W. *History of Orange County*. 1847. Town of Highlands Historical Society.

Eagle, The (Poughkeepsie), 31 July—21 August 1852.

Eaton, Clement. *Henry Clay and the Art of American Politics*. Edited by Oscar Handlin. Eighth printing. Boston and Toronto: Little, Brown and Company, 1957.

Encyclopedia of New York City. New Haven, Connecticut: Yale University Press, 1995.

Ewen, William H. "The Hudson's Blackest Day." *Yonkers Historical Bulletin*. July 1965.

Examiner and Herald, Lancaster, 4 August 1852.

Garraty, John A., and Mark C. Carnes, eds. *American National Biography*. Published under the auspices of the American Council of Learned Societies. Vol. 6. New York: Oxford University Press, 1999.

Gillispie, Charles Coulston, ed. *Dictionary of Scientific Biography*. Vol. 1. New York: Charles Scribner's Sons, 1970.

Goldstone, Harmon H. and Martha Dalrymple. *History Preserved: A Guide to New York City Landmarks and Historic Districts*. New York: Simon and Schuster, 1974.

Guidebook to West Point and Vicinity Containing Descriptive, Historical and Statistical Sketches of the United States Military Academy and of Other Objects of Interest. New York: J.H. Colton, 1844.

Hawthorne, Julian. *Nathaniel Hawthorne and His Wife: A Biography*. Vol. 1. Boston and New York: Houghton Mifflin and Company; Cambridge: The Riverside Press, 1884.

Herald (Rutland, Vermont), 5 August 1852.

Hicksite Friends' Burial Grounds in Dutchess, NY. Part II. Transcribed by Holice B. Young. Listing of graves of Isaac D. Sands and Sylvester P. Sands. *http://www.usgennet.org/usa/ny/county/dutchess/cems/hicksite2.htm*

Hill, Ralph Nading. *Sidewheeler Saga: A Chronicle of Steamboating*. New York and Toronto: Rinehart & Company Inc. 1953.

History of Orange County New York with Illustrations and Biographical Sketches of Many of Its Pioneers and Prominent Men. Compiled by E. M. Ruttenber and L. H. Clark. Philadelphia: Evert & Peck, 1881.

Homberger, Eric. *The Historical Atlas of New York City: A Visual Celebration of Nearly 400 Years of New York City's History*. Alice Hudson, Cartographic Consultant. New York: Henry Holt and Company, 1994.

"Hudson River at West Point." Map marking the Kinsley School on Map of West Point. June 1844. West Point Military Academy Special Collections and Archives.

Information Relating to the Lands Comprising the Military Reservation at West Point N.Y. 1723–1889. U.S.M.A. Press and Bindery, 1891.

"Internments in the St. Luke's Churchyard, Matteawan," from *Old Gravestones of Dutchess County, New York*. By J. W. Poucher, published 1924, items # 62, 63, 92, 458, 459, 460. *http://www.rootsweb.com/~nydutche/cems/stluke.htm*.

Johnson, Allen, ed. *Dictionary of American Biography*. The United States Military Academy Archives. New York: Charles Scribner's Sons.

Keller, Allan. *Life Along the Hudson*. Tarrytown, New York: Sleepy Hollow Restorations, Inc., 1976.

Kinsley family monument notice printed in *News of the Highlands*, 6 August 1891.

Levin, Phyllis Lee. *Abigail Adams: A Biography*. New York: Thomas Dunne Books, St. Martin's Griffin, 2001.

Lossing, Benson J. *The Hudson from Wilderness to the Sea*. Somersworth: New Hampshire Publishing Company, 1972. Originally published Troy, New York: H.B. Nims & Co., 1866.

Mariners' Museum, The. In collaboration with Anthony J. Peluso Jr. *The Bard Brothers: Painting America Under Steam and Sail*. The Mariners' Museum with Harry N. Abrams, Inc. Publishers, 1997.

Mandeville, A. W. "The Burning of the Henry Clay," on file at the Westchester County Archives. Elmsford, New York.

Mellow, James R. *Nathaniel Hawthorne in His Times*. Boston: Houghton Mifflin Company, 1980.

Michaels, Joanne and Mary-Margaret Barile. *The Best of the Hudson Valley & Catskill Mountains: An Explorer's Guide*. Fourth Edition. Woodstock, Vermont: The Countryman Press, 2001.

Miller, Edwin Haviland. *Salem Is My Dwelling Place: A Life of Nathaniel Hawthorne*. Iowa City: University of Iowa Press, 1991.

Morrison, John H. *History of American Steam Navigation*. Forward by Frank O. Braynard. Illustrations by Samuel Ward Stanton. New York: Stephen Daye Press, 1958.

Mylod, John. *Biography of a River: The People & Legends of the Hudson Valley*. Edited by Alec Thomas. New York: Hawthorne Books, Inc. Publishers, 1969.

National Archives and Records Administration, Northeast Region. New York, New York. "Circuit court records for the trial of the officers of the Henry Clay. The United States vs. T. Collyer and others." p. 405–422.

National Archives and Records Administration, Northeast Region. New York, New York. District Court Minutes. "The People vs. Thomas Collyer and Others," and "Copy Indictment for the Manslaughter 1st Degree." E. Wells—District Attorney. State of New York, Westchester County. Filed 24 September 1852.

National Archives and Records Administration, Northeast Region. New York, New York. Grand jury letter dated 2 October 1852.

National Cyclopedia of American Biography, The. Vol. IV. New York: James T. White & Company, 1895.

Newburgh Daily News, 2 April 1888.

Newburgh Sunday Telegram, 29 July—12 August 1905.

Newburgh Telegraph, 5 August—12 August 1852 and 22 August 1914.

New York City Marble Cemetery. Burial for Stephen Allen. *http://home.attbi.com/~ifraser/nycmc/history.html*.

New-York Daily Times. 29 July–5 October 1852 and 18 October–8 November 1853.

New-York Daily Tribune, 29 July–6 August 1852 and 10 October–3 November 1853.

New York Herald, The, 29 July–5 August 1852 and 18 October–3 November 1853.

Obituary notice, *Philadelphia Public Ledger*, 2 August 1852.

O'Brien, Raymond J. *American Sublime: Landscape and Scenery of the Lower Hudson Valley*. New York: Columbia University Press, 1981.

"Orange County Directory 1878–1879." Directory for the Town of Cornwall.

http://www.usgennet.org/usa/ny/county/orange/cornwall/id4.htm.

Orange County Land Records. Orange County, New York. Grantee Index D–H. 1703–1869. DeWint L120 p.165–168. 1853.

Orange County Land Records. Orange County, New York. Grantee Index D—H. 1703—1869. Hubbard L198 p. 368-369. 1867.

Orange County Land Records. Orange County, New York. Grantor Index C–D. 1703–1869. Downing L133 p. 139–142. 1854.

"Personal Papers—The William Whitman Bailey Papers (1867–1904)." The New York Botanical Garden Archives and Manuscript Collections. The LuEsther T. Mertz Library. http://www.nybg.org/bsci/libr/Bailey1.htm.

Princeton Cemetery, The. Burial information for Thompson family. *http://princetonol.com/groups/cemetery/mon.html.*

Proctor Cemetery listing for burial of Harriet Colby. *http://freepages.genealogy.rootsweb.com/~colby/colbyfam/d391.html.*

"Resurrecting A. J. Downing," Newburgh/Revealed. *http://newburghrevealed.org/photo-journalajdowning.htm.*

Ringwald, Donald C. *Hudson River Day Line: The Story of a Great American Steamboat Company.* Berkeley, California: Howell-North Books, 1965.

Rink, Oliver A. *Holland on the Hudson: An Economic and Social History of Dutch New York.* Ithaca and London: Cornell University Press; Cooperstown, New York: New York State Historical Society, 1986.

Records from Newburgh, New Windsor and other Nearby Towns. Vol. 2. Arranged and Indexed for the Orange County Genealogical Society by Marilyn Terry, Dan Burrows, and Helen Benjamin. Orange County Genealogical Society.

Rosenzweig, Roy and Elizabeth Blackmar. *The Park and Its People: A History of Central Park.* Ithaca and London: Cornell University Press, 1992.

Saturday Express, Lancaster, 31 July 1852.

Simpson, Jeffrey. *The Hudson River 1850–1918: A Photographic Portrait.* Sleepy Hollow Press. Prepared for press by Sachem Publications, Inc., Guilford, CT, 1981.

Smithsonian Institution, Horticulture Services Division. Information on the Downing Urn and life of A. J. Downing. *http://www.si.edu/horticulture/gardens/Haupt/Downing/down.html.*

Springside Landscape Restoration. Leaflet "Springside Walking Tour—A National Historic Landmark." Matthew Vassar Estate. Poughkeepsie, New York.

Stanne, Stephen P., Roger G. Panetta, and Brian E. Forist. *The Hudson.* New Brunswick, New Jersey: Rutgers University Press, 1996.

Steuding, Bob. *Rondout–A Hudson River Port.* Fleischmanns, New York: Purple Mountain Press, 1995.

St. Paul's Lutheran Church Cemetery, Town of Durham in the Village of Oak Hill. Ray family burial site. Transcribed by Sylvia Hasenkopf. *www.rootsweb.com/~nygreen2/st_paulschurch_cemetery.htm.*

Town of Gardiner Ulster County New York Cemeteries, "Schoonmaker Family Ground." Copied 15 August 1924 by Dr. J. Wilson Poucher and Byron J. Terwilliger. Items Numbered 10, 11, 28, 29, *http://www.hopefarm.com/gardicem.htm.*

Turner, Arlin. *Nathaniel Hawthorne: A Biography.* New York and Oxford: Oxford University Press, 1980.

United States Census Records for New York State. Village of Cornwall. 1850–1880, Orange County Genealogical Society.

Wade, William. 1848. *Panorama of the Hudson River,* http://www.hhrhighlands.com/wadetext.html.

Wade, William. Master Engraver. 1846. *Virtual Trip Up the Hudson,* http://hhr.highlands.com/virtual.htm.

West Point Military Academy Special Collections and Archives Division. Selected letters of Jacob Whitman Bailey, first professor of chemistry, geology, and mineralogy at the United States Military Academy, West Point, New York, and president (1857) of the American Association for the Advancement of Science together with a series of Jacob Whitman Bailey's letters arranged with commentaries by his son Professor Loring Woart Bailey of the University of New Brunswick, as well as miscellaneous letters and papers relating to the Bailey Family of West Point and the University of New Brunswick. And a note on the Slaughter family of Culpepper, Virginia. Compiled by Alfred G. Bailey, Dean of Arts in the University of New Brunswick, Canada, 1962.

William Whitman Bailey Papers, 1843–1914. Harvard University. Library of the Gray Herbarium Archives. *http://huh.harvard.edu/libraries/archives/BAILEYWW.html.*

Acknowledgements

My sincere thanks to my publishers, Wray and Loni Rominger of Purple Mountain Press. They have been of tremendous assistance through the entire process, kindly answering all of my perhaps silly questions stemming from being a first-time author. They have been kind and patient, understanding and helpful, always with a pleasant demeanor. I am honored to have had the opportunity to work with them on this project.

My husband, Kornel, who is my supporter, encourager, photographer, scanner, designer, editor, chauffeur, photocopier, and computer expert. He accomplished whatever was necessary to bring this book to completion. I am ever thankful and grateful for his assistance, without which this book would not be in its present form.

Janet Dempsey, the Cornwall town historian, who for years has compiled decades of town newspaper clippings and has indexed them for the public library. She found in those archives a newspaper article that acknowledged one of the true heroes in this story.

Claudia Jew, Manager, Photographic Services & Licensing, at The Mariners' Museum in Newport News, Virginia, for her kind and patient assistance in arranging for the rights for use of the three images of the *Henry Clay* in this book.

Sheila Biles, Library Technician for Special Collections and Archives Division, at the West Point Military Academy Library for various records, letters, documents, newspaper clippings, and related items regarding the Kinsley and Bailey families.

Rita Forrester, researcher for the local history room at the Newburgh Free Library, for information on Newburgh and A. J. Downing, and for providing the Hudson River map included in this book.

The librarians and staff at the Wallingford Public Library in Connecticut, especially research librarians Amy Humphries, David Andrews, and Robert Nankin for their kind assistance.

Gregory Plunges, Archivist at the National Archives and Records Administration,

Northeast Region in New York City for finding and photocopying pages of material related to the *Henry Clay* inquest and trial.

The volunteers of the Orange County Genealogical Society in Goshen, New York, especially Jeanne, Marilyn, and Marty, for their research of Orange County census records and other related information.

Jane Walsh and Christine Morin, reference librarians at the Salem Public Library in Salem, Massachusetts, for information regarding Maria Louisa Hawthorne.

Stella Bailey, president of the town of Highlands Historical Society, for information regarding the Kinsley family.

Joseph Ditta, reference librarian, at the New-York Historical Society for information regarding Stephen Allen.

Jerry Bruce, reference librarian, at the Lancaster County Library for information regarding the John L. Thompson family.

Jake Sherman, reference librarian at the Rutland Free Library in Vermont for copies of newspaper clippings related to Isaac McDaniels and his wife.

John McCormick, a commissioner of the Old Town Cemetery Association in Newburgh, for his continued assistance and kindness regarding the Hubbard plot.

Jim Wanamaker of the Old Town Cemetery Association, who searched the cemetery to find the Hubbard plot buried and hidden under decades of brush and overgrowth.

The rector, warden, and vestry of Saint John's Episcopal Church for Saint John's Cemetery in Yonkers, for their permission to photograph the marker for the graves of the unrecognized victims of the *Henry Clay* who were interred there.

Allynne Lange, curator of the Hudson River Maritime Museum, for access to some books in the museum's library and for permitting the photography of the displayed wooden model of the steamboat *Armenia* for use in this book.

Roger Mabie, director of the Hudson River Maritime Museum, for his overview of some aspects of Hudson River steamboat history.

Lisa Baker of the Ulster County Historical Society, for information on Rondout and Kingston, New York.

Roy Jorgensen of the Fishkill Historical Society, for information on the DeWint family of Fishkill.

Public Library of Cincinnati, for information on the Ray Family.

The Free Library of Philadelphia for the copy of the obituaries for Ann Hill and Eliza Smith.

Vassar College in Poughkeepsie for their policy allowing nonstudent researchers access to their library.

The Sojourner Truth Library at the State University of New York at New Paltz, New York, for access to their microfilmed newspaper collection.

Cornwall Public Library, New Rochelle Public Library, Yonkers Public Library, Stamford, Connecticut Public Library, and Ossining Historical Society for various related historical information.

The Newburgh Free Library in Newburgh and the Adriance Library in Pough-keepsie for access to their microfilmed newspaper collection.

The Westchester County Archives for copies of two newspaper articles related to the *Henry Clay* disaster.

National Archives and Records Administration, Northeast Region, in Pittsfield, Massachusetts, for access to various census records.

The reporters, correspondents, editors, and newspapermen of *The New York Herald*, the *New-York Daily Tribune* and especially the *New-York Daily Times* who, over a century and a half ago, diligently reported the news items associated with the *Henry Clay* disaster.